CW01212959

PHILIP JOHNSON

PHILIP JOHNSON
A VISUAL BIOGRAPHY

Introduction
9

01 Son
20

02 Traveler
32

03 Modernist
58

04 Politician
92

05 Architect
122

06 Socialite
192

07 Transformer
230

08 Collector
294

09 Postmodernist
318

10 Icon
346

Notes
383

Bibliography
385

Index
388

This book has two interconnected objectives. The first is to afford a succinct visual overview of the work of Philip Cortelyou Johnson, the architect and curator, whose buildings and museum exhibitions correlated so strongly with the spirit of their times that they practically constitute an aesthetic history of the United States in the twentieth century. The second goal is to allow readers access to primary-source materials about Johnson, the cultural panjandrum, that were previously available only as excerpted in his two formal biographies or in the other books in which Johnson has featured as a central or peripheral character. Since the photographs of the work featured here—as well as the letters, personal effects, and ephemera appearing alongside them—are all dated to Johnson's lifetime, this volume is as much a formal monograph as it is a kind of scrapbook, a peek into the archive.

Revisiting Johnson in this way is rewarding for a number of reasons. First and foremost, there's the particular character of his work: despite his renown, Johnson's design process is somewhat obscure, his buildings often seeming more like pure emanations of his roving mind than quotidian products of sketching and modeling. Looking back at the renderings and models of projects like the 1963 Kreeger House or the 1964 Museum of Modern Art (MoMA) expansion (many of the drawings by John Manley, Johnson's loyal right-hand man and draftsman of five decades), we see Johnson as part of a highly efficient practice, one that enabled him to focus on the big picture without losing sight of details. Susceptible, and quite happily so, to the influence of other designers, Johnson also benefits from a visually oriented treatment by the placement of his own architecture in close proximity to its inspirations, allowing the parallels—between Johnson's apartment for Edward Warburg, for example, and the early interiors of Ludwig Mies van der Rohe, or between his art gallery in New Canaan, Connecticut, and ancient Mycenaean tombs—to emerge organically.

The image-based approach is still more informative when applied to Johnson's broader role as tastemaker. Like no other architect of his time—or any other—Johnson operated as a hierophant for new thinking and new trends, both within his own profession and in adjacent creative fields. He did this through a combination of tactics: through correspondence (with everyone from Sibyl Moholy-Nagy to Donald

Trump), through friendships (with Jacqueline Kennedy Onassis, Andy Warhol, Nelson Rockefeller, and many others), and through the judicious acquisition and donation of artworks, helping to further the careers of generations of artists beginning with Paul Klee in the 1930s and continuing straight through to Keith Haring in the 1980s. Whatever ineffable qualities of charm and persuasion he doubtless possessed, Johnson's influence over individuals and institutions was made possible through bequests, written appeals, public appearances, and newspaper coverage. There can be no better way to apprehend that lifelong cultural stratagem than to see it through the documents and images that chronicle it.

Lastly, there is a quality of the individual himself and the persona he fashioned—or rather the personae, plural—that comes into focus via the quasi-collage presented here. What characterized Johnson's trajectory in architecture and in the culture at large was a capacity for philosophical and artistic quick-changes that came with remarkable regularity but that never failed to have a sensational effect. Alarm, joy, anger, schadenfreude: with every one of Johnson's serial metamorphoses, the reactions from the architecture world and the general public ran the gamut, but were rarely if ever muted. The sheer volume of chatter, along with the constant evolution that engendered it, makes Johnson a daunting object of study, a moving target cloaked in rumor and myth. No written account of Johnson's life, this one included, could claim sufficient objectivity to strip away all the legends that surround him, to reveal the man beneath. Yet with so much already said and written, it seems more than worthwhile to present readers at last with the physical facts of the case—the evidence file behind ten decades of architecture, ideas, and tall tales.

Of that last item there is rather an unusual quantity. Unique among his peers, Philip (and henceforth we will refer to him by his first name, as most people who talked about him did) was a lightning rod for gossip—both about others, which he greedily consumed, and about himself, which for the most part he happily generated. "An intellectual who was also a gossip,"[1] as his most recent biographer, Mark Lamster, described him, Philip was committed to the principle that the two were not so different: gossip *could* be intellectual. Though neither outré with regard to his personal relationships (about which he was fairly tight-lipped) nor uncouth in his public bearing (though he sometimes kept company with those who were) nor even particularly indiscreet when discussing others (he rarely betrayed a real confidence), Philip was nevertheless American architecture's greatest chinwag-exhibitionist. His success in that role can be confirmed by the fact that even now, fifteen years after his death, we still can't stop talking about him. And that is exactly how he would have wanted it.

He was a magnet for criticism and controversy, but he always seemed to turn it to his advantage. Some dismissed him as merely a gentleman architect, a rich man's son who had bought his way into MoMA and Harvard, thanks to his inherited fortune in aluminum stocks. His reply? "I guess I can't be a great architect,"[2] he said, making his dilettantism a virtue and retreating into it whenever the quality of his work came into question. He could make outrageous remarks, such as calling Frank Lloyd Wright "the greatest architect of the nineteenth century"[3]—though in truth, that bit of audacity was mostly for the cameras: behind the scenes, the younger architect spent most of the time trying to placate the old man, weathering Wright's barbs with considerable equanimity. Even the particulars of his business dealings could attract scrutiny, such as when he and longtime firm partner John Burgee—the man who helped build Philip's office into a powerhouse over two decades—fell out in the late 1980s. While he would sometimes minimize Burgee's role as that of "a producer,"[4] Philip could be more than magnanimous toward his former colleague, crediting him with the signature top to their AT&T building. The press frenzy around their acrimonious split gave Philip no pleasure, but when it died down, he was only too happy to bask in the media's perception of him as an unstoppable design dynamo.

Even when it came to the most appalling, most bruited-about episode in his life, Philip was capable of artful public-relations maneuvering. Following his notorious prewar flirtation (closer to a full-blown romance) with Nazism, he was careful to cover his tracks, burning the bulk of his incriminating letters and articles in the brick-clad fireplace of his landmark Glass House in New Canaan. Yet decades later he

"I'm a chameleon, so changeable. I see myself as a gadfly and a questioner."

—Philip to critic Ann Holmes in 1991

granted his first biographer, Franz Schulze, full license to bore into every unseemly aspect of his political period—and then, despite initially insisting that publication be withheld till after his death, Philip allowed the book to go to press. While Schulze exposed much that was previously unknown, including a number of shockingly anti-Semitic statements (comparing Jews to "locusts," for example),[5] Philip took the scrutiny in stride, alternating contrition with a dose of good-humored dismissal. Schulze, he said, had just been "trying to prove what a son-of-a-bitch I am"[6] and had simply paid too little attention to the architecture. As for Philip's more pointed objections, he allowed these to reach Schulze by way of his preferred medium. "I have talked about it ... with my friends," Philip said, "and it will get back to him."[7]

It is worth noting in this context that Philip's private behavior, while not exactly blameless, was in some sense the least gossip-worthy thing about him; Schulze's error, in Philip's view, was in attempting to suggest otherwise. If one thing emerges clearly from the assorted snapshots, press clippings, project photos, and memoranda assembled in this book, it is that Philip had little to hide, in the end. ("When an architect routinely belittles his own work," wrote the New York Times's Herbert Muschamp, "calls himself a whore and makes no secret of the fascist sympathies that overtook him in the 1930s, where's the fun in trying to take him down a peg or two?"[8]) Philip's was very much a public life, and he held on to almost any scrap that documented it. How else to gauge his own impact—on architecture and on the culture at large—but to keep the receipts?

The general perception, during his lifetime and since, is that Philip's career as a "serious" maker of buildings was undercut by his moonlighting as a tabloid staple, a scandal-loving power broker dishing the design-world dirt over lunch at the Four Seasons. But gossip can be serious business: there is value in apocrypha, not when taken as literal truth, but as a glimpse into the profession's subconscious—not what actually happened, but what critics and practitioners want to have happened. In any case, while Philip always insisted that his architecture came first, his innate restlessness made it impossible for him to confine himself within his studio, honing his craft in monkish solitude. Most architects would be content to find what brings them success and mine that vein, peacefully and quietly, for the rest of their lives. Instead, Philip fashioned a permanent place for himself in American life by stoking curiosity and conversation with each change of his stripes. Before the advent of "starchitecture," when buildings would be marketed as commodities and their creators reduced to brands, Philip was free to play one role after another on the national stage, a man of a thousand faces who always kept his audience guessing.

That multifaceted identity furnishes the organizational principle for this magpie collection of Johnsoniana, with each chapter examining another of the sequential (and often overlapping) guises that Philip adopted over the course of his long life. The work of all the scholars who have gone before has given us as much information on the architect as we are likely to get, and as much critical insight as we are likely to need. The great advantage of presenting this selection of raw data, of spreading it out across these pages with as little accompanying exposition as possible, is the quasi-voyeuristic pleasure of looking at it—a suitable approach to the subject, as it happens. "The idea of a glass house," Philip once told an interviewer, "where somebody just might be looking—naturally you don't *want* them to be looking. But what about it? That little edge of danger ... "[9]

From the austere Miesian reserve of the Glass House, to the wild Expressionism of Da Monsta, the final addition to the New Canaan campus; from the groundbreaking success of the 1947 Mies exhibition at MoMA, to the critical punching bag that was the Deconstructivist show at the same museum over forty years later; from the mid-career stylistic excursions that yielded such varied products as the Beck House and the Kline Biology Tower, to the return to order of the AT&T Building at the end of the 1970s: with each new phase of his career, Philip seemed determined to plot a new course for American architecture. His transformations never wanted for drama.

As early as 1959, twelve years after organizing a groundbreaking MoMA exhibition on his original architectural sensei, Philip would announce his first major act of apostasy: "My stand today is violently *anti*-Miesian,"[10] he declared. In the so-called television windows of the first MoMA expansion, with their rounded corners, and in the Gothic echoes of the proposed (though never built) portico for Lincoln Center, Philip set about trying to soften the hard edges of Modernism as it had developed in the United States. If any people were surprised by this sudden turn, they shouldn't have been—Philip had given his heart to Mies only after entertaining other Modernist suitors, in particular J. J. P. Oud and Walter Gropius, both of whose work he had encountered during his trips abroad in the late 1920s. The same promiscuity would characterize his work in the years that followed, and though his stylistic switches sometimes seemed calculated to shock, there is every reason to believe they were motivated largely by instinct. "There is only one absolute," he wrote in 1961, "and that is change."[11] The line could almost serve as his personal motto.

The reproach most frequently levied against his work—part and parcel, really, of the rap against Philip's love of the media spotlight—is that his apparent caprice was evidence of a lack of moral and intellectual conviction. Certainly the architect who insisted that "social responsibility" was "boring"[12] and who could behave as Philip did in the 1930s could not exactly be faulted for his unyielding devotion to principle. Yet beside its sheer variability, there is another connecting thread that ties together Philip's extraordinary opus. Even in such modest projects as the early residential commissions (the 1952 Wiley House in New Canaan, for example, with its rustic base and glass lantern), as much as in the grandiose commercial undertakings of his later career (like the 1972 IDS Center, an office tower in Minneapolis), the buildings insist on their own presence, their own monumental singularity. Even when professing himself a postmodernist, Philip abjured the notion that architecture can and should produce buildings "appropriate" to their environs, contextually suited to the historic urban fabric, which was a key tenet of the movement's intellectual godparents, Robert Venturi and Denise Scott Brown. Whether in his supersized homage to Claude-Nicolas Ledoux for the University of Houston's architecture school or in his cathedral-like headquarters for Pittsburgh Plate Glass, he appropriated tradition with gusto, but used it to create projects that utterly refused to recede into the background. If that made the buildings fatter targets for critical disdain, so be it: he intended his buildings to be seen.

The result (and this much *does* seem calculated) is that architecture was seen—and not just seen but argued about and written about. In hindsight, Philip's greatest contribution to the American design scene was his capacity to act as an ambassador for the profession as a whole, at a time when the nation's economic power and prestige meant that its architecture was poised to become the global standard. Philip was, as critic Paul Goldberger once observed, "by no means the greatest architect of his time" but "surely the greatest architectural figure."[13] That may sound like a slight to the buildings, but in truth it only places them on a different tier, instruments in a wildly ambitious cultural project: with his designs, Philip would announce a new direction for the field; then, using his status as arbiter extraordinaire, he would set about fulfilling his own prophesy, inveigling wealthy patrons and promoting younger architects who would advance the cause. In Philip's absence, it is unclear whether American architecture in the twentieth century could truly have come into its own, with as much diversity and creative vigor as it did.

Whether staging exhibitions at MoMA, appearing at a landmarks-preservation gala with Onassis, or just sitting around a table at the Four Seasons with a group of younger architects—telling them perhaps how Blanchette Rockefeller never knew "anything about architecture"[14]—Philip always made architecture seem like something worth paying attention to. In a country where the so-called mother of the arts has often been treated more like a neglected stepchild, that is an accomplishment as towering as any of Philip's lofty skyscrapers. Spread the word.

1. Mark Lamster, *The Man in the Glass House: Philip Johnson, Architect of the Modern Century* (New York: Little, Brown and Company, 2018), xiii.
2. Alexandra Lange, "Philip Johnson's Not Glass Houses." *New York Times*, February 13, 2015. < www.nytimes.com/2015/02/13/t-magazine/philip-johnson-david-whitney-glass-house>.
3. Algis Valiunas, "Master Builder." *Claremont Review of Books* 17 (Summer 2017): 71.
4. Benjamin Forgey, "The Towering Obsessions of Philip Johnson." *Washington Post*, July 8, 1986.
5. Richard Hurowitz, "Don't forget Philip Johnson's Nazi past." *Jerusalem Post*, September 26, 2016.
6. Philip Johnson, interview by Sharon Zane, *Museum of Modern Art Oral History Program*, December 18, 1990. <www.moma.org/momaorg/shared/pdfs/docs/learn/archives/transcript_johnson.pdf>.
7. Ibid.
8. Herbert Muschamp, "A Man Who Lives in Two Glass Houses." *New York Times*, October 17, 1993.
9. Alice T. Friedman, *Women and the Making of the Modern House: A Social and Architectural History* (New Haven: Yale University Press, 2007), 147.
10. Frank D. Welch, *Philip Johnson & Texas* (Austin: University of Texas Press), 90.
11. Lee Radziwill, "Fancy Speaking." *Esquire*, December 1974.
12. Michael Z. Wise, "Review of 'The Man in the Glass House: Philip Johnson, Architect of the Modern Century.'" *Architectural Record*, January 8, 2019. <www.architecturalrecord.com/articles/13809-review-of-the-man-in-the-glass-house-philip-johnson-architect-of-the-modern-century>.
13. Paul Goldberger, "Philip Johnson's Glass House." Lecture, National Trust for Historic Preservation, Board of Trustees Meeting, the Glass House, New Canaan, CT, May 24, 2006.
14. Lamster, *The Man in the Glass House*, 222.

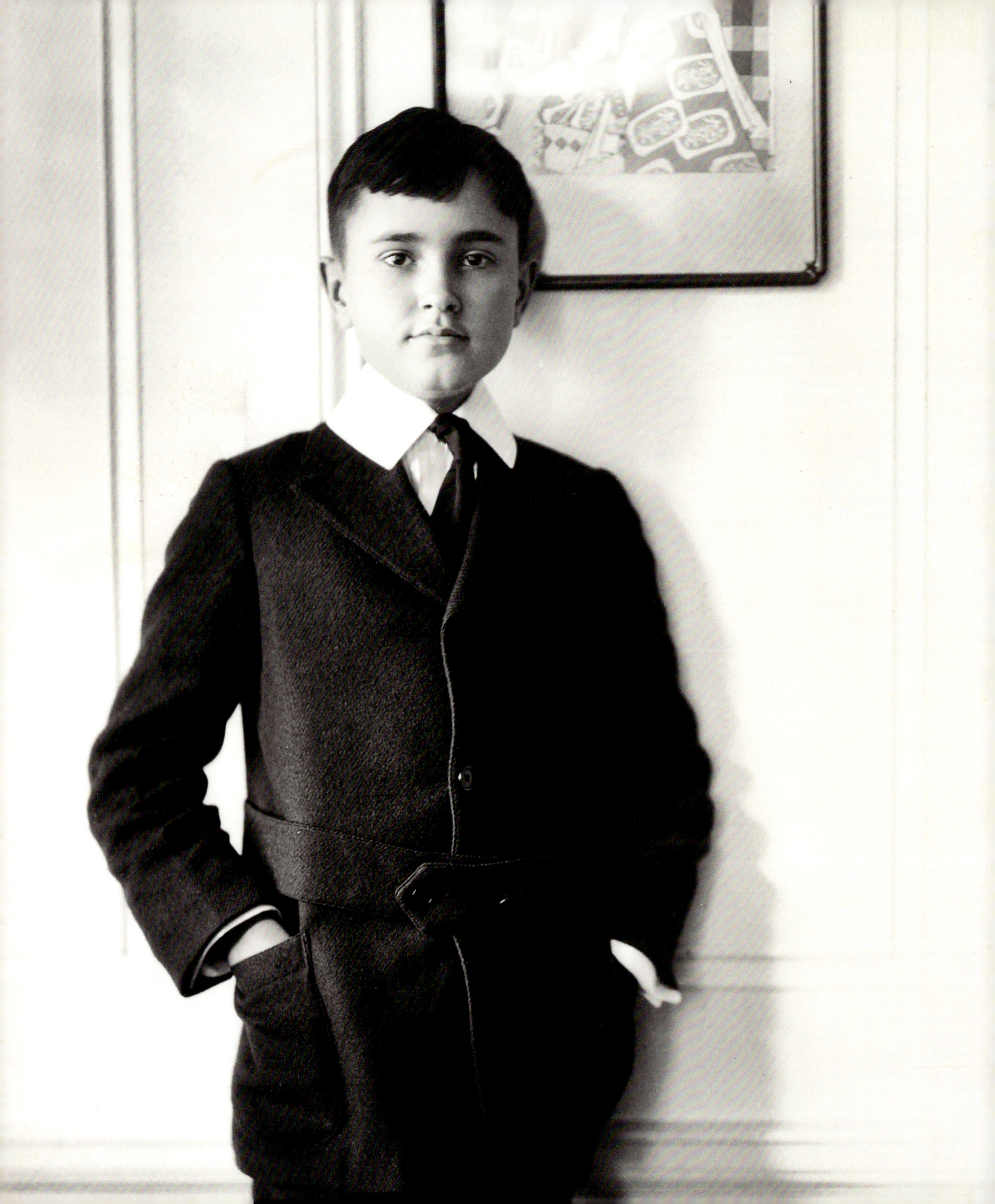

01 Son

Son

Nothing in Philip Cortelyou Johnson's birth and background marked him for a career at the summit of art and society in America. His parents, Homer and Louise, were prosperous but hardly gilded millionaires, residing in Cleveland, Ohio. Born in 1906, Philip was the third of four children, behind sister Jeannette and brother Alfred, and before younger sister Theodate (to whom he was always closest). Philip's parents expected little more from him than a life of respectability, hard work, study, and creature comforts. Over the next ten decades, he would either outstrip or abandon all of these.

Though in some ways simply an escape from the complacency of his Ohio upbringing, Philip's subsequent trajectory would follow several lines that had been laid down long before. Education and culture were the lodestars of his mother's upbringing: born Louise Pope, she descended from a wealthy Cleveland industrial family, and she had gone east to attend Wellesley College before traveling to Europe to continue her studies, a rarity for an American woman in the nineteenth century. Her artistic sensibility was as well-informed as it was progressive, and shortly after her (rather late, at the age of thirty-two) marriage to Homer, she briefly considered commissioning a new house for the two of them from a still relatively obscure Chicago architect—Frank Lloyd Wright. The project was derailed, but the family home was always a stylish affair, with Louise's taste guiding the way. Though Philip would sometimes typify his mother as a "cold fish," he learned much from her example.

Homer's outlook, by most accounts, was a bit more circumscribed. A Harvard-trained lawyer from the small Ohio town of New London, Philip's father was most in his element in boardrooms and clubrooms; even when home, his strained relationship with his youngest son (Homer always ascribed a weak, even girlish quality to the boy) meant that he exerted far less influence than the ever-present Louise. But Homer's default conservatism did not mean he was altogether provincial, and at least one of his decisions as paterfamilias had a lasting effect on Philip: after World War I, Homer brought his little brood to Europe, where he had been given a position with the U.S. government assisting in the demobilization of American armed forces on the Continent. Eleven-year-old Philip got his first taste of life abroad, strolling the parks and boulevards of Paris, riding the Metro by himself, and then enrolling in a boarding school in Geneva where he could improve his foreign-language skills, returning to Cleveland after six months.

One other major childhood development was also to prove decisive. In 1908, when Philip was only two, his brother Alfred—then five—died suddenly of what today would be an easily curable ear infection. This left Philip as the best and only vehicle for achieving his mother's cultural aspirations, and she poured all of her knowledge and energy into his intellectual formation. It also meant that Philip would have one fewer heirs to contend with, with a larger portion of the family's inheritance settling on him. Fortuitous investments by Homer would eventually ensure that Philip need never work a day in his life. But by the time the money was his, Philip had already struck out on a far more active, far more challenging path.

His late teens and early twenties had seen to that. High school and especially attending Harvard were trying experiences for Philip, times when his sense of self was undergoing rapid and sometimes painful evolution, a transition that his sheltered upbringing had done little to prepare him for. He was seized by bouts of depression that he could feel, he later said, "like a storm approaching over the mountains, within sight."[1] Part of this may have been a struggle with his emerging sexuality, but a larger part seemed to be philosophical, a burgeoning uncertainty about his place in the world. "The only thing I lack just now is, strange to say, self-confidence,"[2] the twenty-two-year-old wrote Homer (one of the relatively few letters between father and son, compared to the voluminous correspondence with his mother and Theodate). As he came to terms with his identity—and his limits—Philip discovered a reserve of strength that was to serve him throughout his life. After college, his self-confidence was never again in doubt.

"If you gaze long into an abyss," wrote Friedrich Nietzsche, one of Philip's early intellectual heroes, "the abyss gazes into you."[3] Having taken his own measure, Philip left behind the introspection and quietude of his youth, turning his face resolutely forward. He would rarely look back again.

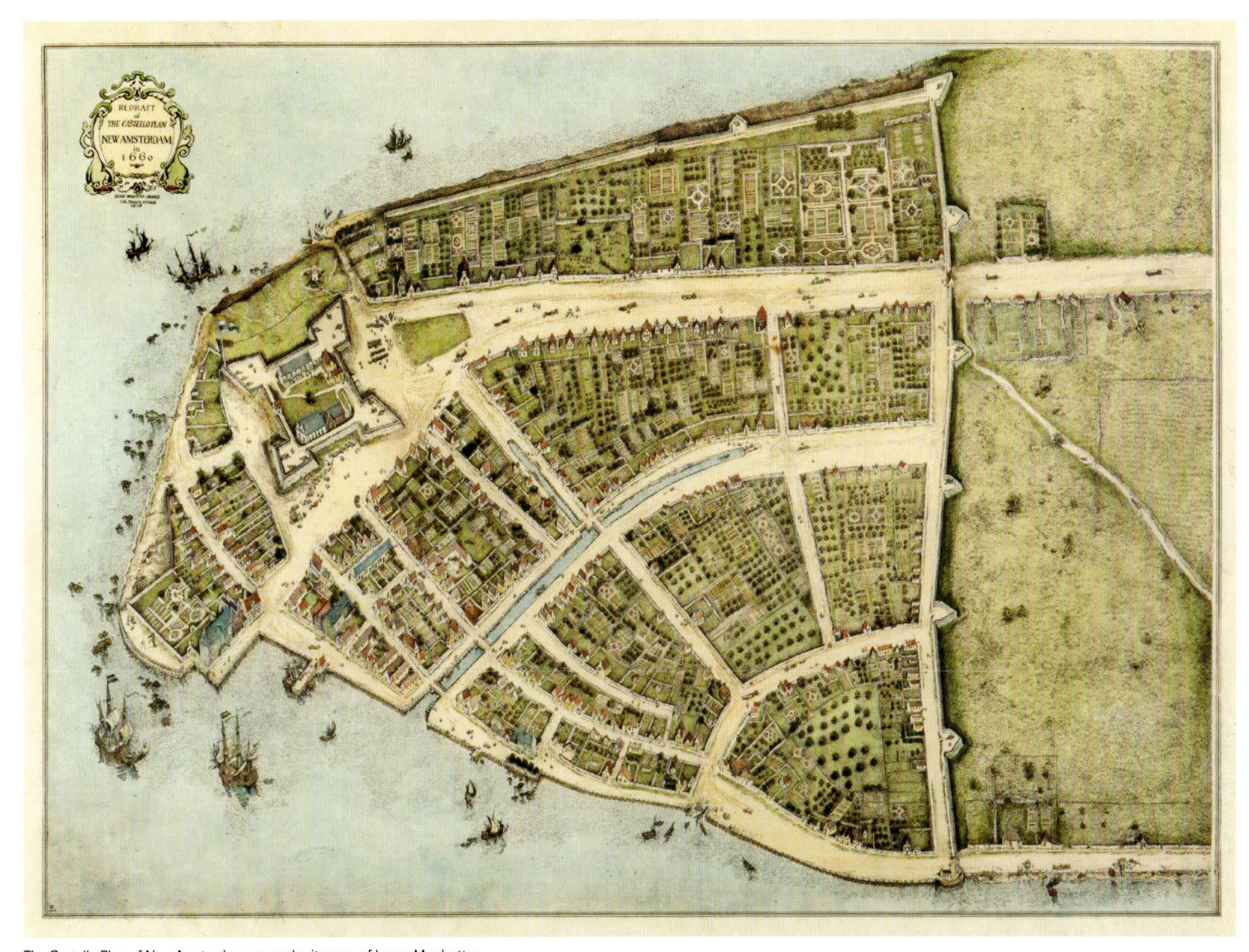

The Castello Plan of New Amsterdam, an early city map of Lower Manhattan in 1660, redrawn in 1916. The original map was created by Jacques Cortelyou, a seventeenth-century ancestor of Philip, who became a successful real-estate speculator in the New World. As surveyor to New Amsterdam's famous Governor Peter Stuyvesant, Cortelyou not only created one of the city's earliest maps but also helped build its first wall, now known as Wall Street. The Johnsons took some pride in their ancient lineage (by American standards), and so they named their son Philip Cortelyou in recognition of the long-ago New Yorker—the first of his family, though not the last, to build great things in Manhattan.

Public Square, Cleveland, Ohio, c. 1916.

"The Sixth City." Cleveland, Ohio, in the late nineteenth and early twentieth centuries was a city on the move. Even before John D. Rockefeller founded Standard Oil there in 1870, it had already become a major locus of American industry, one of the country's largest and fastest-growing urban centers. By the time Philip was born in 1906, it had also become a hub for immigrant labor and progressive politics, though the Johnson family would have little connection with the messy vitality of their hometown.

"We got along alright... Most of the time he talked pieties. Noble thoughts. Clichés."

—Philip on his father

Homer Johnson with Alfred and Jeannette, 1904.

Greek Revival house at Townsend Farm, c. 1913.

Townsend Farm, New London, Ohio. The Johnsons (originally Jansens, of Dutch heritage) had moved to Ohio in the eighteenth century, settling in the town of New London, about 50 miles (80 km) west of Cleveland. Homer grew up here and, though he quickly proved an inept farmhand, he continued to come back to the family homestead long after he had launched his legal practice and settled down in Cleveland. Philip and his sisters would spend some of their happiest childhood hours in New London, the eleventh generation of Johnsons to do so.

Son

Portrait of Philip and his sister Theodate.

Portrait of Philip with his mother, Louise, and sisters, Jeannette and Theodate.

Child of privilege. Homer's practice prospered in the 1910s, and the Johnson clan belonged to the upper tier of Cleveland society. They were hardly society figures: Louise did not keep alcohol in the house, and they rarely entertained. But Philip nonetheless grew up in fairly plush surroundings and enjoyed the best of both city and country, shuttling between his family's home in the Cleveland Heights neighborhood, the New London farm, and an additional home that Homer acquired in Pinehurst, North Carolina, where the family spent most winters.

"Marry a woman with brains. I did, and I've never regretted it. It is a little hard at home. I like to see people. Your mother doesn't. But her intelligence makes up for it."

—Homer to Philip

25

Hackley School, Tarrytown, New York, 1920.

School days. Following Philip's early years under his mother's tutelage (she had founded a school in Pinehurst so that he could study there in the winter), it was decided in 1920 that Philip should move to the East Coast for the first time, and he matriculated at the prestigious Hackley School in Tarrytown, New York. The life of a boarder seemed to suit him: he lost a stutter he'd had since childhood, joined clubs, acted in theatricals, and impressed his school chums with his verbal wit and talented musicianship at the piano. He was among the top two students in his class and seemed to thrive among the sons of the eastern establishment, though he made few friends while there.

> "'Phil' is the intellectual type, rather than the athletic… How we envy that youth (he's only sixteen, too) his brains."
>
> —Philip's high school yearbook

Son

Top: "The Annual," the Hackley School yearbook, 1923. Bottom: School photo, with Philip third from right in the bottom row.

Philip to his mother, from Harvard, October 1925.

Philip to his sister Jeannette, from Harvard, October 1925.

Letters home. Philip developed an epistolary habit early on, exchanging long letters with his mother, younger sister, and (less frequently) his father. Continuing in the cerebral vein that had always characterized their relationship, his letters to Louise often featured long discursive asides on whatever he happened to be reading. Only rarely, or in sidelong glimpses, did Philip hint at the psychological turmoil he was then undergoing.

Son

HARVARD UNIVERSITY
CAMBRIDGE, MASS.

Nov. 1925

Wednesday

Dear mother,
What a shocking thing nt to have written for weeks it must be, but I have beenso busy thinking that I have not done a thing. Now, however, I seem to have recovered my sane mind and enjoy life and college once more. Sometimes, I get very sick of having to do things that will not help me any and not having the things to do that would. In other words our system of education is a sort of forceful feeding, and irks me. But when I think how good it is that I have to do certainkindsof work that I don't like doig, Irealize that I am getting something out of the place.

Just now my passion for Philosophy is unbounded. Mr. Demos who is our section instructor and my tutor, whosee inspiring talks made me change my field, is very nice to me and I am learning a lot. Then too, Peter has decided that he likes philosophy and sometimes we sit up until twelve o'clock discussing metaphysics, psychology etc. Just now I am in arms against Behaviorism and scientific psychology in general. That Dr. Hinkall down at Cousin Theo's is just another example of how not to be a psychologist. They have got the bug that theirs can be an exact science, so they have divorced all interest inhuman nature from them and are truly a narrow lot. Gove me the philosophical psychology of William James. I don't wish to be narrow minded however, so I am engaged inreading the standard apology of Behaviorism.

I was very interested to see what effect music would have on me when I was ina tragic mood. I found out. Sunday when I came back from Cousin Theo's I went to Paderewski. I was feeling very low, not depressed but tragic, if you know what I mean. The music was the most glorious that I have ever heard. It accentuated the feeling that I had to a great degree, and yet exalted me. It was quite as much as I have ever got from a concert. Paderewski certainly deserves his reputation. He is the most thrilling of jusicians. My theory is that to be a great musician youmust be a man first, just as to be a gret teacher, you must be a man first. Paderewski is certainly that.

Philip to his mother, from Harvard, November 1925.

HARVARD UNIVERSITY
CAMBRIDGE, MASS.

Feb. 19-

Dear mother,
I have not written for so long, a week or so, because I have not had a thought to put do-wn. I have been very blue about nothing in particular, and have not done a thing inany way, except go t concerts which I have done onan awerage of once a day. Yes, these should have cheered me up, but the cheeriness I got from them did n t last. Last night I hear the Gled Club concert, which I did not sing inon account of too many cuts, with Dr. and Mrs. Holbrock. They are much superior to the son and I enjoyed the evening very much. I was rather surprised at the invitation to dinner which Sandy gave me, since I have hardly set eyes on him this year. He is one among those that haved seemed more boring than they are worth. Now everybody is that way except Demos and Peter. The former is too busy and the latter is going in a few days to New York to get a job. He was fired this mooning. He does not care much so the blow was not so much but he would like to stay and I did not realize how much I would like to have him stay until I actually knew he was going. What will I do here all alone! I am so used to coming home in the evening and comparing notes with Peter that I shall be lost without him. I must have company and if I don't have some one as nice as he is I will have to go farther and I am sure fare worse. I haven't been to a Greek class for a week or so andthe thrifty pages of trnslation that has piled up does not add to the joy of living. Of course I never will make them up but I'll have to do some of it. Te philosophy courses are depressing in their excellence. Demos is so good that he discourages me utterly from ever getting anywhere. Everybody seems to know so much and to be able to think so logically except me. The thought that I am suffering mostly from an injury to my amour propre does not lessen feeling, it makes me all the madder. I have spent all my life in broadening, as it is called, in other words finding out all the thinfgs I don't know, and what a hopeless amount of things there are to know and be. All the vistas which I may have mentioned ina previous letter which are continually opnjeing out before me depress me with their number and size. Descartes is discouraging. he set out to think about something and did it so successfully that he invented the science of analytical geometry. I start out at the same age to think about something, and the first thing I know is that I am dreaming about some thing, perhaps relevant but not usually, but the point is dreaming and notthinking. I give up. It's too much work to worry about getting anywhere. As I said to Theo, I think I'll have a convenient nervous breakdown next month and come to Pinehurst, where at least the emphasis would not be on tryig to think, or trying not to either.

Philip to his mother, from Harvard, February 1926.

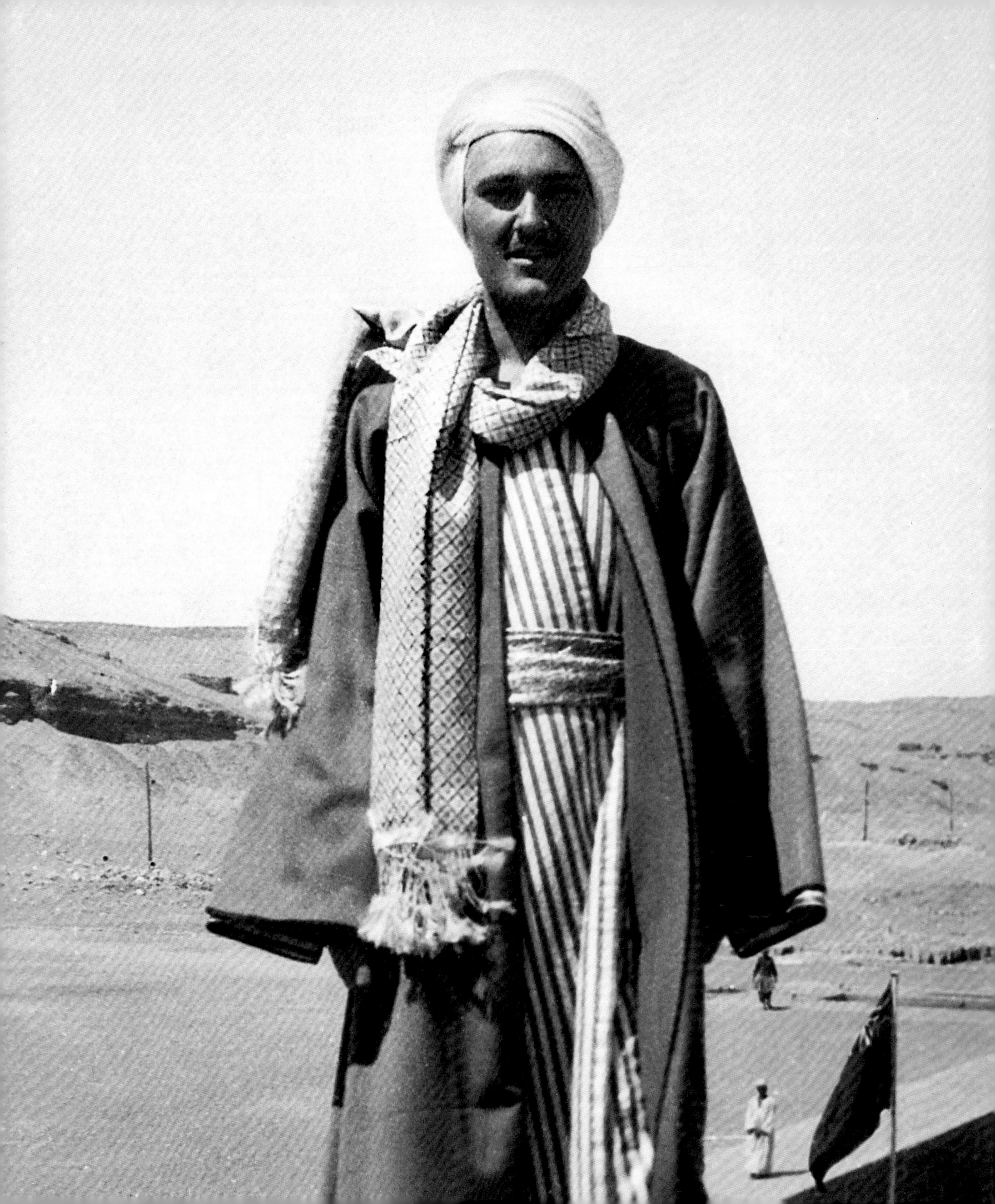

02 Traveler

Traveler

A certain regard for the Old World was with Philip from the start. His foreign-language training began when he was still a small boy, under the tutelage of German governesses hired by his parents. His first journeys abroad, also conducted under parental auspices, were intended as typical exercises in mind broadening, the sort of forced acculturation often undertaken by the young scions of moneyed families at the time. But the future architect took to Europe with singular gusto: he would return again and again, becoming a devotee of its great treasure houses of art, its cathedrals, and its walled cities with their narrow medieval streets. In time, Philip's attention would also be caught by monuments of more recent vintage.

As an undergraduate at Harvard, he developed a kind of psychological need for travel, using it as an escape hatch from the ongoing troubles of his early adulthood. The warmth and ease of the Mediterranean, as well as the pomp and richness of *Mitteleuropa*, seemed to grant Philip a degree of license, allowing him to feel more himself; more precisely, it allowed him to try on alternate *versions* of himself, some of which would become permanent features of his personality. It was overseas where Philip would have his first romantic tryst, formulate his first political sentiments, and elaborate the philosophical ideas that he had only encountered in books into something like a personal code. He would find still more books and ideas—assimilating some of them, discarding others—and he would do something not dissimilar with people: meeting many and cultivating a few relationships, including a number of prominent and soon-to-be-prominent figures whose thinking would inform Philip's own and his future career as an architect.

His decision to pursue that profession was also made, at least provisionally, during his earliest and most intense period of travel. But it was already evident that he would not be any ordinary designer. It was while traveling that Philip first began to collect art, especially Modern art (an endeavor much facilitated by the soaring value of shares gifted to him by his father), and to position himself as not only a connoisseur but also an impresario of architecture, leveraging his personal wealth to commission (or at least flirt with commissioning) works of Modern design that would bring the movement to the United States. This nascent desire to act as a conduit between the hemispheres—to bring the European avant-garde home—would make Philip something more than just an ordinary patron to the designers and artists whom he most admired. He would become a sort of one-man relief committee, dispensing aid to favored individuals caught in the social and economic maelstrom of the 1930s.

More important than any of the individual roles that he took on during his travels was the habit of self-reinvention. In Philip's later years, the press would frequently attach the epithet "chameleonlike" to his name, and in no small measure, his seemingly infinite mutability dates to his early forays abroad. Unmoored from the strictures of Cleveland, Ohio, and Cambridge, Massachusetts, Philip found that he could be anyone he pleased—an Arab sheikh, a Parisian bohemian, an earnest young scholar of German *Kultur*—and that his quick intelligence and ready charm would make almost anyone game to get in on the act. On top of everything there was his raw enthusiasm for art and design, which only became stronger under the stimulus of travel. "He was wildly impatient; he could not sit down," said Marga Scolari Barr, one of his regular travel companions. He was "raring to race."[1]

Philip would never stop traveling, though in the postwar years he would certainly become more deeply immersed in the American scene. This was in part because of a shift he himself had helped bring about: having successfully brought European architecture to the States, he no longer needed to look abroad in search of it. Politics played a role as well—particularly in the diminution of Philip's Germanophilia, for reasons that will become obvious later. But his affection for all things foreign never died, and as his stature grew in the United States, he would seek out commissions around the world and find a warm reception in at least a few quarters. His conception of architecture had always been global in scope, and he lived long enough to see globalism become a reality by the dawn of the twenty-first century—a gratifying turn, no doubt, for an instinctive cultural nomad who was able to take whatever he found, wherever he found it, and make it his own.

Philip (left) and Alfred H. Barr, Jr. (right), Lake Maggiore, Italy, April 1933.

Top: Postcard from Cairo, Egypt, showing the pyramids of Giza.
Bottom: Postcard from Nubia, Egypt, showing the Temple of Dendur.

Postcard from Mycenae, Greece, showing the Lion Gate.

Grand tours. Greece, North Africa, Italy... Wherever Philip wandered, he encountered buildings that, even before he chose architecture, would work their way into his visual imagination. He had learned to be a flâneur at the source, riding the Paris Metro unattended as a child—though he never much liked the city, viewing it as "never that *gastfreundlich* [welcoming]." Germany would be his preferred destination through the mid-1920s, as Philip staged a number of excursions, increasingly under his own steam rather than at the direction of his mother. In all his meanderings of the 1920s and 1930s, he would be aided by the extraordinary increase in the value of his ALCOA stocks (an aluminum supplier): soaring far above anything his father had imagined when he gifted them, they made Philip the prototypical wealthy American abroad, staying in the best hotels, keeping the best company.

Traveler

Postcards from Rome, August 1924.

Philip and Jeannette, Nice, France, 1928.

"I would not live in any of his houses, but they are certainly exciting to see."

—Philip on Le Corbusier

Le Corbusier. The experimental Weissenhofsiedlung—a suburb outside Stuttgart, Germany, composed entirely of Modernist buildings by various architects—had been completed only two years before Philip arrived there during a 1929 trip. It was there that he saw the work of Le Corbusier for the first time, and while it did not excite him the way the Germans—particularly Walter Gropius—had, he would deem Le Corbusier "unquestionably a genius," albeit (after meeting him in Paris a year later) "an objectionable man."

Top: Villa Savoye by Le Corbusier and Pierre Jeanneret, Poissy-sur-Seine, France, 1930. Bottom: First page of letter from Philip to his mother, Élysée Palace Hotel, Paris, June 1930. He describes his time in Paris, with particular attention to the quality of the furniture, and informs her that he will soon be going to Germany with architectural historian Henry-Russell Hitchcock.

Berlin
Nov. 8.

Dear mother,

I got your wonderful letter just after I sent off my last to you. I don't think I have ever had so much good news all at once. Of course I have known for months of Barr's appointment and strange that in my letter that crossed yours I should tell you about the same thing. I cannot of course credit what Miss somebody told Theo who told you who told me, but just the same it is exciting! I would rather be connected with that Museum and especially with Barr than anything I could think of. I will have to hump myself and learn something in a hurry though.

And then of course, I am terribly thrilled with your enthusiasm about my pet color scheme. I am not at all sure that it would be really livable. I have now the idea of going to the leading modern interior decorator here, and talk things over with him and have him make plans which I can buy "off" him. That way I shall get lots of new ideas, and the plans too. With the Barrett house, I shall have really lots of fun. I really don't see why a wing to the east is necessary at all, surely an ell is as good as two wings, especially when the house is so high as this one, but we shall see. The red door was John's idea, and I really would like to have him help me. We have talked together so much, we can hardly disentangle our separate ideas. I think of doing the house inside slowly. It may be more expensive than doing it all at once, but it will be better for experimental purposes, and in such a thing as architecture, practice is the only teacher. Drawings can be made ad infinitum, but you must have practice.

Here I am in Berlin, doing everything but learning German. It is disgraceful, but I suppose in my usual manner I attack it hard at first and get pretty good, and then call that enough. Just as I get petty good at writing on the typewriter but never really good. It is too discouraging. But Berlin is so fascinating. There is a series of the best films now being shown and of course I cannot miss any of those, then there are more modern and Gluck things at the opera, and concerts all the time. I just don't look at the affiches any more. Tonight I am going to the theater for the first time. They seem very proud of it and I really must take some in. Then there are the galleries with different exhibitions all the time, and in the background there is always the Kaiser Friedrich's. But really I almost dread to go in there because it is such a tiring procedure, this seeing things in a gallery, especially when they are so good.

I must run now, I have a lunch date with a young stage designer. I really have met the nicest assortment of people. Ruhtenberg family is too charming. I have fallen quite in love with the children, ages between four and eight. I am already Onkel Philip, which means to them of course the Philip in the Struwelpeter book who always fidgeted and meddled. Was that why you named me Philip? In spite of this nice country, I shall be glad to sail on the sixth. I am dying to see you all.

Love, Phil

Philip to his mother, 9 November c. 1929, describing his time in Berlin and his collaboration with British architect John McAndrew. He writes, "in such a thing as architecture, practice is the only teacher."

Back of postcard from Philip to his mother, 18 October 1929. It describes his impression of the Bauhaus building by Walter Gropius. The front of the postcard (opposite, top) shows that building, constructed in Dessau, Germany, 1926.

The German scene. On his momentous 1929 excursion to Germany, Philip followed an itinerary laid down by his new friend Alfred H. Barr, Jr. and shortly made contact with a Berlin-based architect called Jan Ruhtenberg. The young German insisted on taking him to Dessau to see Gropius's Bauhaus building; the experience confirmed Philip's initial impression that Gropius "may be the greatest of them all."

Traveler

38

Above: Note on a clipping from a German newspaper. The clipping is about the most modern form of car, and the note says, "How would you like me to call on you in this? The best car I have seen yet."

Portrait of Ludwig Mies van der Rohe in the doorway of the Riehl House, Potsdam-Neubabelsberg, Germany, c. 1910.

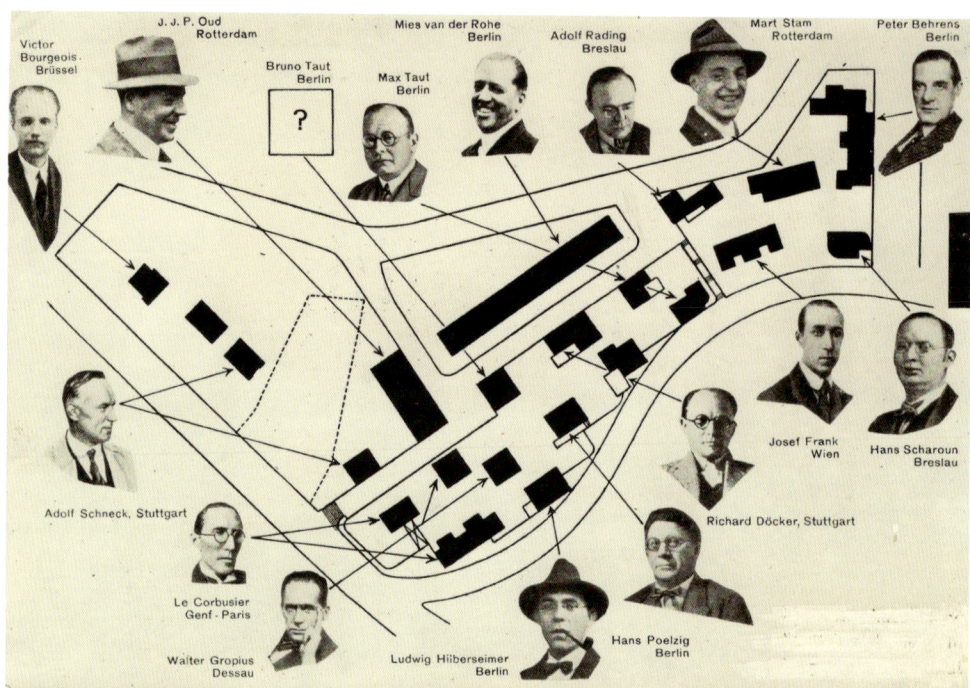

Top: Plan of the Weissenhofsiedlung site, Stuttgart, Germany, with portraits of participating architects keyed to their respective projects. Bottom: Aerial view of the estate, with Le Corbusier's two houses at upper left.

Traveler 40

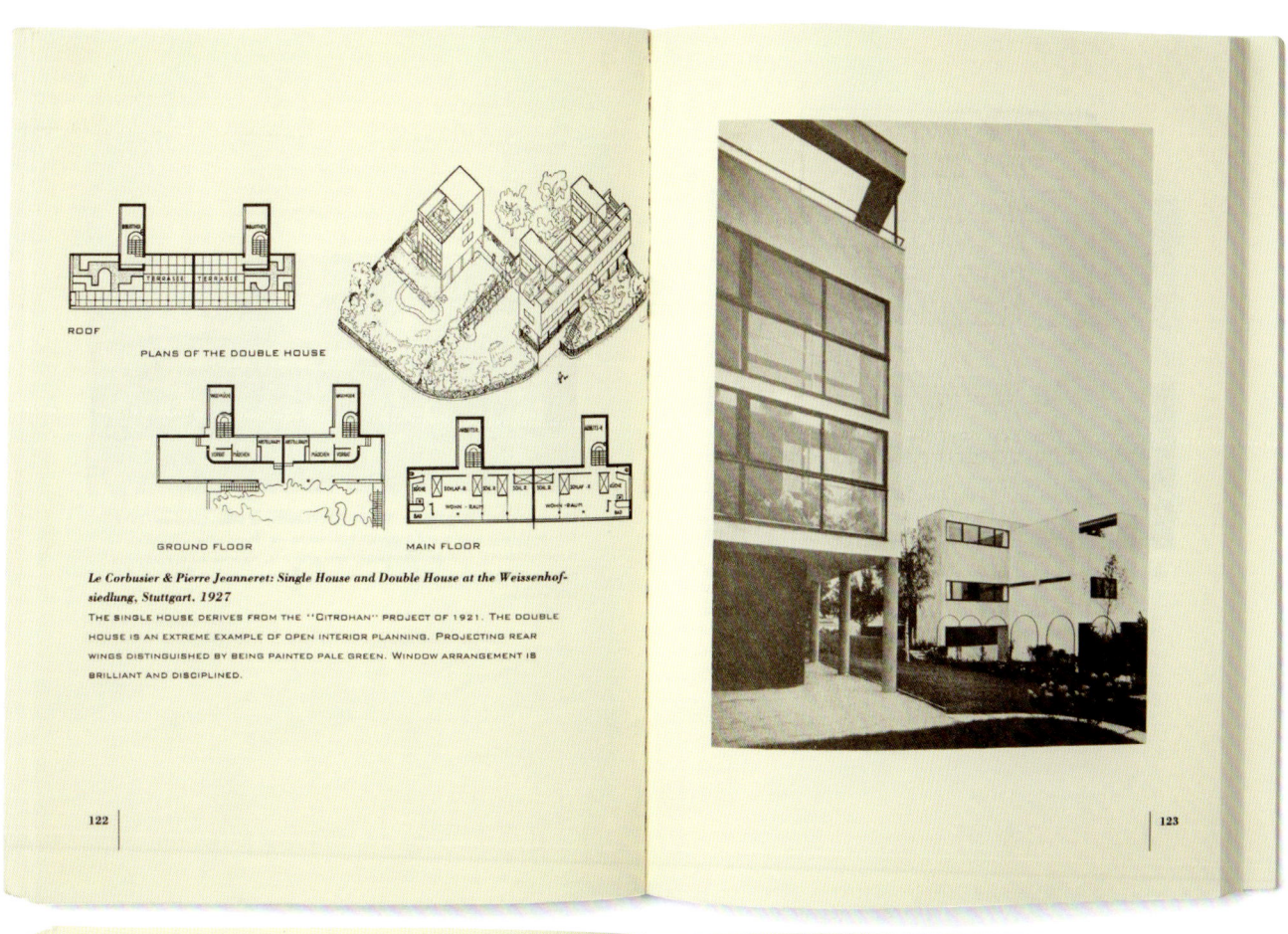

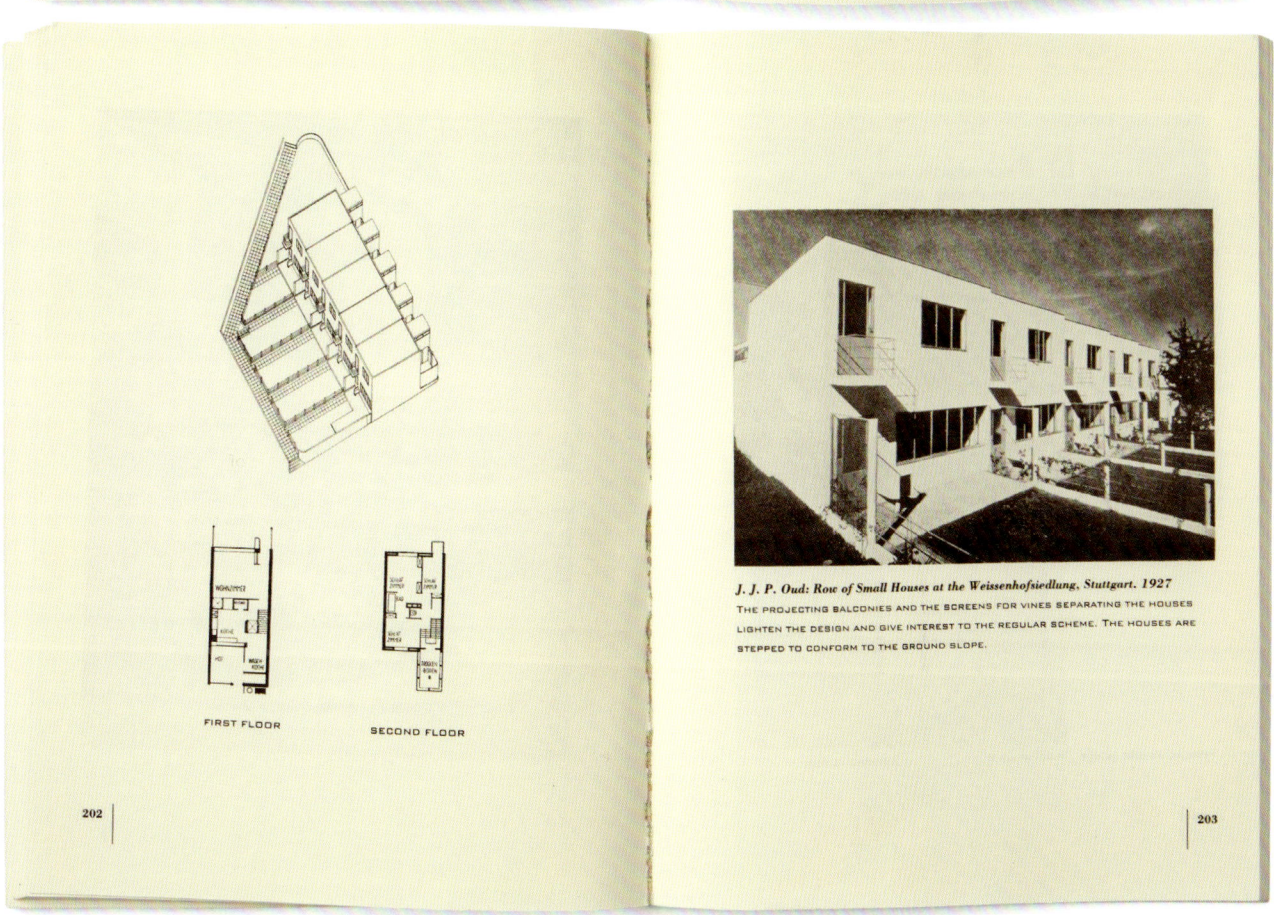

Single House and Double House by Le Corbusier and Pierre Jeanneret (top) and row of Small Houses by J. J. P. Oud (bottom), Weissenhofsiedlung, Stuttgart, Germany, 1927.

Housing block in the Weissenhofsiedlung by Ludwig Mies van der Rohe, Stuttgart, Germany, 1927.

Traveler 42

West facades of the Single House and Double House by Le Corbusier and Pierre Jeanneret, Weissenhofsiedlung, Stuttgart, Germany, 1927.

Top: Kroll Opera House by Ludwig Persius and Eduard Knoblauch, Berlin, 1844. Bottom: Heilandskirche by Ludwig Persius, Potsdam, Germany, 1842.

I am a camera. For a 1932 jaunt through Germany, Philip commissioned a large German-built view camera and set out in search of the work of Ludwig Persius, an early nineteenth-century architect who trained under the illustrious Karl Friedrich Schinkel and about whom Philip intended to compose a detailed monograph. The project never reached completion, a fate not uncommon with some of Philip's early flights of fancy.

Traveler

Top: Wirtshaus Moorlake by Ludwig Persius, Berlin, 1841. Bottom: Orangery Palace by Ludwig Persius, Potsdam, 1862.

Portrait of Ludwig Mies van der Rohe in his Berlin studio, c. 1927.

Interior views of living area with library beyond (top) and dining area (bottom), Tugendhat House by Ludwig Mies van der Rohe, Brno, Czech Republic, 1930.

Mies. The fateful meeting of Ludwig Mies van der Rohe and Philip occurred in the summer of 1930 in Berlin. It would be difficult to imagine two less compatible personalities: Philip, excitable, charming, and verbose; Mies, sedate, stony, and at times nearly monosyllabic. And yet the pair had an unlikely rapport from the start, and they quickly set out to see Mies's Tugendhat House in Brno, now in the Czech Republic—Philip's first glimpse of it, and Mies's as well, since he had never visited the actual site.

Tugendhat House by Ludwig Mies van der Rohe, Brno, Czech Republic, 1930.

"Mies is the greatest man we or I have met... He is a pure architect."

—Philip on Ludwig Mies van der Rohe

> The Hague
> Sept 22
>
> Dear mother,
>
> I wrote you from Koln the other day but I think th t I forgot to m il the letter andso you have not heard from me for a long long time. The truth is we have been traveling so fast that there has not been time to sit down to do anything. I know you will be thinking that I am traveling too fast and that I am getting tired, but I really am not. I have never enjoyed anything so much. Today we have discovered the worlds greatest architect, J. JL.PP. Oud, the city architect of Rotterdam. For the time being we are quite fanatic about him; we shall probably come to our senses and our critical faculties will reassert themselves, but today we are quite under his spell. Having someone to travel with like this makes traxgxingx writing letters very hard. If ever I have a feeling I canshare it immediately and we pass on to more, so I won't go into all the architecture we have been enjoying the past few days because we are in far too deep to make anythingclear and it would all soundsilly without pictures. Our latest plan is to make a book, a fact-picture book, with a minimum of metaphysics and aesthttcs in it. We shall name the priniclemen in each country and the styles of that country and picture and place their good works. But expecially will we have good pictures. Sacrifice the best buildings if they don't photograph well. Don't you think that would be a very good thing. Also we hope to include a short article of belief by each ofth the big men that will do it.
>
> We have such grandiose ideas, because we had such luck in the charming town of Essen. We walked right up to the Stadtbauamt, which has charge not only of architectur e but of city planning in general, and got a very nice young architect to take us around and show us the recent things. He turned out to know quite a lot, and we learned immense amounts from him, though of course I had to do all the talking since John doesn't understand a word of German. No, he understand a little but just enough to understand what I say without quite getting the answer. Well this young man, Hermann Weiser, was an Austrian and has studied with the best men, and had wonderful ideas. We are going to keep in touch with him, for new books and new articles. We may even write on the City planning of Essen, because of its contrast to American methods, in so far as architecture is concerned. Tomorrow we have an exciting day. We hope to meet Oud himself, we are like schooldhildren meeting King George, and to talk with him about things. I hope he speaks English, because John must do some of the talking.
>
> John, by the way, is a perfect traveling companion. He knows much more than I, but is very modest, just as enthusiastic as I. but less prejudiced, less apt to be a fanatic. I am learning a lot from him. He is nly two years ol er and doesn't look a bit older, but he was three years

Philip to his mother, The Hague, 22 September 1929. He writes of his discovery of influential architect J. J. P. Oud. "Today we have discovered the world's greatest architect, J. JL. PP. Oud [sic] … We hope to meet Oud himself, we are like schoolchildren [sic] meeting King George."

Oud. While still an undergraduate, Philip discovered the work of Dutch architect J. J. P. Oud. Having seen Oud's contribution to the Weissenhofsiedlung, Philip sought him out, the pair meeting in the summer of 1930. Immediately the two took a shine to one another. In the years that followed, Oud would turn to Philip for counsel and material support, in addition to designing the abortive Pinehurst project—a house for Philip's mother.

Traveler

Top and bottom, left: Kiefhoek Housing Development by J. J. P. Oud, Rotterdam, Netherlands, 1929.

Above: Workers' Housing Estate by J. J. P. Oud, Hook of Holland, Netherlands, 1927.

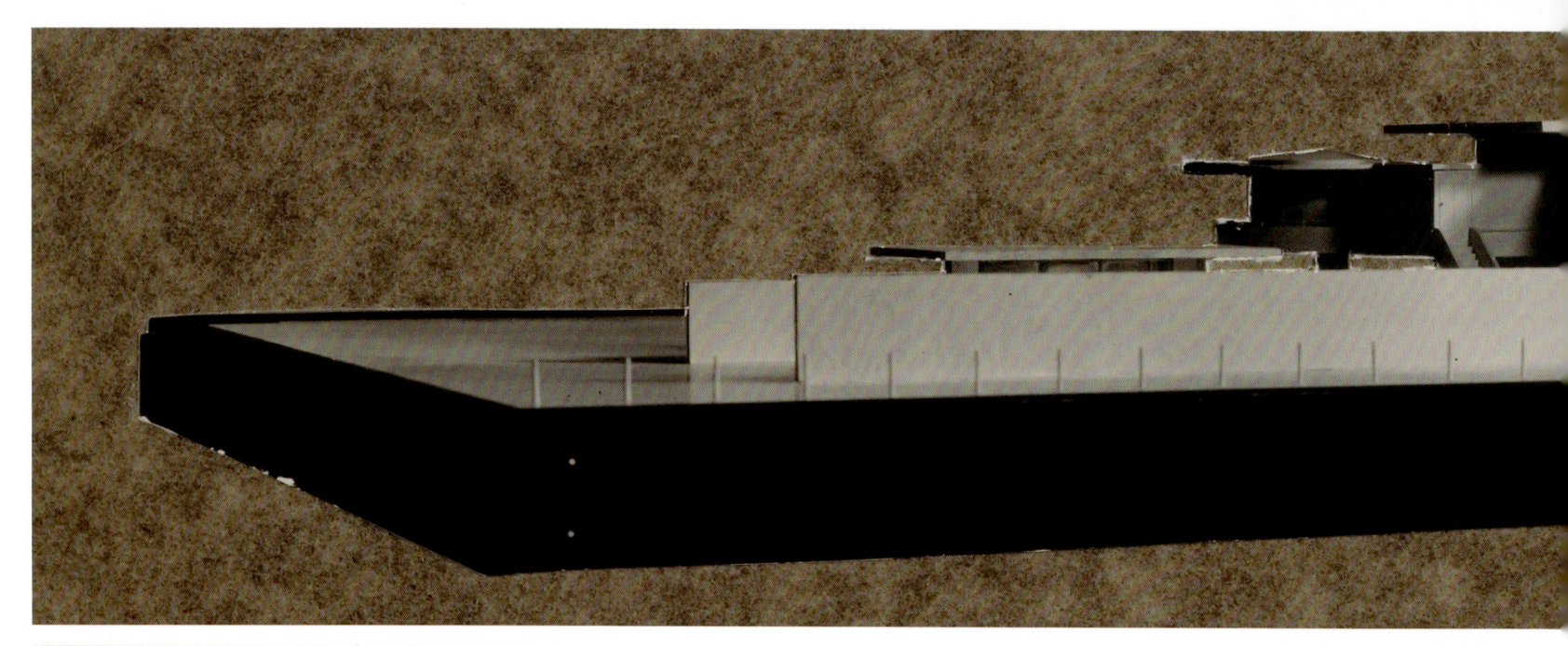

Top: Model for the unbuilt Johnson House by J. J. P. Oud, Pinehurst, North Carolina, c. 1931. Bottom: Oud's sketch for Johnson House, 1925.

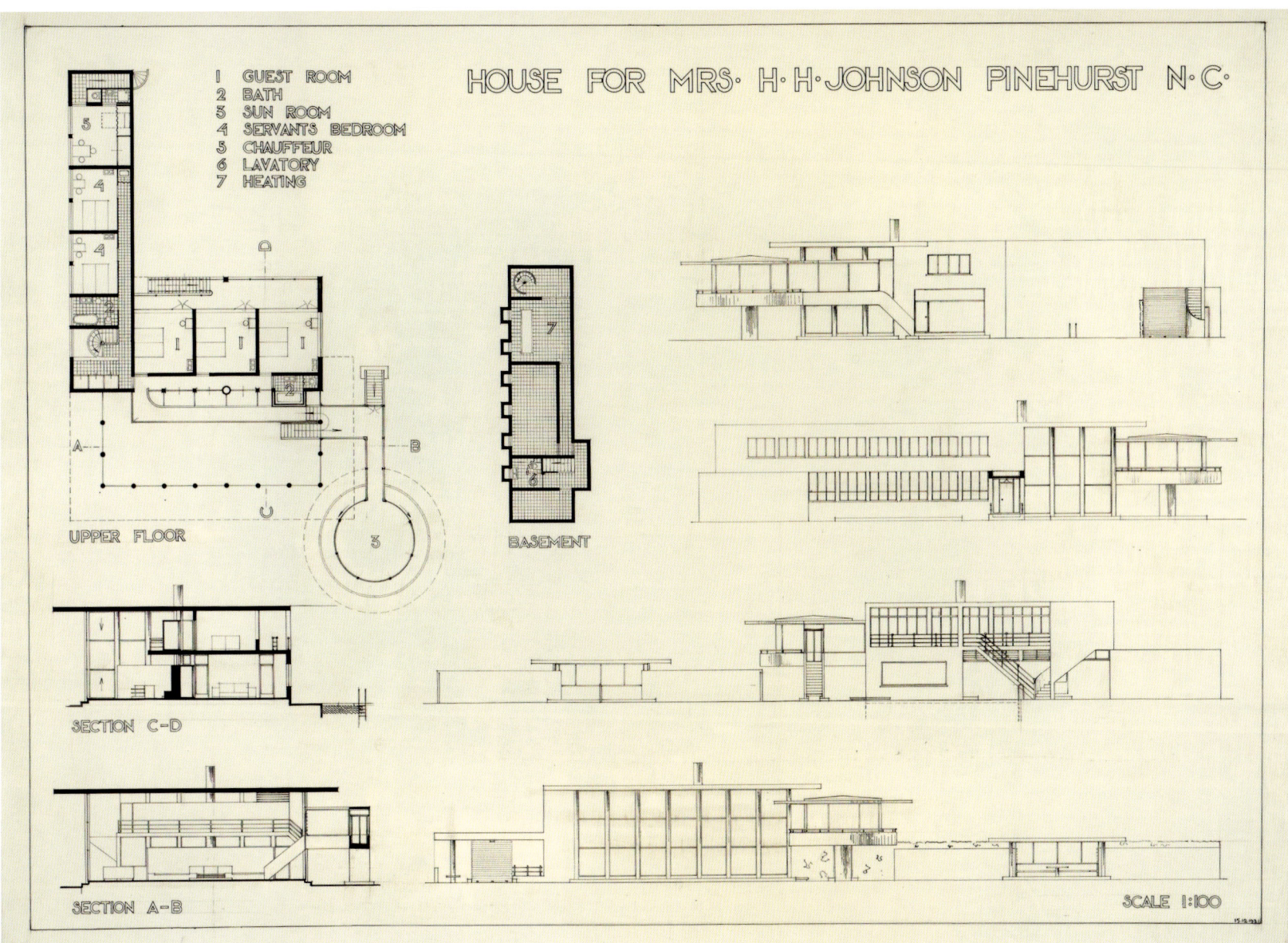

Above: Plans, sections, and elevations of the unbuilt Johnson House,
Pinehurst, North Carolina, 1931.

Paradise Restaurant by Erik Gunnar Asplund and Nils Einar Eriksson, Stockholm, Sweden, 1930.

Companions. Philip occasionally traveled alone, but more often in the company of friends and colleagues—in particular Barr, his friend at the newly launched Museum of Modern Art in New York.

Traveler

Top (from left to right): Alfred H. Barr, Jr., Philip, and Marga Scolari Barr, Cortona, Italy, 1932. Bottom: Philip (right) with Marga and Alfred outside Siena's cathedral, Italy, 1932.

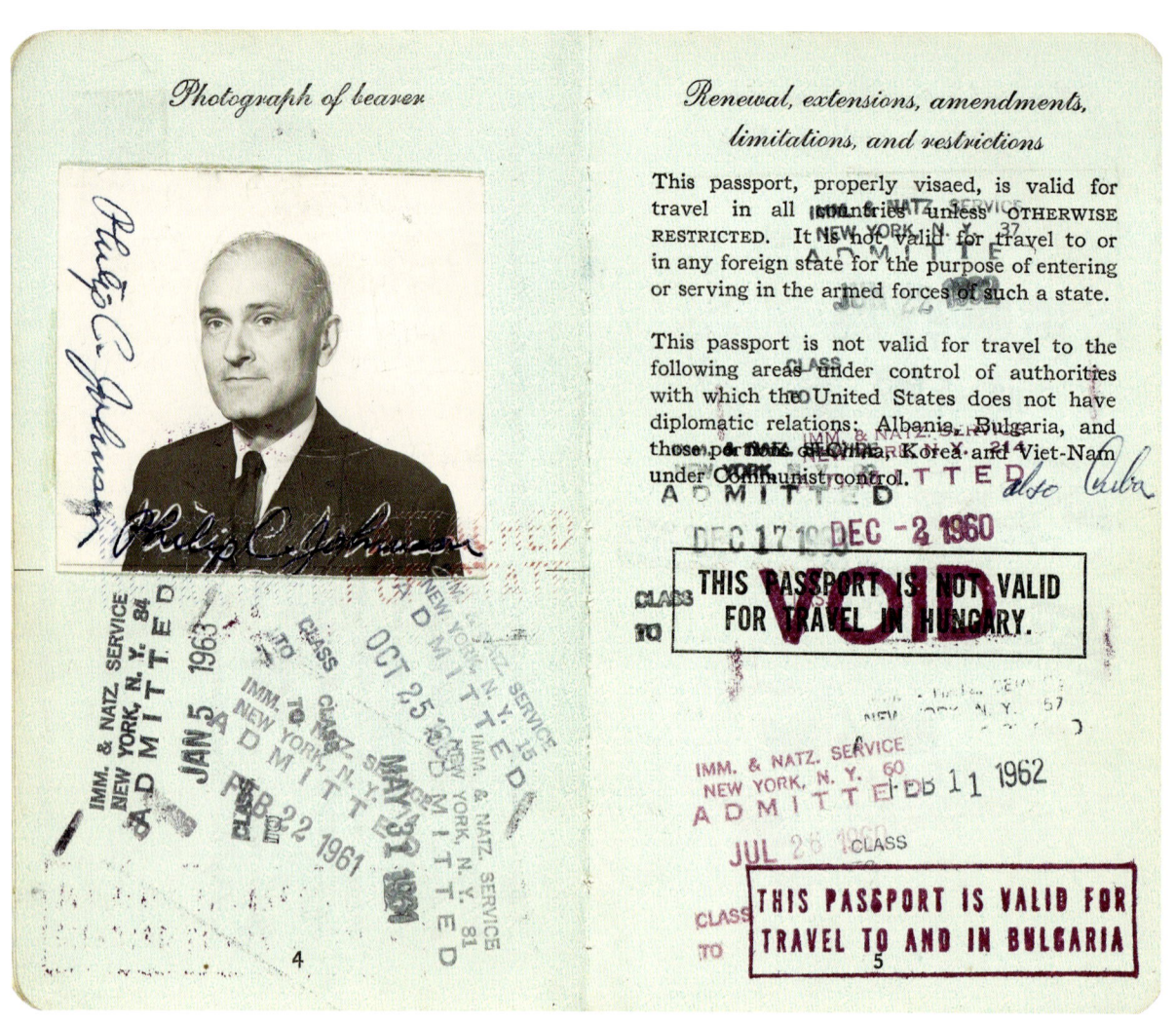

Above and opposite: A collection of Philip's American passports.

Man in motion. Philip rarely let a day lapse between the expiration of one passport and the receipt of another.

Traveler

WARNING—ALTERATION, ADDITION OR MUTILATION OF ENTRIES IS PROHIBITED. ANY UNOFFICIAL CHANGE WILL RENDER THIS PASSPORT INVALID.

NAME
PHILIP CORTELYOU JOHNSON

BIRTH DATE
JULY 8, 1906

BIRTHPLACE
OHIO, U.S.A.

HEIGHT
5 FEET 10 INCHES

HAIR
GREY

EYES
GREY

WIFE
X X X

ISSUE DATE
DEC. 10, 1964

MINORS
X X X

PASSPORT RENEWAL

CANCELED

SIGNATURE OF BEARER

IMPORTANT: UNLESS OTHERWISE LIMITED THIS PASSPORT EXPIRES THREE YEARS FROM ISSUE DATE. IF RENEWED, IT EXPIRES FIVE YEARS FROM ISSUE DATE.

U. S. IMMIGRATION
NEW YORK, N. Y. 313
JUL 3 1967

IMM. & NATZ. SERVICE
NEW YORK, N. Y. 71
ADMITTED
JUL 1 1965

OCT 1 1968

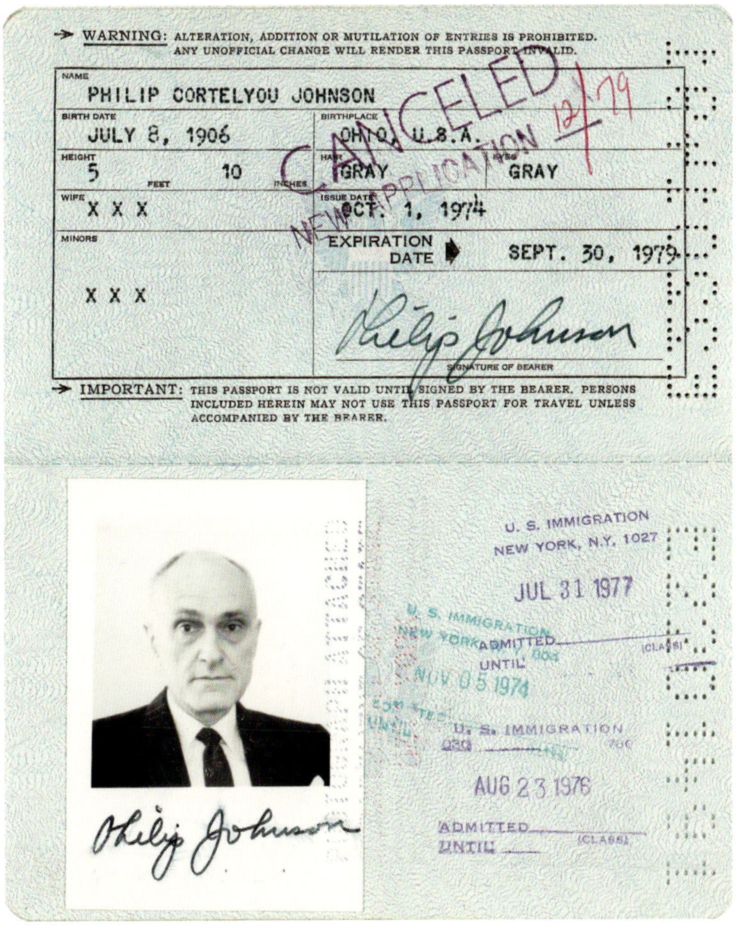
WARNING: ALTERATION, ADDITION OR MUTILATION OF ENTRIES IS PROHIBITED. ANY UNOFFICIAL CHANGE WILL RENDER THIS PASSPORT INVALID.

NAME
PHILIP CORTELYOU JOHNSON

BIRTH DATE
JULY 8, 1906

BIRTHPLACE
OHIO, U.S.A.

HEIGHT
5 FEET 10 INCHES

HAIR
GRAY

EYES
GRAY

WIFE
X X X

ISSUE DATE
OCT. 1, 1974

MINORS
X X X

EXPIRATION DATE
SEPT. 30, 1979

CANCELED
NEW APPLICATION 12/79

SIGNATURE OF BEARER

IMPORTANT: THIS PASSPORT IS NOT VALID UNTIL SIGNED BY THE BEARER. PERSONS INCLUDED HEREIN MAY NOT USE THIS PASSPORT FOR TRAVEL UNLESS ACCOMPANIED BY THE BEARER.

PHOTOGRAPH ATTACHED

U. S. IMMIGRATION
NEW YORK, N.Y. 1027
JUL 31 1977

NOV 05 1974

U. S. IMMIGRATION
AUG 23 1976
ADMITTED
UNTIL
(CLASS)

WARNING: ALTERATION, ADDITION OR MUTILATION OF ENTRIES IS PROHIBITED. ANY UNOFFICIAL CHANGE WILL RENDER THIS PASSPORT INVALID.

NAME—NOM
PHILIP CORTELYOU JOHNSON

SEX—SEXE
M

BIRTHPLACE—LIEU DE NAISSANCE
OHIO, U.S.A.

BIRTH DATE—DATE DE NAISSANCE
JULY 8, 1906

ISSUE DATE—DATE DE DELIVRANCE
DEC. 13, 1979

WIFE/HUSBAND—EPOUSE/EPOUX
X X X

EXPIRES ON—EXPIRE LE
DEC. 12, 1984

MINORS—ENFANTS MINEURS
X X X

CANCELED
NEW APPLICATION 1/30/85

SIGNATURE OF BEARER—SIGNATURE DU TITULAIRE

IMPORTANT: THIS PASSPORT IS NOT VALID UNTIL SIGNED BY THE BEARER. PERSONS INCLUDED HEREIN MAY NOT USE THIS PASSPORT FOR TRAVEL UNLESS ACCOMPANIED BY THE BEARER.

ADMITTED
U. S. CUSTOMS
U. S. IMMIGRATION
JFK AIRPORT
DATE

1887

FROM MASONRY TO

03 Modernist

Modernist

In later years, it would be said of curator and historian Alfred H. Barr, Jr. that he was "the champion of contemporary things before they become respectable."[1] Without question, Barr's embrace of the modern in art and design—and his evangelism on Modernism's behalf—was essential to its subsequent success in America. Philip just happened to be among his earliest converts.

The two had met in 1929 at Wellesley College—where one of Philip's sisters was a student—while Barr was on the faculty there, teaching a course (the first of its kind in the United States) on new European and American painting and sculpture. The rapport between the two men was instantaneous, and within months—following Philip's visit, at Barr's instruction, to Modernist sites in Europe—the young acolyte was hired at the Museum of Modern Art (MoMA) in New York, still being organized by Barr, as its de facto architectural curator. The unofficial role was one into which Philip would have to grow: outside of what he'd gleaned during his travels, he had no formal training in the subject, and his interest rather outstripped his expertise. But his burgeoning friendships with Ludwig Mies van der Rohe, J. J. P. Oud, and others put him at the forefront of the Modern movement, while his boundless energy suited an institution where the atmosphere was "absolutely electric,"[2] as Barr's wife, Marga, described it.

Alongside Barr, the second lodestar of Philip's early Modernist phase was the architecture historian Henry-Russell Hitchcock. A vocal polemicist on behalf of new design, Hitchcock could bring to bear all the knowledge and methodological rigor that Philip so sorely lacked; he was also unkempt, uncouth, even "slightly disgusting," in the view of his fastidious counterpart. Together, however, the two made a surprisingly effective team, and in short order they set about laying the groundwork for a new book that would chronicle the latest developments in Europe. What began as a modest treatise to be published in German became MoMA's, and Philip's, first architecture show—and the watershed moment for Modernism in America.

By the debut of *Modern Architecture: International Exhibition* in February 1934, Philip had already set himself up as a kind of one-stop shop for all things Modern. He had hired Mies and his then collaborator Lilly Reich to design his private apartment in New York; he had cowritten and arranged for the publication of the show's catalog, as well as the no-less-influential book *The International Style* with Hitchcock; he had helped foster two other, smaller architecture exhibitions, one in New York and the other in Cambridge, Massachusetts; and he had succeeded, largely by force of personality, in persuading the wealthy and conservative board members of the just-opened MoMA to embrace architecture as a permanent fixture of its programming. In scarcely a year and a half, Philip had gone from a novice without so much as an undergraduate degree—"silly" and "gossipy," as another of his Modernist mentors, Lincoln Kirstein, had called him—to an influential authority in national and even international design circles.

His transformation was not without its defects. For as much as Philip had contributed logistically to the creation of the seminal book (including, arguably, its title), the writing was mostly Hitchcock's, not his. The creation of the exhibition was very much Philip's work—and its execution had been brought about with the maximum amount of acrimony, both from participants and the excluded, earning Philip and the museum the lasting enmity of such distinguished figures as Frank Lloyd Wright. And then there was the whole premise of both the show and the book: in declaring their work a "style," Philip had taken a diverse group of architects and reduced them to practitioners of a single anodyne aesthetic. In doing so, he had obscured one of the prime factors that had actuated architects as distinct as Le Corbusier and Walter Gropius: their commitment to the pressing social problems facing a continent devastated by World War I. The MoMA show did have a discrete section dedicated to housing; but it was curated separately, by the critic Lewis Mumford, and treated as something of an afterthought. To Philip, political do-goodism was of significantly less interest than the stark surfaces, elemental geometries, and striking asymmetries of the new buildings he liked best.

No matter. The exhibition—along with its idiosyncratic sequel, *Machine Art*—set the boundaries of Modern design in the United States for a generation, and what Philip was then calling "my style" would soon start popping up in cities all across America. He could not yet claim direct responsibility for any major projects: his efforts to attract a commission of his own (from the Rockefellers, most notably) had come to nothing; would-be American commissions for Oud and Mies (on behalf of his parents) were likewise smothered in the cradle. And yet, through Philip's agency, such once-exotic phenomena as the German Bauhaus and French *esprit nouveau* now held real currency among the East Coast elite. This, as much as the sensual appeal of the new architecture, might just be what had drawn him to Modernism in the first place: for a restless spirit, the still-unsung movement represented a cause that he could fight for, and in which his affluence and charisma could make him a leader. What he most wanted, Philip declared in 1931, was to "be influential."[3] Now he was, and he would remain so for the rest of his life.

Installation view of *Modern Architecture: International Exhibition*, Museum of Modern Art, New York, 9 February–23 March 1932.

Interior view of Philip Johnson Apartment by Ludwig Mies van der Rohe and
Lilly Reich, New York, 1930.

Modernism begins at home. Designed by Mies van der Rohe and (mostly) Lilly Reich, Philip's apartment at 424 E. 52nd Street was completed in 1930. Philip intended the space to be a "show apartment,"[4] demonstrating to American audiences the superiority of new European design; quickly, it also became a meeting ground for like-minded culturati—especially once the Barrs moved into the same building.

Modernist

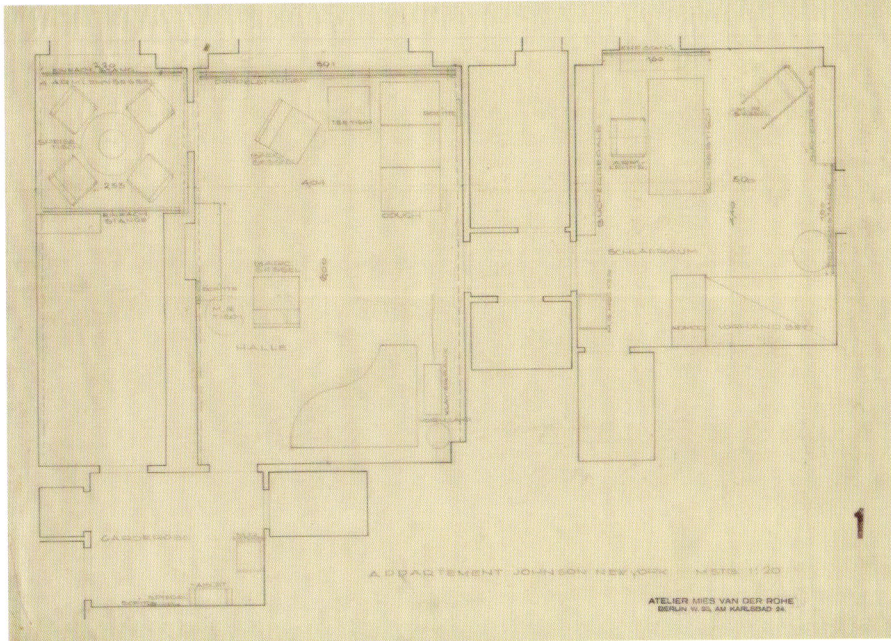

Interior view of Philip Johnson Apartment (top) and floorplan (bottom) by
Ludwig Mies van der Rohe and Lilly Reich, New York, 1930.

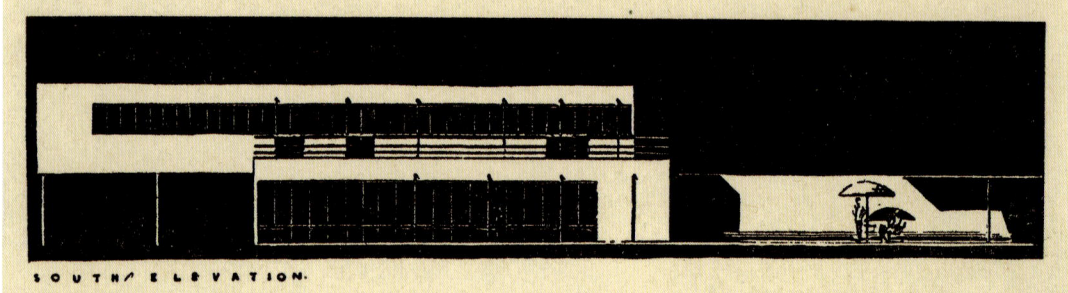

Flyer for *Rejected Architects: Models, Projects, Photos*, New York, 21 April–5 May 1931.

Salon des Refusés. It was 1931, and the work on view at the Architectural League of New York's yearly design show ran heavily toward Art Deco, Moderne, and the jazzy "Modernistic" style that Philip in particular loathed. In response, he and a group of collaborators launched a counterexhibition, *Rejected Architects*, in midtown Manhattan; organized in scarcely a month, it was a small affair featuring mostly lesser-known architects. But it was Philip's first outing as a curator and a prelude of what was to follow.

Cover of *The International Style: Architecture Since 1922* by Henry-Russell Hitchcock and Philip Johnson (New York: W. W. Norton, 1932).

Modern Architecture: International Exhibition. As early as 1929, Hitchcock had expressed the values he thought essential to anything deserving the name Modern architecture: "The simplicity of the massing, the clean flat treatment of the surfaces, and the all but complete avoidance of ornament." Three years later, he and Philip—after extensive research abroad, importunate letters to architects both foreign and domestic, and a successful campaign of persuasion aimed at the board members of MoMA—succeeded in bringing their shared vision to the public, with a six-room, six-week show (not counting a subsequent nationwide tour) that would change the face of American architecture.

Philip to his mother, The Hague, 20 June 1930, describing architectural historian Henry-Russell Hitchcock in detail.

Reception. Never one to shy from publicity, Philip promoted the *Modern Architecture: International Exhibition* show with characteristic zeal. His efforts paid off: 30,000 visitors traipsed through the narrow, windowless rooms of the Heckscher Building, then home to MoMA. If the reception was mixed ("absorbingly vital and important," declared the *New York Times*; "monotonous" and "repetitious," said *ARTnews*), at least it was emphatic.

"I am inclined now to say of the book that it was less remarkable for what it said than for the point in time when we said it."

—Henry-Russell Hitchcock, looking back on *The International Style* three decades later

ARCHITECTURE STYLED "INTERNATIONAL"

Its Principles Set Forth in Models Displayed in a New York Exhibition

On Wednesday there will open at the Gallery of the Museum of Modern Art an exhibition—the most inclusive this country has so far had—of so-called "Modern" or "International" architecture, exemplifying the horizontal principle of construction which Europe has been developing since the World War, while we have continued vertical expression in our skyscrapers. There has been much controversy over this European style. The following article endeavors to place the "International" program in the whole architectural perspective.

By H. I. BROCK

THE architecture usually called "Modern" has reached a stage where it must be treated at least as a present phenomenon. By its votaries it is described as the first definite style since the Gothic to be "created on the basis of a new type of construction." In other words, it is a logical outcome of the substitution of steel cages for supporting walls and of reinforced concrete for the old-fashioned materials of floors and roofs. As such, its advocates proclaim it the only logical form of building for this age. Any other form is an anachronism.

Because steel and concrete are used in building all over the civilized world, the commercial manner of building induced by these materials is internationally distributed. Therefore, the propagandists of that manner have of late undertaken to substitute for the label "Modern" (which obviously means nothing permanently) that of "International."

Much acrimony has been expended, both by architects and lay critics, in discussing the question whether "Modern" or "International" architecture is, or is not, architecture at all in the esthetic sense. On this point, even the people who actually build, or plan to build, in the fashion to which these words are applied as labels, are themselves divided into two camps. In one camp are those—and these do 90 per cent of the building—who call themselves "functionalists" or words to that effect, who build merely for maximum use at minimum cost, and who do not care whether or not what they turn out is "architecture" from the esthetic point of view. If it is, it is an accident. These practical people are not concerned with beauty. And they say so right out.

In the other camp are those who profess to be super-esthetes, who discover in precisely this same new manner of building, based strictly on economy in the use of new materials, a style of architecture more chaste and beautiful, elegant and sincere, than the world has ever known. Naturally, it is from this second camp that the articulate promoters of the cause proceed. Between what the builders have structurally produced and what the esthetes have proclaimed, the world has been considerably impressed—and more than a little puzzled.

* * *

AS it happens, we in America are strong conservatives in architecture as in other fields. We are, in spite of the prodigious crop of our steel-cage skyscrapers, in spite of having produced decades ago Frank Lloyd Wright, who is an acknowledged prophet of the new school, though he refuses to submit to the "rigid discipline" of the sacrosanct style to which his disciples have committed their fortunes. Such conservatives are we, indeed, that we have extant in the year 1932 almost nothing in the way of the architecture which alone is acceptably "Modern" to the "Modernists."

This architecture loftily rejects the verticality which has been the pride of our tower builders. It scouts the great tower builders and flouts the tall towers as mighty spurious imitations of what they are not. It has grown up in Europe—in France, Holland and Germany, principally—since the war. Observe that what the Swedes have done is as clearly out of the picture as our towers. The hierarchs of the movement are the French-Swiss, Le Corbusier, arch-propagandist, the Germans Gropius and Mies van der Rohe, and the Hollander Oud.

Examples of the thing they do (and preach the gospel of) exist in European countries as remote from the seat of authority and inspiration as England, Spain and Czechoslovakia. Examples may also be found in Brazil and Japan—even on our Pacific Coast.

But New York has nothing nearer the real thing than Raymond Hood's blue-green McGraw-Hill building, which, though a skyscraper, emphasizes the horizontals. Notoriously Hood will try anything in the way of a building—once. Besides, he had just the year before gone the limit of the vertical in The Daily News Building, with its effect of a coop of giant palings or palisades.

Hence the value of assembling here in this city models and plans of all the "Moderns" who are recognized as authentically such by the insiders in the movement. Those who have not been able to get to Europe to see the new buildings—or who, getting to Europe in spite of the depression, have found the old place full of things more interesting, tempting or important and have not taken time off to look at the new buildings—all those may this week go to the Museum of Modern Art in Fifth Avenue, just a block from the plaza of the Grand Army, and see at least the models and the pictures and the plans.

After six weeks in New York the exhibition is advertised to go on a three-year tour of the country, so that our principal cities, North, South, East and West—all the way to Los Angeles—may have a chance to see what (we are told) we are coming to in the way of the new housing accommodations.

In the group are factories, department stores, schools, town and country houses, and wholesale housing developments on a great scale — including one partly executed in Cassel in Germany and one projected for the recently devastated area between Chrystie and Forsyth Streets on the lower east side of Manhattan. Each of these last projects, by the way, is represented by an elaborate model and each is doubly interesting—first, as a piece of ingenious machinery and second, as an index to what the standardized tenant of the future (the fellow who has to pay minimum rent) is expected "internationally" to be like. In New York, as in Germany, he is expected to be tame and neat. In Germany he has three times as much space to be tame and neat in. Even churches and gasoline service stations are included in the show. Every item is done in the new ferro-concrete manner and each item is presented as an authentic example of that authentic manner. This is true even where the architects have professed to be no more than hard-boiled executants of a complex engineering job.

* * *

HOOD is included in the group—not with the McGraw-Hill Building, but with an experiment in spaced skyscrapers for garden suburbs (a sort of variant on the Radio City formula) with which he has been playing for some time. Wright also is included. But (it is explained) he really counts only as the greatest and most incorrigible of the individualists whose experiments opened the way for a style professing to be thoroughly integral and disciplined. Discipline is a watchword of this school, whereas Wright is a rebel to all discipline. Howe and Lescaze are responsible for the very interesting Chrystie and Forsyth Streets wholesale housing plan. Otto Haesler for the Cassel plan.

The material—mostly from Europe—has been assembled by Philip Johnson of Cleveland, after a careful survey of the actual buildings in situ in the various countries where they have been built. The photographs and plans tell something. But "Modern" architecture has been so touted that a great many of the photographs can hardly be new to magazine and newspaper readers in this country. Most can be learned from the models. Indeed, models in three dimensions are almost indispensable elements of such a show. "Modern" or "International" architecture, being the architecture of the functioning machine, can hardly be judged from

(Continued on Page 22)

New Architecture for Commerce—The Façade of a German Department Store. — Erich Mendelsohn, Architect.

New Architecture for Dwelling—A Steel Construction House in Los Angeles. — Richard J. Neutra, Architect. Luckhaus Photo.

"Architecture Styled 'International'" by H. I. Brock, *New York Times*, 7 February 1932. The article reports on the *Modern Architecture: International Exhibition*, Museum of Modern Art, New York, 10 February–23 March 1932. It describes Modern architecture as the first definite style since the Gothic to be "created on the basis of a new type of construction."

Cover of catalog for *Modern Architecture: International Exhibition*, Museum of Modern Art, New York, 10 February–23 March 1932. It features the garden elevation of the Tugendhat House.

The International Style. Representing sixteen countries from as far afield as Finland and Japan, the fifty-plus architects featured in the show were a mixed bunch, both aesthetically and ideologically. But in large measure, their differences were effectively steamrolled by the curators: as Philip and Hitchcock put it in the show's catalog, the designers all shared the basic principles of "modern engineering [and] modern provision for function," resulting in a "general convergence" toward a single unerring aesthetic. From Le Corbusier to J. J. P. Oud to Walter Gropius, all were lumped together, whether they liked it or not. (Many didn't.)

Images of models from *Modern Architecture: International Exhibition*,
Museum of Modern Art, New York, 10 February–23 March 1932.

Installation view, *Modern Architecture: International Exhibition*,
Museum of Modern Art, New York, 10 February–23 March 1932.

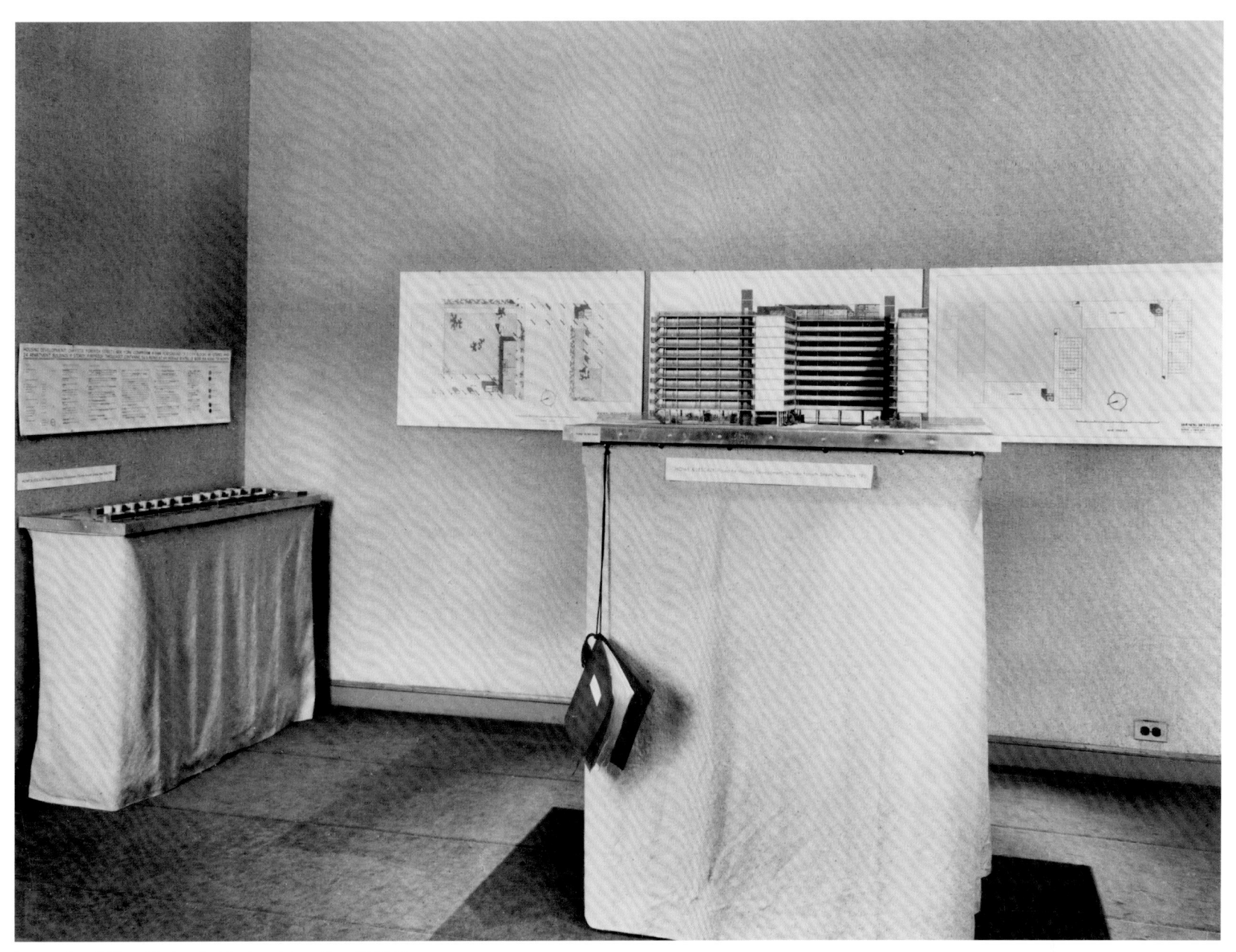

Image of model from *Modern Architecture: International Exhibition*,
Museum of Modern Art, New York, 10 February–23 March 1932.

Installation view, *Modern Architecture: International Exhibition*,
Museum of Modern Art, New York, 10 February–23 March 1932.

Anatomy of a show. To date, save for his outing with the *Rejected Architects*, Philip had little or no experience mounting a full-on exhibition about Modern design. On the other hand, no one else had any either. "The New York boys," as Wright dubbed Philip and Hitchcock, simply made it up as they went along: entrusting the (rather marginalized) section on social housing to Mumford, cribbing much of the show design from Mies and Reich, installing the photos and models at the last possible instant before the February 10 opening, they managed to present a surprisingly cogent image of a "style" that hadn't really existed until they willed it into being. Along the way, they alienated everyone from Gropius (they relegated the Bauhaus to an anteroom) to Wright himself, who mocked them as an "amateur" and a "salesman" and repeatedly threatened to pull out of the whole endeavor.

Modernist

Image of model from *Modern Architecture: International Exhibition*,
Museum of Modern Art, New York, 10 February–23 March 1932.

Master Copy

November 27, 1931.

Museum of Modern Art
Architectural Exhibition

FOR RELEASE ....

The President and Trustees of the Museum of Modern Art today extended a formal invitation to the members of President Hoover's Conference on Home Ownership and Home Building in Washington, D.C., to attend the opening at the Museum of an Exhibition of Modern Architecture on Wednesday, February 10, 1932. The Exhibition will continue at the Museum's quarters at 730 Fifth Avenue for six weeks.

In extending the invitation, Stephen C. Clark, said: "It is the sincere belief of the Museum that the Exhibition of Modern Architecture will exert a most beneficial influence on architecture and building in the United States and particularly in the field of multiple dwelling developments both urban and suburban."

The Exhibition will show by means of models by American and European architects and by enlarged photographs of their executed work the latest and most modern developments in architecture throughout the world. Almost all the models have been designed and constructed especially for the Exhibition which, under the direction of Philip Johnson of Cleveland, has been in preparation since December, 1930. The Exhibition, after its closing in New York, will make a three year tour of the most important cities in the United States. In Los Angeles it will open coincident with the Olympiade on July 15.

2.

There will be two main divisions of the Exhibition, the second of which has, in the opinion of the Director, particular significance for those attending the Washington conference. This section is devoted to the most recent solution of multiple dwelling problems by leading architects of the world. Howe & Lescaze of New York have designed a model showing their plans for utilization of the Chrystie-Forsyte Development in the Lower East Side just above Manhattan Bridge. Raymond Hood's model illustrates graphically a new scheme of suburban apartment-skyscrapers which preserve the natural beauty of the countryside by vertical arrangement of the houses instead of complete horizontal coverage of the original site. Otto Haesler, leading community planner of Germany, will be represented by a model of a "Siedlung" - a project for minimum wage earners already under construction at Cassel in Germany.

Housing of minimum wage earners is a subject claiming the attention of the nation. Private enterprise, under existing construction methods, realizes a return of but 2% on capital invested. The State and City governments are faced with the problem of subsidizing this type of building. The model solutions take into account lower construction costs while maintaining a high standard of living conditions.

Alfred Barr, Director of the Museum, states one of the purposes of the Exhibition: "Never in this country or abroad has an International Exhibition of this nature been held. Obviously, it is by far the best way of presenting effectively to the public every aspect of the new movement.

This page and opposite: Draft press release for *Modern Architecture: International Exhibition*. The press release, dated 27 November 1931, invites the members of President Hoover's Conference on Home Ownership and Home Building to attend the exhibition and describes its content.

3.

The hope of developing really intelligent criticism and discussion depends on furnishing the public a knowledge of contemporary accomplishments in the field. Our present limited vision in this respect is caused by the very lack of those examples which the Exhibition will supply. The stimulation and direction which an exhibition of this type can give to contemporary architectural thought and practice is incalculable. It is desirable that we view and ponder the new mode of building which fits so decidedly into our methods of standardized construction, our economics and our life."

The Museum of Modern Art was founded in the summer of 1929 by a group of American art patrons, principally New Yorkers, but including trustees from Boston, Chicago and Washington. The present Trustees are:

    A. Conger Goodyear, President
    Mrs. John D. Rockefeller, Jr., Treasurer
    Samuel A. Lewisohn, Secretary
    William T. Aldrich,
    James W. Barney,
    Frederick C. Bartlett,
    Cornelius N. Bliss
    Stephen C. Clark,
    Mrs. W. Murray Crane,
    Frank Crowninshield,
    ~~Chester Dale~~,
    Duncan Phillips,
    Mrs. Rainey Rogers,

4.

    Mrs. Charles C. Rumsey,
    ~~Arthur Sachs,~~
    Paul J. Sachs,
    John T. Spaulding,
    Mrs. Cornelius J. Sullivan,
    John Hay Whitney.

They believed that the art of our time was not receiving adequate presentation in existing institutions. Since the fall of the same year exhibitions have been regularly held at the Museum's quarters. During the two years of its services approximately 315,000 people have visited the galleries, almost 1/4 the attendance at the Metropolitan Museum during the same period.

The Museum has closely followed the international activity in architecture and has long felt the need for a comprehensive exhibition of modern architecture. The present Committee of the Exhibition includes:

    Stephen C. Clark, Chairman
    Samuel A. Lewisohn, Treasurer
    Homer H. Johnson,
    W. W Norton,
    Dr. G. F. Reber,
    Alfred H. Barr, Jr.
    Philip Johnson.

The present exhibition of works by Henri Matisse the famous Dutch Painter closes on Sunday, Nov. 6.

> THE MUSEUM OF MODERN ART
> 11 WEST 53RD STREET, NEW YORK
> TELEPHONE CIRCLE 7-7471
>
> For Immediate Release.
>
> "Chicago and not New York is the birthplace of the skyscraper", declares Philip Johnson, Director of the Department of Architecture of the Museum of Modern Art, as announcement was made today of the next exhibition, "Early Modern Architecture: Chicago 1870-1910, to open to the public at the Museum of Modern Art, 11 West 53d Street on Wednesday, January 18. Few people realize that on the ashes of the Chicago fire of 1871 there was built the only architecture that can truly be called American." The Museum will present for the first time an exhibition of this architrcture.
>
> "The great names in the building of the frontier city, "Mr. Johnson states, "were three architects, H.H.Richardson, Louis Sullivan and Frank Lloyd Wright, who with their followers made the end of the nineteenth century the greatest epoch in the architectural development of our country. They created a native product not indebted to English or continental precedent. To these men goes the credit of bridging the gap between the Crystal Palace of steel and glass in London in 1851 and the skyscraper of today. They were the first to take advantage of the shift from masonry to cast iron and from cast iron to steel. This independent American architecture finally succumbed to the wave of classical revivalism which the World's Fair first brought to Chicago in 1893."
>
> The Museum's exhibition will therefore be the first record of a great architecture which is vanishing rapidly under the sledgehammer of the housewrecker.
>
> Mr. Johnson who also directed the Exhibition of Modern Architecture, held at the Museum of Modern Art in February and March 1932, and now on tour throughout the country, spent the summer in the middle West with Professor Henry Russell Hitchcock of Wesleyan University collecting information from the source and photographing important buildings still standing.
>
> FOR INFORMATION AFTER MUSEUM HOURS :
> TELEPHONE : A. R. BLACKBURN, JR. REGENT 4-5758 OR HELEN F. McMILLIN : CIRCLE 7-5434

> The Exhibition "Early Modern Architecture: Chicago 1870-1910 "will follow the Exhibition of "The Art of the Common Man in America", now on view at the Muséum of Modern Art and continuing to January 14. The Exhibition of American Painting and Sculpture, which includes the famous painting "Portrait of the Artist's Mother" by James McNeil Whistler, will remain on view on the first three floors of the Museum until January 29.

Press release for *Early Modern Architecture: Chicago 1870–1910*, Museum of Modern Art, New York, 18 January–23 February 1933.

Looking back. For their second act, Philip and Hitchcock took on nineteenth- and early-twentieth-century Chicago and its contributions to Modernist architecture. A less ambitious show than what had come before (and what would follow), it nonetheless marked an important precedent for Philip: his interest in the future of architecture would always be rooted in its past.

Modernist

74

FROM MASONRY TO STEEL

STAGES IN THE EVOLUTION OF THE SKYSCRAPER: PHILIP JOHNSON of the Museum of Modern Art, New York, Displaying Models Which Show the Development of Modern Architecture From the Low, Heavy Dark Masonry Building to the Light, Airy Steel Tower of Today.

Philip with models demonstrating the evolution of the skyscraper from masonry to steel. These models were shown at *Early Modern Architecture: Chicago 1870–1910*, Museum of Modern Art, New York, 18 January–23 February 1933.

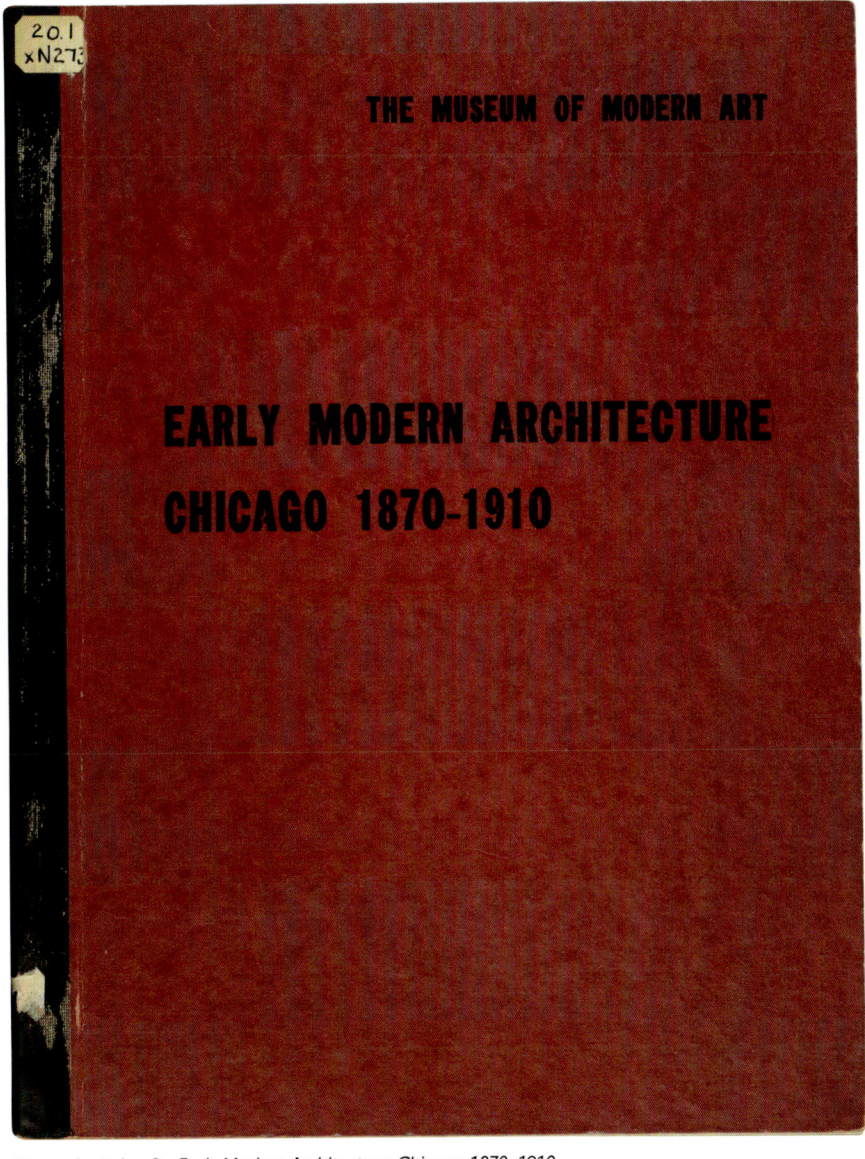

THE MUSEUM OF MODERN ART

EARLY MODERN ARCHITECTURE
CHICAGO 1870-1910

Cover of catalog for *Early Modern Architecture: Chicago 1870–1910*.

75

A map of Harlem Prohibition speakeasies and nightclubs drawn by E. Simms Campbell. It was created for the first issue of *Manhattan* magazine, 1932, and republished nine months later in *Esquire*.

Uptown nights. In the 1920s and 1930s, fashionable New Yorkers looking for an after-hours thrill would drive north by way of Central Park, arriving in the bustling nightlife district of Central Harlem. On one such evening, in one of the many clubs where black performers entertained an almost exclusively white clientele, Philip met Jimmie Daniels, a singer and actor who would go on to a Zelig-like career on the international stage. The relationship lasted about a year; Philip, in his words, "was naughty," alternately pushing Daniels away and demanding his attention. In some sense, the relationship may have been little more than an expression of their shared Modernist sensibilities—an avant-garde act, calculated to *épater les bourgeois*. Still, it was serious enough that Philip would always remember Daniels as "the first Mrs. Johnson."

Modernist

Top: Photographs of Jimmie Daniels and James Cross from an album by British photographer Barbara Ker-Seymer, 1944. James "Stumpy" Cross was part of the dance and comedy duo Stump and Stumpy. Bottom: George Platt Lynes, *Jimmie Daniels, Singer at Le Ruban Bleu*, 1933.

Cover of catalog for *Objects: 1900 and Today*, Museum of Modern Art, New York, 10–25 April 1933.

First page of the exhibition catalog for *Objects: 1900 and Today*. Philip writes, "This exhibition of decorative and useful objects is arranged with the purpose of contrasting the design … of two modern periods. One is not necessarily better than the other."

Curator. Now firmly established in his role at MoMA, Philip undertook a sequence of influential exhibitions, continuing to proselytize on behalf of the Modern movement. *Objects: 1900 and Today*, *The Work of Young Architects of the Middle West*, and *Machine Art* not only made a strong case for new design, but also cemented design as a permanent fixture of MoMA's curriculum. As with the *Modern Architecture: International Exhibition* show, they were inspired improvisations (objects included items pilfered from Philip's mother's house), and they drew ire from critics who, as one reporter wrote, saw the museum "drifting … in the direction of the crafts." But they also earned praise for their creator: the *New York Sun* called Philip "our best showman," inaugurating his reputation as America's premier architectural emcee.

Modernist

Installation view, *Objects: 1900 and Today*, Museum of Modern Art,
New York, 10–25 April 1933.

Installation view, *Objects: 1900 and Today*, Museum of Modern Art,
New York, 10–25 April 1933.

Modernist

Installation views, *Objects: 1900 and Today*, Museum of Modern Art,
New York, 10–25 April 1933.

81

THE MUSEUM OF MODERN ART
1 WEST 53RD STREET, NEW YORK
TELEPHONE: CIRCLE 7-7470

FOR RELEASE Thursday, March 1, 1934.

Walls are moving, ceilings dropping, lights changing as a day-and-night shift of workmen transforms the Museum of Modern Art, 11 West 53 Street into a completely new modern background for the Exhibition of Machine Art, which opens Wednesday, March 7. For the first time, the Museum is giving as much importance to the installation as to the Exhibition itself. The background against which the objects will be displayed is not general but specific and has been designed to concentrate maximum attention on each object individually, yet to give a certain coherence to a display of more than a thousand items. In this way the diffusion of interest so confusing in the usual museum display will be avoided. As the installation has been planned from the point of view of the observer, the Museum is keenly interested in the reaction of the public.

False ceilings are being constructed of muslin, through which overhead lighting will diffuse evenly. The entire floor plan of the Museum and the surfaces of the walls are being changed by movable screens, panels, and spur walls of aluminum, stainless steel, and micarta, and by coverings of oilcloth, natural Belgian linen, and canvas painted pastel blue, pink and gray. Stands and display tables are being built of aromatic cedar and Circassian walnut, shelves of black and white Carrara glass.

Three methods of display will be employed: isolation--a water faucet, for example, will be exhibited like a Greek statue on a pedestal; grouping--the massing of series of objects such as saucepans, water glasses and electric light bulbs; and variation--a different type of stand, pedestal, table and background for each object or series of objects.

Springs, gears, cables, chemical capsules, carpet sweepers, and kitchen cabinets are among the useful objects that will be shown. They have been selected for the Exhibition not on the basis of their usefulness but for their beauty of form, finish and material. On the third floor will be a "jewel room" where shining precision instruments, sections of wire, watch springs, and tiny ball bearings will be displayed on black velvet.

2.

Mr. Philip Johnson, Chairman of the Architectural Department of the Museum, is directing the Exhibition of Machine Art. He is responsible for the creation of the installation, all of which is being built by the Museum's own workmen. Mr. Johnson is widely known for his original ideas in museum display. His installations of previous exhibitions, notably "Objects: 1900 and Today" held at the Museum of Modern Art in the Spring of 1933 and "Modern Architecture" in 1932, have had influence not only in the museum field but in commercial display as well.

The Museum will be closed to the public until the opening of the Exhibition of Machine Art on March 7, which will continue until April 16.

Press release for *Machine Art*, Museum of Modern Art, New York, 6 March–30 April 1934. It is dated 1 March 1934.

Cover of catalog for *Machine Art*, Museum of Modern Art, New York, 6 March–30 April 1934. The cover art was designed by Josef Albers.

Bearing spring, American Steel & Wire Co., Subsidiary United States Steel Corp. (left) and a large boat propeller, Sullivan Shipyards, Inc. (right), displayed at *Machine Art*, Museum of Modern Art, New York, 6 March–30 April 1934.

"The show was a great *succès de scandale*. I mean, why would you want to show pots and pans?"

—Philip on the *Machine Art* exhibition

Modernist

Installation views, *Machine Art*, Museum of Modern Art, New York,
6 March–30 April 1934.

85

Hydrometer jars, Eimer & Amend, displayed at *Machine Art*, Museum of Modern Art, New York, 6 March–30 April 1934.

Glass vase designed by P. T. Frankl and manufactured by the Frankl Galleries, New York (right) and a section of copper tubing manufactured by the Chase Brass & Copper Co., Waterbury, Connecticut (left), displayed at *Machine Art*, Museum of Modern Art, New York, 6 March–30 April 1934.

Modernist

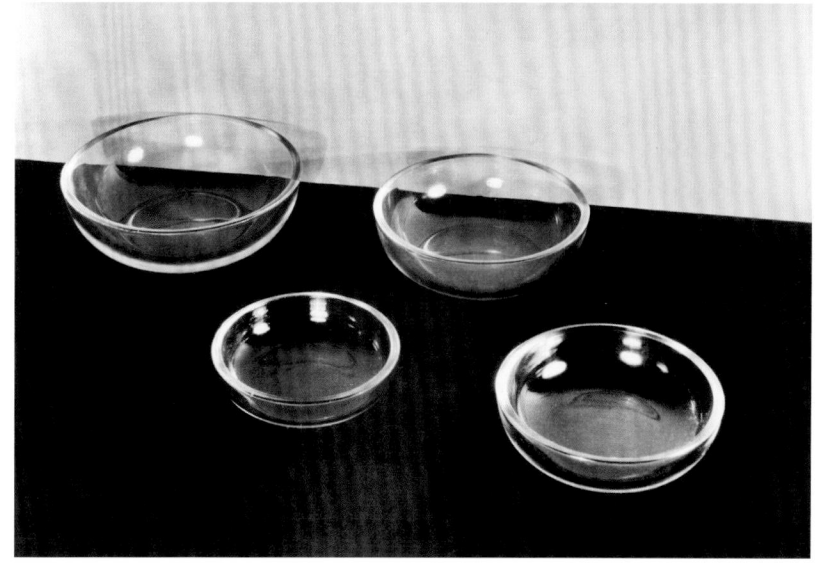

Clockwise from top left: Bomb humidor, Distillers Products Corp.; crusader hotel sauce pots, Lalance & Grosjean Mfg. Co.; ash tray set, Fostoria Glass Co.; and silver ice (for chilling drinks), lent by Saks Fifth Avenue, displayed at *Machine Art*, Museum of Modern Art, New York, 6 March–30 April 1934.

"The quality of instruction, however, remained high both in the official academies and the one-man studios. It is in the field of education that the United States has most profited architecturally from the European war. Expatriates returned and émigrés came to teach. Walter Gropius and Marcel Breuer of the Bauhaus teach at Harvard. Moholy-Nagy has started a new Bauhaus in Chicago. Mies van der Rohe is the Director of Architecture at the Illinois Institute of Technology. Erich Mendelsohn of Palestine and Serge Chermayeff of London are now active here."

—Philip on education

ARCHITECTURE in 1941
by Philip C. Johnson

In the year of war 1941 the art of architecture took on, as was inevitable, a more public character. By the end of the year indeed it was obvious that private building for private purposes was nearly at an end. The period of skyscrapers, suburban residences, country clubs and even churches, museums and schools was, temporarily at least, over. The energy of architects all over the country was absorbed more and more by public commissions.

Official Architecture

Among the public works of the year there were some peacetime buildings still being built. The most anachronistic were the Mellon Gallery in Washington and the Jefferson Memorial in the same city. The minds of the country were on less monumental problems and on less classical and eclectic design. Both buildings looked old fashioned even before they were open to the public. Also in Washington stands the new National Airport which belongs, with its out of scale reminiscences of Mt. Vernon, and with much less justification, also in the category of old fashioned new buildings.

New York, our second capital city, fared better. Brilliant Commissioner Robert Moses continued his road building, making art out of traffic lanes. Most of his parkways and bridges are good architecture; the East River Drive winding in and out and up and down, crossed by light concrete footways, is very good architecture. Even the New York Asphalt Plant which Mr. Moses had to move away from the river front for his Drive is now a work of art. Its startling parabola is a welcome relief among New York's endless rows of walk ups.

Except for New York, however, municipal architecture during the year was meagre. The Federal Agencies did better. Most memorable will be the work of The Tennessee Valley Authority under the general architectural supervision of Roland Wank. Massive in scale and straightforward in detail, the dams, dynamo rooms and control houses of the Tennessee Valley are much more nearly symbolic of our times than the correct dullness of official Washington.

Socially perhaps even more important is the work of the San Francisco office of the Farm Security Administration. Besides making a dent in the migrant labor problem of the far west, young architect Vernon De Mars has made a dent in the central problem of architecture-town planning. The FSA camps at Chandler, Arizona; Woodville, California; and Granger, Washington, though they owe something in design to the great Swiss pioneer of contemporary architecture, Le Corbusier, are very clean, very neat, and very American.

Housing.

The big new step in architecture for 1941 was public housing. Never before in our country have we seen governmental planning and architectural creativeness combined in the building of whole communities. Heretofore, our housing developments have been built speculatively, crowdedly, hit-or-miss, and, more often than not, entirely without benefit of architect. In 1941 the combination of necessity and leadership put the United States far in advance of the whole housing world. The necessity was the dislocation caused by defense requirements. Workers were suddenly needed where none had been needed before. The leadership came from the Federal Works Agency, especially from Defense Housing Chief, Clarke Foreman. The result is a whole series of planned communities. They are discouragingly inadequate to the problem, but they are a beginning.

Architecturally the most important is the New Kensington, Pa. project designed by two Harvard professors, Walter Gropius and Marcel Breuer. Here a new pattern of city planning takes the place both of the dull grid-iron system of the nineteenth century, and of the romantic scattered house type of the "suburban" period. The houses are connected in rows of four to eight units and these rows are grouped, carefully following a steeply sloping site, in a free asymmetrical arrangement. The project will undoubtedly have a great influence on future housing. The largest project of the year was architect William Wurster's 1600 units at Vallejo, California. Site prefabrication cut costs and proved the desirability of large scale undertaking in the field of housing.

Among the projects having free standing single houses, Hugh Stubbins of Cambridge did the most interesting work. The best organized office for handling big work was probably George Howe's in Philadelphia. The most distinguished name among housing architects of the year was that of America's foremost architect, Frank Lloyd Wright, whose project at Pittsfield, Massachusetts had not been completed at the end of the year.

1941 may be known in our architectural history as the year when community planning started in the United States—the year when the field of activity of the architect widened from the single building to congeries of buildings.

Prefabrication

With defense housing rose the demand for prefabricated houses; that is the adaptation to housing of the mass production methods of such industries as the automotive. It was only partially answered in 1941. Engineer-architect Buckminster Fuller produced a house made by a corncrib manufacturer. The Pierce Foundation for the Glenn Martin Plant near Baltimore built many houses using an insulating sandwich. The Pierce house is however not fully prefabricated. Others proposed plywood panel construction and one man built an experimental house near Washington of "gunite" concrete sprayed onto a balloon held framework of reinforcing rods. The only attempt at erecting a test community of prefabricated houses was a Government project at River Head, Maryland. It was not a success.

Design

The trend in design during the year continued the direction of the past decade toward what used to be called "modern". Holabird and Root of Chicago in their work

Excerpts from Philip's unpublished manuscript, *Architecture in 1941*, 1942. It reveals Philip's distaste for John Russell Pope's Neo-Classical style in Washington, D.C. and his preference for New York's municipal architecture.

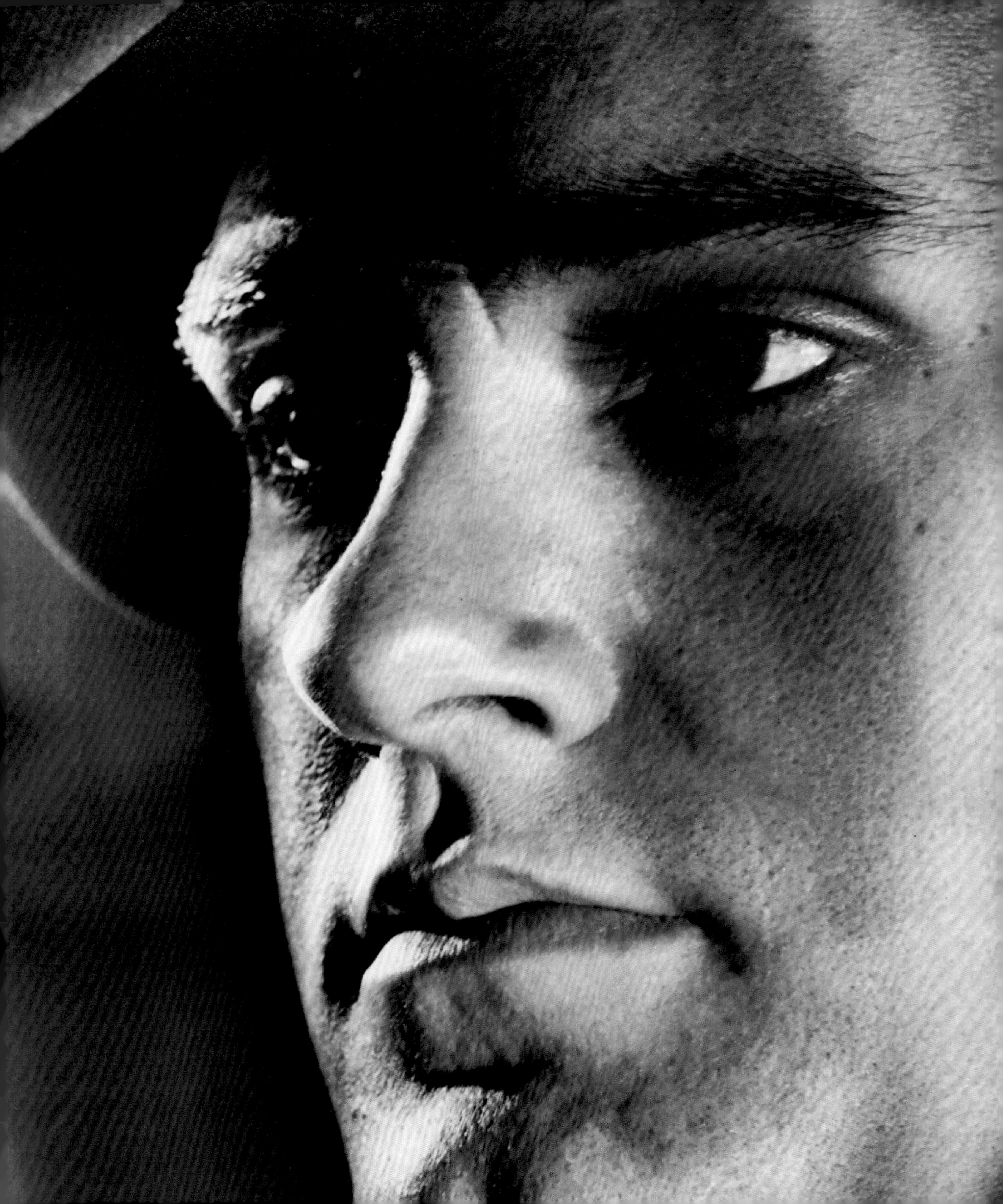

04 Politician

Politician

"You simply could not fail to be caught up in the excitement of it, by the marching songs, by the crescendo and climax of the whole thing, as Hitler came on last to harangue the crowd," Philip said in 1932, in Nuremberg, of the new and terrible order arising in Germany. The bizarre interlude of Philip's political period in the 1930s has been among the most hotly debated episodes in the history of American architecture. In some ways, it still seems inexplicable: how could such a cultivated, intelligent man, with so many friends who were either Jewish or socialists or both, possibly embrace fascism? There is no definitive answer, though the particular vices and virtues that marked Philip's personality and architecture—his indifference to social concerns, his love of show and grand spectacle—all came into play. In a way, the whole business was absurd, an errant bit of dilettantism. It was also unpardonable, and it was to remain a black mark on his record that time would never quite efface.

When did it start? As early as 1927, while in Heidelberg, Germany, Philip had been in close proximity to the growing National Socialist movement, which staged the first of its rallies that summer in Nuremberg. His Germanophilia was already well in place by that point—an attraction that went far beyond the intellectual. (As he once said of the language, "I learned it the best way: the horizontal method.") In addition, there was the philosophical strain that had worked its way into Philip's thinking during his college years, the whole Nietzschean apparatus of individuality and greatness, all of it so appetizing to a young man possessed at once by lofty aspirations and dispiriting doubts as to his own place in the world. Commonplace morality, Nietzsche had written in *Beyond Good and Evil* (1886), stunts humankind, rendering a man "a herd animal, something eager to please, sickly and mediocre." The alternative was a self-glorifying will to power, and this Hitler turned into a practical political program.

Though it grossly traduced Nietzsche (who was never an anti-Semite), Nazism arrived at precisely the right moment for Philip. The reception of the Museum of Modern Art (MoMA) shows, though emphatic, had not yet afforded him the personal exultation he had sought: he was still constrained in his curatorial role by the Rockefellers and their ilk, while his fledgling design career had been limited to apartment interiors for himself, his sister, and his art-collector friend Edward Warburg. With waning enthusiasm for being an impresario, and realizing that he might "never be a Mies or a Le Corbusier or a Wright,"[1] he proffered his resignation to the MoMA board just a few weeks before the new year of 1935.

Over the next four years, the Johnsonian trick of trying on multiple personae would kick into overdrive, only now with a political theme. First there was the organizational gambit: along with his Harvard roommate and former MoMA assistant Alan Blackburn, Philip announced the formation of the National Party, a sort of fascism lite organization—replete with symbol and dark-colored shirts—in which the pair tried to enlist the support of Louisiana's populist governor, Huey Long. When Long proved unamenable, the two moved on—first to the Johnson homestead at New London, Ohio, where Philip flirted with a candidacy for public office, and then to Detroit, Michigan, where they presented their services to the virulently anti-Semitic radio priest Charles Edward Coughlin, whose movement soon sputtered. They tried radio speechifying, hectoring listeners about the twin perils of communists and capitalists "organized to sell out America," before at last parting ways—at which point Philip changed course again, looking to publishing (either by buying an existing organ or starting his own), hosting political salons (primarily at his own New York home, some of them held even before his departure from MoMA), and most importantly journalism—Philip would file multiple approving dispatches about the new Germany and even tour the Continent on the outbreak of war.

His friends, particularly Alfred H. Barr, Jr., looked on in horror; his family, especially Theodate, disapproved of what she termed the "riffraff" with which her prodigal brother was associating himself. Yet Philip steamed ahead undaunted—right up to the very moment when his activities would have categorized him as an unqualified traitor. Then, just as abruptly as he had taken it up, he dropped politics and walked back into the architecture world, as though nothing had happened.

Or almost nothing. What Franz Schulze, his first biographer, termed Philip's "inglorious detour"[2] led to a wartime investigation that might have sent Philip to prison. As the decades rolled by, his most ardent detractors in the media would dredge up the episode, and even today it casts a long shadow over his reputation. Many mysteries remain unresolved—was Philip ever in the formal employ of the German government? Did he have a closer relationship with any high-ranking Nazis than is currently known? But perhaps the more pressing questions are the ones that today's architects, and the architectural public, must pose themselves: how should we interpret the legacy of Philip in view of his political transgressions? And could a designer in our time make the same mistake again?

Sports Youth during the Nazi Party Congress in Nuremberg, Germany, 1938.

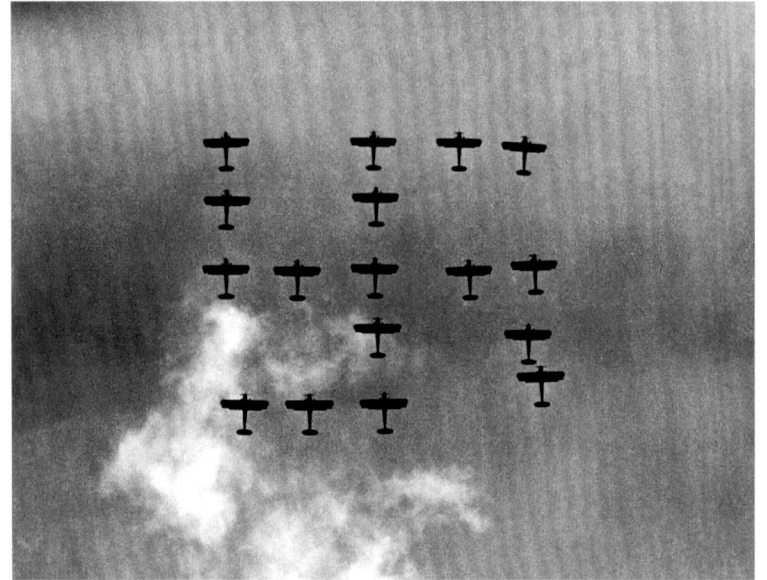

Nuremberg Rally, September 1937. Lighting was used to dramatic effect during these annual late-night rallies—designed by Albert Speer.

Top: Planes in swastika formation at the eleventh Nuremberg Rally, 5 September 1937. Bottom: The German Luftwaffe bombs Warsaw, Poland, 1939.

Spectacle of the Will. "I just felt excitement," Philip recalled, referring to the outbreak of the war. Nazi rhetoric and bloodlust compelled him, it seemed, as much out of lurid curiosity as genuine political belief; Germany was where the action was, and that was where Philip was determined to be. Cultivating (and being cultivated by) a coterie of Nazi sympathizers, like the American art critic Helen Appleton Read, Philip enjoyed a view of fascism from the top, a privileged vantage point from which its unseemlier aspects were obscured behind a patrician veneer and the visual theatrics of Joseph Goebbels's propaganda machine. Philip's growing interest did not go unnoticed, either by the Nazis or by the American government: his extensive FBI file would note that during his sojourns in the Third Reich—of which there were several—"the Germans were quite solicitous about his welfare."

Politician

Top: Nuremberg Rally, September 1938. Bottom: Swastikas hanging in the streets of Munich, c. 1935.

Architecture in the Third Reich

Philip Johnson

IT WOULD be false to speak of the architectural situation in national socialist Germany. The new state is faced with such tremendous problems of re-organization that a program of art and architecture has not been worked out. Only a few points are certain. First *Die Neue Sachlichkeit* is over. Houses that look like hospitals and factories are taboo. But also the row houses which have become almost the distinguishing feature of German cities are doomed. They all look too much alike, stifling individualism. Second, architecture will be monumental. That is, instead of bath-houses, Siedlungen, employment offices and the like, there will be official railroad stations, memorial museums, monuments. The present regime is more intent on leaving a visible mark of its greatness than in providing sanitary equipment for workers.

But what these new buildings will look like is as yet completely unknown. Germany as the birthplace of modern architecture can hardly go back to Revivalism since there exist no architects who could or would design in styles. Nor is it possible that they will adopt the Bauhaus style. It is not monumental enough and it has irretrievably the stamp of Communism and Marxism, Internationalism, all the "isms" not in vogue in Germany today. Somewhere between the extremes is the key; and within the Party are three distinct movements each of which may win out.

First and up till recently the strongest are the forces of reaction, with Paul Schulze-Naumburg at the head. He is the enemy of anything which has happened in the last thirty years. His book *Art and Race*, contains the most stupid attacks on modern art which he considers mere interest in the abnormal, a point of view which he defends by showing juxtaposed clinical photographs of physical abnormalities and modern paintings. In architecture, he approves of nothing since the War, and is himself the architect of many simplified but Baroque country houses including the Crown Prince's

Excerpt from "Architecture in the Third Reich," *Hound & Horn* literary quarterly, published late in 1933. In this essay Philip hypothesizes about the future of architecture in the Third Reich.

Demagogues. What Philip and Blackburn were looking for in the mid-1930s was a figurehead to sell their version of right-wing populism. Lawrence Dennis, author of the book *The Coming American Fascism* (1936), was a personal mentor to Philip, but his parlor politics (and secret identity as a person of color) made him poorly suited to electoral grandstanding. Long seemed a likely enough wagon to hitch to, but he needed no advice from a pair of East Coast elites; Coughlin's handlers found the pair more useful but largely brushed them aside, dubbing them "the Gold Dust Twins."[3]

Huey Long waves his hat in the air as he steps off a train, 1932.

Top: Portrait of Lawrence Dennis, 1941. Bottom: Charles Edward Coughlin speaking at an event in 1938.

97

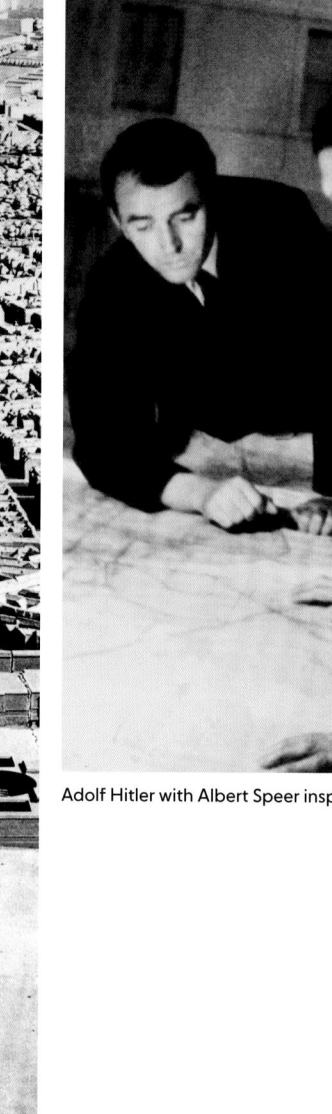

Model of Welthauptstadt Germania ("World Capital Germania"), the projected renewal of the German capital overseen by architect Albert Speer. View from the planned Südbahnhof ("South Station") over the Triumphbogen ("Arch of Triumph") to the Große Halle ("Great Hall") (north–south axis), Berlin, 1939.

Adolf Hitler with Albert Speer inspecting building plans, 1938.

Speer. Unfortunately for Philip (or, as the case may be, fortunately), the Nazis had as little use for architectural Modernism as Americans had for right-wing rabble-rousing. Albert Speer would occupy the role of the Führer's favorite *Baumeister*: "His relationship to Hitler," as journalist Chester Wilmot described it, was that of "one artist to another," and their grandiose architectural vision bore no resemblance to the lean Miesian poetics that Philip idolized. His disappointment with Nazi architecture did not cool his political ardor, and in fact his own later work would exhibit more than a soupçon of Speer's historicism. Speer himself, still alive and well and living in Heidelberg, was appreciative.

Politician

Albert Speer   Heidelberg

MAY 3 1 1978

Dear Philip,

    I have just finished a day's work interviewing Speer, a most interesting experience which gave me much to ponder on ; rather than try and write it all down, I shall recount it to you over lunch when I get back and, if you would like to hear them, play you some of the tapes. Anyway, Speer talks of you with great affection and respect ; I am directed, so to speak, to send the compliments of the Masterbuilder to the Formgiver. He inscribed a copy of the new book on his architecture to you, and I have it in my suitcase. He asked me to write an essay for his next book, which I shall certainly do, although God knows what the reaction in the better-thinking circles of New York will be ; as the researcher on our film crew remarked, on hearing of this, "First gays, now Nazis — what next ?" He is very curious about AT & T and thought it more in the spirit of his own work than anything he had seen by an American architect since 1945. (I will _try_ not to put this story into circulation, or would you prefer a straight cash arrangement ?)

    I left New York in rather a rush, so I didn't have the chance to tell you that I had lunch with Carleton Smith ; we got on well, although I scarcely had a chance to get a word in between the rolling thunder of names that he kept dropping. If you hadn't told me otherwise, I would have thought he was as mad as a March hare, but I shall go along with him and see what happens.

6900 Heidelberg 1   Schloß-Wolfsbrunnenweg 50   Tel. 26501

-2-

    The series is going well. I have taken three months off from the magazine to work on it, without interruption ; it must go to air in March 1980, first in England, and then later — assuming we find a firm sponsor — in America. Then I have to work like a non-white person to turn the scripts into a book. Then I can finish my house in Italy, and its attendant gazebo, which I still hope you will design for me ; if you won't, I shall ask Speer to, and I don't think I would be able to afford the masonry for _him_.

    I'll ring you when I get back, around May 7.

Best wishes,

Bob Hughes

From art critic Robert Hughes to Philip, (likely May) 1978, describing an interview with Nazi war criminal and architect Albert Speer. Hughes recounts that Speer "talks of [Philip] with great affection and respect."

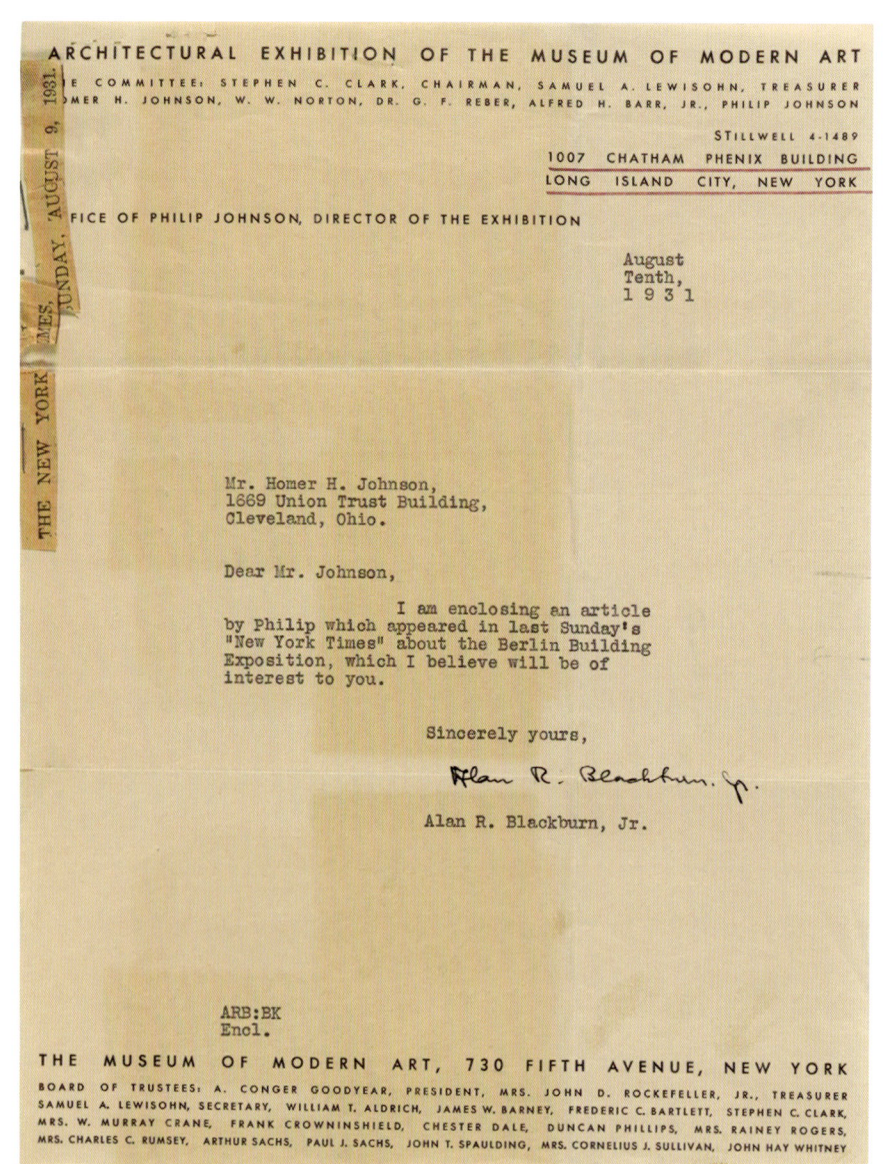

From Alan Blackburn to Philip's father, New York, 10 August 1931, enclosing an article by Philip that appeared in the *New York Times*.

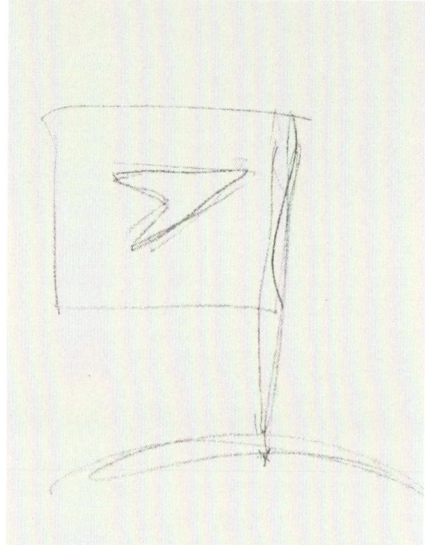

Philip's drawing of the flying wedge, the symbol of the Young Nationalists, the political group he founded with Alan Blackburn in Ohio during the late 1930s.

Architecture or revolution? Though abrupt, Philip's withdrawal from MoMA in 1934 was also the product of a long string of incidents and encounters. His journeys to Germany, while nominally in pursuit of the country's new architecture, had brought him into contact with the country's right-wing insurgency. With his resignation, his deputy at the museum Blackburn was transformed from a glorified secretary (charged with sending news clippings to Philip's mother) into the cochairman of the newly declared National Party, or Young Nationalists: membership never rose above a couple hundred, though Philip did design them a fetching little insignia.

Politician 100

Turn From Modern Art to Ultra-Modern Politics

Herald Tribune photo—Steffen

Philip Johnson, at left, and Alan Blackburn

Two Quit Modern Art Museum For Sur-Realist Political Venture

Blackburn and Johnson, With No Program but One Party for Nation, Start Saturday, for Louisiana to Study the Interesting, to Them, Huey Long

Alan Blackburn, executive director of the Museum of Modern Art, and Philip Johnson, chairman of the museum's Architectural Department, have deserted art for politics, it was learned yesterday. They have resigned their posts at the museum, and on Saturday they will leave for Louisiana, to begin the task of building up their private political party by getting a line on the antics of Senator Huey Pierce Long.

Both Mr. Blackburn and Mr. Johnson have been admirers of the sur-realist school of painting, and their politics are not without a certain sur-realist flavor. Their party, to be called quite simply "The National Party," is distinguished from all other political aggregations, juntas, parties or groups, past and present, by a complete lack of platform or program. They plan to pick one up as they go along, possibly in Louisiana.

Mr. Blackburn and Mr. Johnson jointly outlined their plans in Mr. Johnson's little office at the Modern Museum, 11 West Fifty-third Street, where catalogues of firearms and advanced art publications were piled everywhere.

...

The adventure begins on Saturday, after Mr. Blackburn and Mr. Johnson have taken leave of the museum, for which they expressed great admiration, and after they have collected necessary supplies. They were attacking the problem of firearms yesterday. Mr. Johnson favored a submachine gun, but Mr. Blackburn preferred one of the larger types of pistol. When such difficulties are settled the baggage will be packed in Mr. Johnson's large Packard touring car and they will set off.

Clipping from the *Herald Tribune*. The photograph shows Philip (left) and Alan Blackburn (right).

Otto Dix, *Dr. Mayer-Hermann*, 1926.

Monuments Man. In the last days of the war, Philip's old friend Lincoln Kirstein, the American writer, helped recover priceless works of art as one of the famed "Monuments Men," combing Europe for masterpieces looted by the very Nazis to whom Philip had shown such favor. And yet even in the early 1930s, while his fascist phase was still in full blossom, Philip had managed a few rescues of his own: two paintings by artists condemned by the Nazis, Oskar Schlemmer and Otto Dix, that might well have been destroyed had Philip not purchased them. Both were donated to MoMA, among the first of more than two thousand works Philip would give the museum in his lifetime.

Oskar Schlemmer, *Bauhaus Stairway*, 1932.

Portrait of Philip, c. 1944.

Quick change. Even before Pearl Harbor, Philip recognized which way the winds were blowing. He had toured the Polish front at the outbreak of the war, writing approving dispatches on the Wehrmacht; but on his return home, he found himself isolated—"twiddling my thumbs," as he said later, a would-be fascist hierophant in a country now keenly aware of the Nazi menace. Quietly, almost surreptitiously, he applied to Harvard in 1940 for graduate studies in architecture. In 1942 he attempted to enter the navy as an officer—and was denied. His political record now exposed him to serious scrutiny, and he was lucky to be accepted as a buck private a year later.

Top: Philip's letter of rejection from the U.S. Naval Reserves, Chicago, 20 October 1942, citing a lack of mobilization billets for his qualifications and substandard physical record—though it is largely understood he was in fact rejected for his politics. Bottom: Philip's Separation Qualification Record, which details his work as a draftsman in the U.S. Army, 9 December 1944. It states that he "drew topographical maps in the Army Engineer Corps."

Top: Letter from architect George Howe, Washington, D.C., 19 June 1942, recommending Philip for the position of officer. Bottom: Philip's Enlistment Record detailing his service in the U.S. Army from 12 March 1943 to 9 December 1944. The record is stamped 9 December 1944.

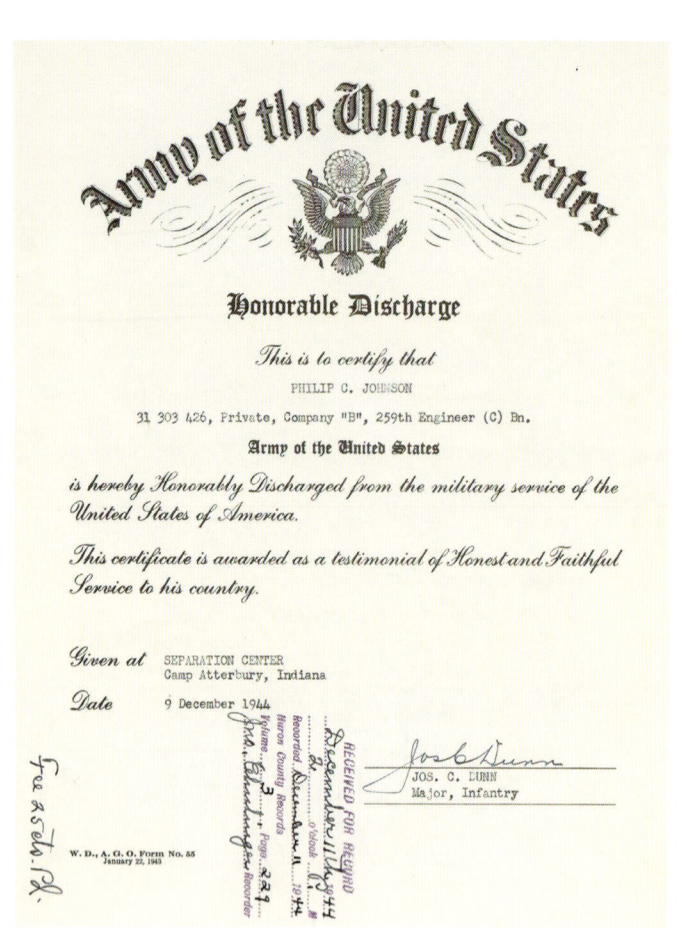

Philip's Certificate of Honorable Discharge from the U.S. Army, 9 December 1944, Camp Atterbury, Indiana.

"Keep your eyes on Mr. Philip Johnson about to build a modern house on the corner of Ash Street & Acathia Street, Cambridge, Mass. Studying under Mr. Gropius at the Harvard Architecture School."

—From an anonymous communication received at the Federal Bureau of Investigation, postmarked 15 July 1941

Politician

106

Top: First page of a letter from Philip to his sister, Theodate. He describes his social life in Washington, D.C. while based at Fort Belvoir, and in particular his meeting with journalist Kay Halle. Bottom: From Philip to Theodate, from Fort Belvoir, Virginia. He describes his time while under investigation by the FBI, asking, "What is to come? What will it be? Naturally all sorts of horrid things come to mind."

Top: From Philip to Theodate, from Fort Belvoir, Virginia (where Philip was held while being investigated by the FBI). He writes to ask her to send candy "in quantity." Bottom: A letter from Philip to Theodate describing his menial work at Fort Belvoir. The letter opens with him thanking her for the candy she sent him ("The fudge was perfect") and goes on to complain about "the uneducated around here."

Where Was PHILIP?

BY MICHAEL SORKIN

"YOU CANNOT NOT KNOW HISTORY." —Philip Johnson

"I do not believe in principles, in case you haven't noticed." —Philip Johnson

POLITICS

It seems that *everyone's* an ex-Fascist nowadays. There's Kurt Waldheim, the well-known Austrian ex-Nazi, and Herbert von Karajan, the well-known German ex-Nazi. Then there's Paul de Man, the renowned Yale professor, recently deceased, who, it turns out, wrote pro-Fascist articles for Belgian newspapers during the war. And of course there's always Martin Heidegger, the late philosopher, Nazi Party member and prominent ex-friend of the *Führerprinzip*.

These creeps have been getting a lot of print lately, and the question everyone seems to be asking is, what difference does it make? Do we have to reconsider *Blindness and Insight* (De Man) or *Being and Time* (Heidegger) or the UN resolution on Afghanistan (Waldheim) just because their authors might also have abetted the mass extermination of certain unfit persons? And should we expect some kind of apology?

The *Times* gave ample space last summer to the revelations about De Man, but nobody ever seems to ask these questions about that raffish old ex-Fascist Philip Johnson —arts patron, museum trustee, friend of the mighty, dean of American architecture and designer most recently of William Paley's new building to house the Museum of Broadcasting. Of course, it's not exactly as if his work could seem any *more* opportunistic. And, it's true, nobody has produced any pictures of the elegant tastemaker sporting in the Balkans in SS drag. Still, to coin a phrase, *where was Philip?* Let's return to the 1930s, when the young Museum of Modern Art curator had more on his mind than promoting a new architectural style and himself.

In 1934 the beginning of Johnson's political career was heralded by the following four-line headline in the *Times*: TWO FORSAKE ART TO FOUND A PARTY/MUSEUM MODERNISTS PREPARE TO GO TO LOUISIANA AT ONCE TO STUDY HUEY LONG'S WAYS/ GRAY SHIRT THEIR SYMBOL/YOUNG HARVARD GRADUATES THINK POLITICS NEEDS MORE 'EMOTION' AND LESS 'INTELLECTUALISM'. What a lark for the self-styled disciples of self-styled American Fascist Lawrence Dennis. "We shall try to develop ourselves," declared Johnson's friend and MoMA colleague Alan Blackburn, "by doing the sort of things that everybody in New York would like to do but never finds time for. We may learn to shoot, fly airplanes and take contemplative walks in the woods."

There was, to be sure, some vagueness about the program of and membership in the new party. "We have no definite political program to offer," declared Blackburn, the party mouthpiece. The two also declined to reveal membership data (an estimated high-water mark was fewer than 150). The one thing that was certain was the choice of shirting. Imagine the conversation when this was decided. *Brown is too...seasonal. Black? Like those Italians? Silver? Déclassé! Gray? Gray! Wire Turnbull & Asser!*

Tiring rapidly of Louisiana and the Kingfish (whose embrace of the two-man volunteer brain trust from New York City was apparently less than effusive), the pair switched crypto-Fascist demagogues, now sucking up to the revolting anti-Semites and right-wingers William Lemke and Father Charles Coughlin, donating at least $5,000 to their activities. In his book *Demagogues in the Depression*, David Bennett describes the two fellow travelers in 1936: "Johnson and Blackburn...appeared at the Coughlin convention, ostensibly representing the 'Youth Division of the NUSJ [National Union for Social Justice—Coughlin's organization].' Although inactive in Union affairs, they were fascinated by radical politics and their financial aid gave them access to party organizers. Later they were to form the quasi-fascistic National Party." Indeed, Johnson, who grew up in Cleveland, even attempted a run at the Ohio state legislature in the mid-1930s. Such an irony: just as the world might have been spared years of carnage if Hitler had only been admitted to architecture school, imagine the architecture that might have been avoided if the electorate had had the prescience to make young Philip a

---

may borrow a page from Krieger's book: Retain public-relations counsel, issue a press release and announce that you have established an educational foundation; call it the Karma Foundation. Announce a new entrepreneurial venture; name it after yourself. Is it necessary to mention in the press release that your leave-taking was not wholly amicable? Must one allude to the firing thing, or to disputes with one's employer over the advisability of one's trading style? Krieger chose to emphasize the constructive elements of his situation:

"Options trading specialist Andrew Krieger announced today he will leave the investment firm of Soros Fund Management on June 30, 1988 to pursue two personal interests, Krieger & Associates Ltd. and the Karma Foundation...."

"'Increasingly over the last several months [he was quoted in his own press release as saying] I have been receiving substantial and unsolicited offers from major institutions and individuals that I manage their investment trading portfolios. Simultaneously, I have been studying how I could better manage my own funds and my growing philanthropic objectives. The decision... ensures me the time and freedom to accommodate that investor interest and still have a means for participating more actively in various socially responsible endeavors.'"

The release, antedating the restatement of foreign-exchange earnings by Bankers Trust, mentioned the $338 million booked by the firm in last year's fourth quarter. It was an understandable error—if Bankers Trust didn't understand Krieger's positions, Krieger himself, so long gone from the bank, could hardly be expected to know.

In truth, the press release raised as many questions as it answered. If it was true that Krieger wanted to manage money, why was he in such a hurry to leave a place that had so much of it? Why would he freely choose to leave the payroll of a man who is known to pay top dollar for talented traders? Krieger, when reached on the telephone, reiterated, "I was not fired. I resigned." Likewise a Soros spokesman: "It was an amicable parting." Amicable, no doubt. George Soros, risk-taker extraordinaire, is once again able to sleep at night, and Krieger, Bankers Trust trading ace, is able to raise new money for his own fund. "I'm not worried about having sufficient capital," Krieger has said. "I'm concerned that we don't accept too much." Anyway, there will always be lepers.

138 SPY OCTOBER 1988

Above and opposite: "Where Was Philip?" by Michael Sorkin, *Spy* magazine, October 1988. The article collates a number of Philip's explicit quotations supporting fascism and anti-Semitism, as well as his association with fascist figures.

Fallout. Decades after the government investigation into his prewar activities, Philip's politics were again the subject of heated debate. In the 1980s, architect Peter Eisenman (a sometime Johnsonian acolyte) had discussed the matter at length with Philip during a series of interviews for a proposed biography—never to be completed, after Philip decided he didn't care to publicize his past misdeeds. It was to no avail: writer Michael Sorkin relayed the episode in a banner exposé for *Spy* magazine, reopening a chapter Philip thought he had closed.

legislator.

As the 1930s progressed Johnson began to sign his name to a variety of articles for the publications of the lunatic fringe, quickening the pace of his pro-German maunderings as world war approached. For instance, in a 1939 issue of *Today's Challenge*, an article titled "Are We a Dying People?" offered the latent master builder's views on the master race. "The United States of America is committing race suicide," he warned. Deploying statistical evidence of the precipitous decline of the "white" race, he rebuked the "philosophy of Individualism and Materialism" as "eugenically bad" for failing to fulfill "the imperatives of racial maintenance."

Then, in a mighty peroration subtitled "The Will to Live," Johnson offered a truly chilling metaphor to describe the way in which this will is to be exercised. "Human will is a part of the biological process," he declared. "Our will...interferes constantly in the world of the lower animals. When English sparrows threaten to drive out our songbirds, we shoot the sparrows, rather than letting nature and Darwin take their course. Thus the songbirds, thanks to our will, become the 'fittest' and survive."

This was written in *1939*.

As it turns out, the national origin of those sparrows was not meant entirely metaphorically. Credentialed as European correspondent for Father Coughlin's scurrilous, Jew-baiting paper *Social Justice*, Johnson filed, as war accelerated, a stream of tacitly pro-Nazi dispatches mocking the English. (And his fine aesthete's eye and celebrated wit were fully operational even in the midst of war. "It is said, with how much truth I am unable to say," he wired in a dispatch from the summer of 1939, "that a large London hospital had had to add to its staff because of the increased accidents caused by the 'volunteer' nurses. I can only vouch for the fact that most of these volunteers look very bad indeed in their baggy uniforms; I have heard Paris audiences laugh out loud at them.")

Likewise, his anti-Semitism is filtered through his refined sense of what really matters. Back in Paris, he wrote, "Another serious split in French opinion is that caused by the Jewish question, a problem much aggravated just at present by the multitude of émigrés in Paris. Even I, as a stranger in the city, could not help noticing how much German was being spoken, especially in the better restaurants. Such an influx naturally makes the French wonder, not only about these incoming Jews, but also about their co-religionists who live and work here and call themselves French. The facts that [Léon] Blum and the men around him are Jews, that there are two Jews in the present cabinet, Messrs. Zay and Mandel, and that the Jewish bankers Mannheimer, de Rothschild and Lazard Freres are known to stand behind the present government all complicate the situation." Philip made the danger in this complication clear in another *Social Justice* article, published in July 1939: "Lack of leadership and direction in the [French] State has let the one group get control who always gain power in a nation's time of weakness — the Jews."

The undoubted high point of Philip's career as a journalist came as he accompanied the Nazi blitzkrieg to Poland in September. Arriving in Berlin shortly before the invasion, Johnson crossed into Poland to get the story. In a dispatch in the September 11 edition of *Social Justice*, he found the Poles "so excited and so worried about the crisis which they feel is at hand, that they arrested me at the border merely for taking pictures." Later he ridiculed the defensive efforts being undertaken by that hapless nation, puny measures that, he related, caused his German pals to roar with laughter when he reported them.

The Polish police weren't the only ones suspicious of Philip's activities at the border. Near Danzig he encountered William Shirer, who describes their meeting in *Berlin Diary*: "Dr. Boehmer, press chief of the Propaganda Ministry in charge of this trip, insisted that I share a double room in the hotel here with Philip Johnson, an American fascist who says he represents Father Coughlin's *Social Justice*. None of us can stand the fellow and suspect he is spying on us for the Nazis. For the last hour in our room here he has been posing as an anti-Nazi and trying to pump me for my attitude. I have given him no more than a few bored grunts." (Johnson responded to this in a 1973 interview in a British architectural journal, saying about Shirer, "[He is] a very irresponsible journalist... very third rate writer.")

Meanwhile, back on the Polish beat during the Nazi invasion, Philip proclaimed his "shock" at his first visit to the country of "Chopin, Paderewski and Copernicus." Under the subhead JEWS DOMINATE POLISH SCENE he wrote, "The boundaries of Europe seem to the traveller to [*sic*] the most part arbitrary lines. But here was a real boundary. Once on the Polish side I thought at first that I must be in the region of some awful plague....In the towns there were no shops, no automobiles, no pavements and again no trees. There were not even any Poles to be seen in the streets, only Jews!" Later Philip visited Lodz, "a slum without a city attached to it." It didn't take long to find out who was to blame; it was the 35 percent of the population who happened to be Jewish and who, "dressed in their black robes and black skull-caps and with their long beards... seem more like 85 per cent." Philip retained his fine sartorial eye. No gray shirts here.

At the end of 1939 Philip returned to the U.S., where he lectured to the American Fellowship Forum, the Nazi-front group behind *Today's Challenge*. Then, late in 1940, he went back to Harvard to study architecture. In 1943 he was drafted, and he served two years. At the end of the war he resumed his curatorship at MoMA and shortly thereafter began his architectural practice, going on to become the most celebrated designer in America.

And what about some sort of apology? Some version of the Waldheim grovel? There never has been one from Johnson — not publicly, at any rate. However, apology or no, he has been forgiven. When Philip was up for election to MoMA's board of trustees in 1957, someone had the bad taste to mention that the man had spent years as, er...a Jew-bashing Fascist. John D. Rockefeller's wife, Blanchette, already a museum trustee, rose to the occasion with suitable noblesse oblige. "Every young man," she said, "should be allowed to make one large mistake." ❯

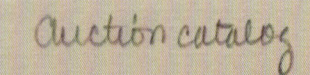

auction catalog

Paintings and Sculptures

INCLUDING IMPORTANT EXAMPLES
OF IMPRESSIONIST, POST-IMPRESSIONIST
AND CONTEMPORARY AMERICAN ART

For the benefit of the
ISRAEL EMERGENCY FUND
OF THE UNITED JEWISH APPEAL

Public Auction • Tuesday, June 11 at 8 P.M.

PARKE-BERNET GALLERIES, INC.
980 Madison Avenue • New York • 1968

Cover of an auction catalog for *Paintings and Sculptures*, aiding the Israel Emergency Fund of the United Jewish Appeal, New York, 1968. The catalog includes a foreword written by Philip.

The Jews and Mr. Johnson. So was Philip a bona fide Jew hater? Casual anti-Semitism was not uncommon among American intellectuals of the era (evidenced by T. S. Eliot and Ernest Hemingway, both of them of the same haute-bourgeois Midwest extraction as Philip). But few were led by their prejudices as far as sedition, and fewer still left a paper trail as long as Philip's, with letters and newspaper items detailing his feelings about Jews "[gaining] control in a nation's time of weakness."[4] In later life, Philip would attempt to atone: he designed a synagogue, sold portions of his art collection to benefit Jewish causes, and even befriended then Israeli defense minister Shimon Peres, on whose behalf he designed a nuclear power facility. Given his relationships with Jewish designers and artists throughout his life, one could conclude of Philip's anti-Jewish phase that it was nothing more than that, a passing fancy like so many others in his checkered career. By the same token, his purported contrition may have been equally disingenuous, undertaken, as one of his clients put it when advising him to take on the pro bono synagogue design, merely to "help you with your past."

THE NEW YORK TIMES, FRIDAY, FEBRUARY 26, 1971

An Open Letter to Mayor Kollek

By PHILIP JOHNSON

Dear Mayor Kollek,

Nothing in history has prepared you for your present dilemma in the planning of Jerusalem. At once the most sacred of spiritual sites, the most torn and disputed area of modern times, the capital of a new and forceful country, the agglomeration of centuries of different ownerships with differing ideologies. In other words, you have a mess.

At the same time, opportunity. Before a complete modern impasse develops you can still plan a new Jerusalem. Too late New York, Tokyo, Moscow; our future is behind us. Yours is still ahead.

One modern specter already looms: I see by the paper that your City Council has approved housing on sites like Mount Samuel and Government House Hill. Politics aside, this is esthetic criminality. The bare Judean Hills are your backdrop, your greatest visual asset. I know that we have ruined our cityscapes with sprawl, but must you follow our bad example?

I am aware of many insolubles—insoluble not only to you but the rest of us unfortunates in a technological and world capitalist era. To name three: Traffic—you can never provide enough car space, so do the best you can; Housing—housing will, in all likelihood, forever be substandard; provide whatever your national purse will allow you; for Heaven's sake don't let your minorities ruin the beautiful Judean Hills; Speculative building—remember the golden rule: He who has the money makes the rules, but fight it. Even money will respect rules (height restrictions? stone facing?) when forced.

I am not writing you on these subjects, but rather on the subject of the aspect of Jerusalem, the physical place-design which will make Jerusalem either great or trivial. What use traffic clover-leaves if there is no grandeur for the traffic to get to? What point square miles of low cost (and low esthetic quality) housing if there is no center of life for the thousands to visit, to shop in, to worship in? What if you successfully keep down the Hiltons, the Sheratons and the skyscrapers, if nothing takes their place?

Right now, in 1971, Jerusalem has no place. Though within its Turkish walls the Old City has many, outside there is nothing. Jerusalem awaits its 20th century, its Israeli shape.

Jerusalem today has the problems that Rome had in the 16th century. Rome was a mess of alleys with great buildings (the churches) scattered, its hills masked with hovels. The ambitions of the papacy changed all that. Sixtus V sliced roads and crossroads through Rome (each crossing marked with its obelisk) clarifying the processionals, creating a network which still constitutes the arteries and veins of modern Rome. Rome since Sixtus has had a plan.

Other great capitals created their particular sense of place in other centuries. Paris: the Tuileries, the Concorde, the Place Vendôme. Berlin, its Unter den Linden. Venice: its Piazza San Marco. New York's great Central Park. All have an artistic architectural, sentimental "place;" a recognizable center where one can say, I am here when I am "here."

All these city centers are now old. Your plan will be different, new. It will be the first 20th-century urban place, and the only one in the world with a history like Jerusalem.

I realize, Mr. Mayor, that my dream is easy for me since I am so far away and have none of the responsibilty. And yet, there are no insuperable difficulties. Control you must have, money you must have. The first, I imagine, you have. Money is, or could be, the tax on the finished city of the future. Who, after all, paid for Haussmann's Paris? The third ingredient, after control and money, is imagination. Yours and your architects. I know you and I know your architects—no problem.

The direction is laid out in the excellent framework produced by your team's preliminary report: you need a new city center north of the Jaffa Gate. And you need a way from Mount Herzl to Mount Scopus.

The new center will be the end of the new rapid transit from Jerusalem, the Grand Central of the City. In a megastructure, around and over and under the station, will be hotels, car parks, bus stations, shopping malls, enclosed plazas, all the beauties of a modern concentration. The center cannot be tall, lest it interfere with the Jaffa Gate, but it can be spatially a new experience of plazas, malls, varying levels, all with their own microclimate, at once the agora, transportation node, souk—the heart of the New City.

You will have the way, a processional from Mount Scopus to Mount Herzl passing the Jaffa Gate with its new center in the east and the universities in the west. This will be the great life-giver, the Champs Elysées, the Oxford Street, Unter den Linden, the Corso, all rolled into one.

But it will be 20th century, in other words, much superior. Minibuses running free of charge; tree-shaded pedestrian medians; reduced car traffic, not overly wide. And what vistas! What city has so many hills, so much visible history to be enjoyed from one way. A road joining the Old City and the universities, the business district and the Government center and museum. The way will be a chain of beauty, a city creator. And the New Jerusalem will have its sense of place.

Philip Johnson, a leading American architect, participated in the recent Congress of Engineers and Architects in Jerusalem.

"An Open Letter to Mayor Kollek" by Philip, *New York Times*, 26 February 1971.

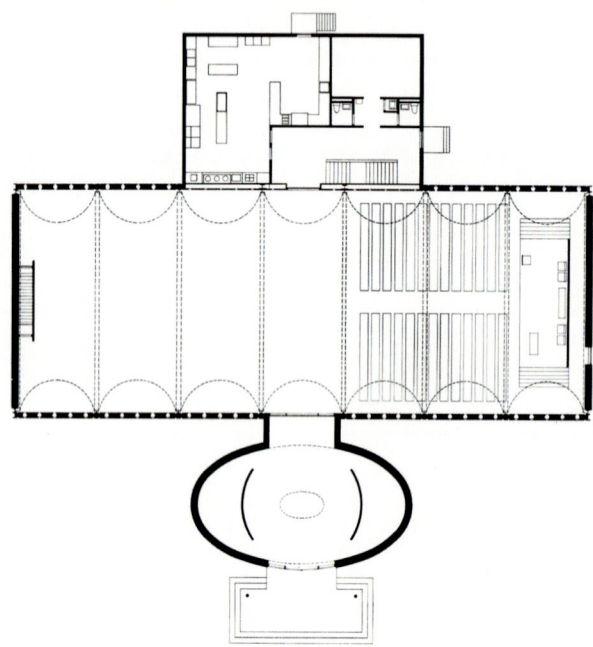

Top: Interior perspective sketch of Kneses Tifereth Israel Synagogue, Port Chester, New York, 1956. Bottom: Plan of the synagogue.

Imperfect atonement. The synagogue (in Port Chester, New York) was generally considered a success—even if some of the members found its narrow windows to be alarmingly prison-like; the Israeli nuclear facility was even more remarkable, although its highly secretive nature meant that few people would ever get to see it in person.

Politician 112

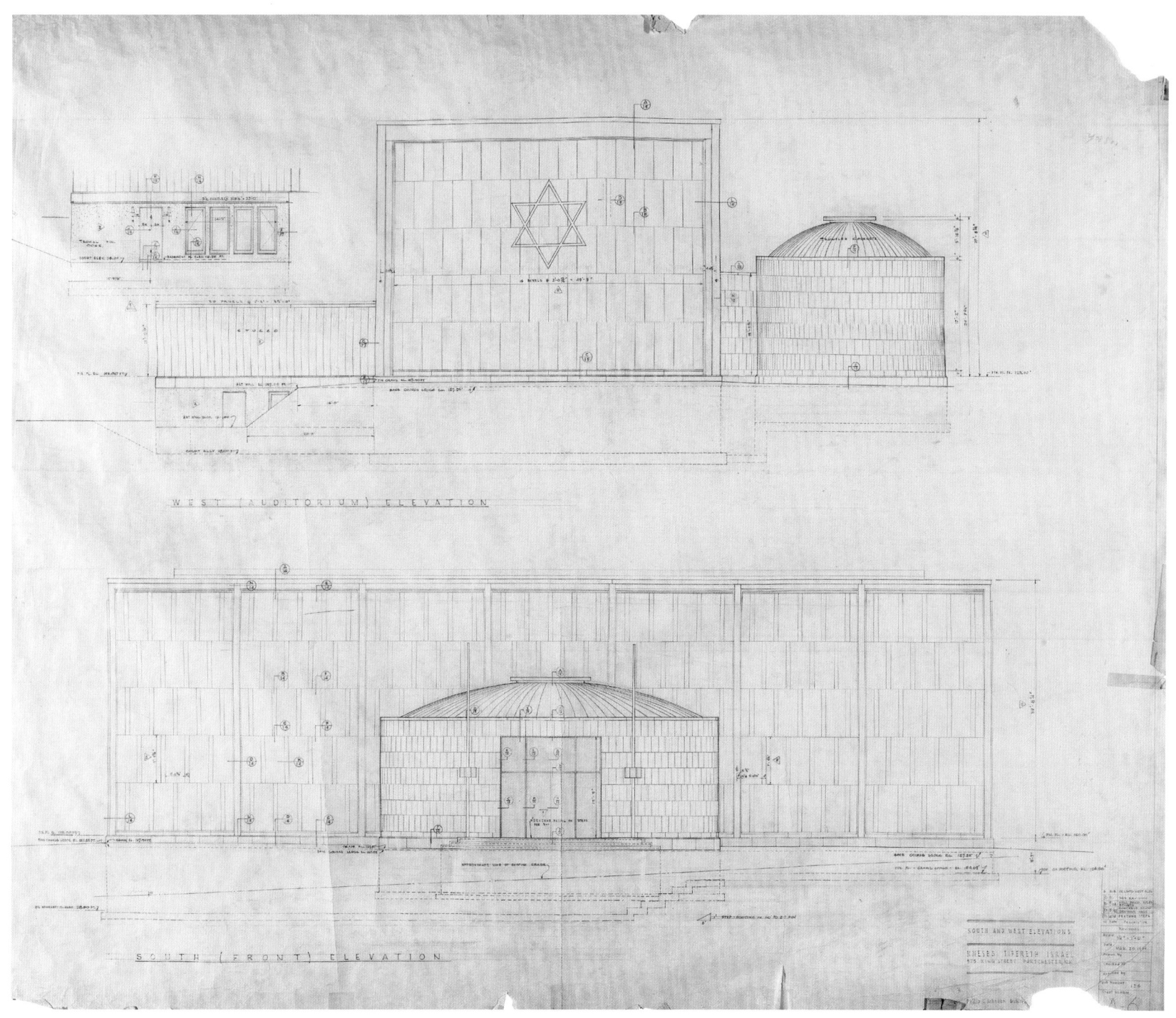

Elevation of Kneses Tifereth Israel Synagogue, Port Chester, New York, 1956.

Interior view of Kneses Tifereth Israel Synagogue, Port Chester, New York, 1956.

Exterior view of Kneses Tifereth Israel Synagogue, Port Chester, New York, 1956.

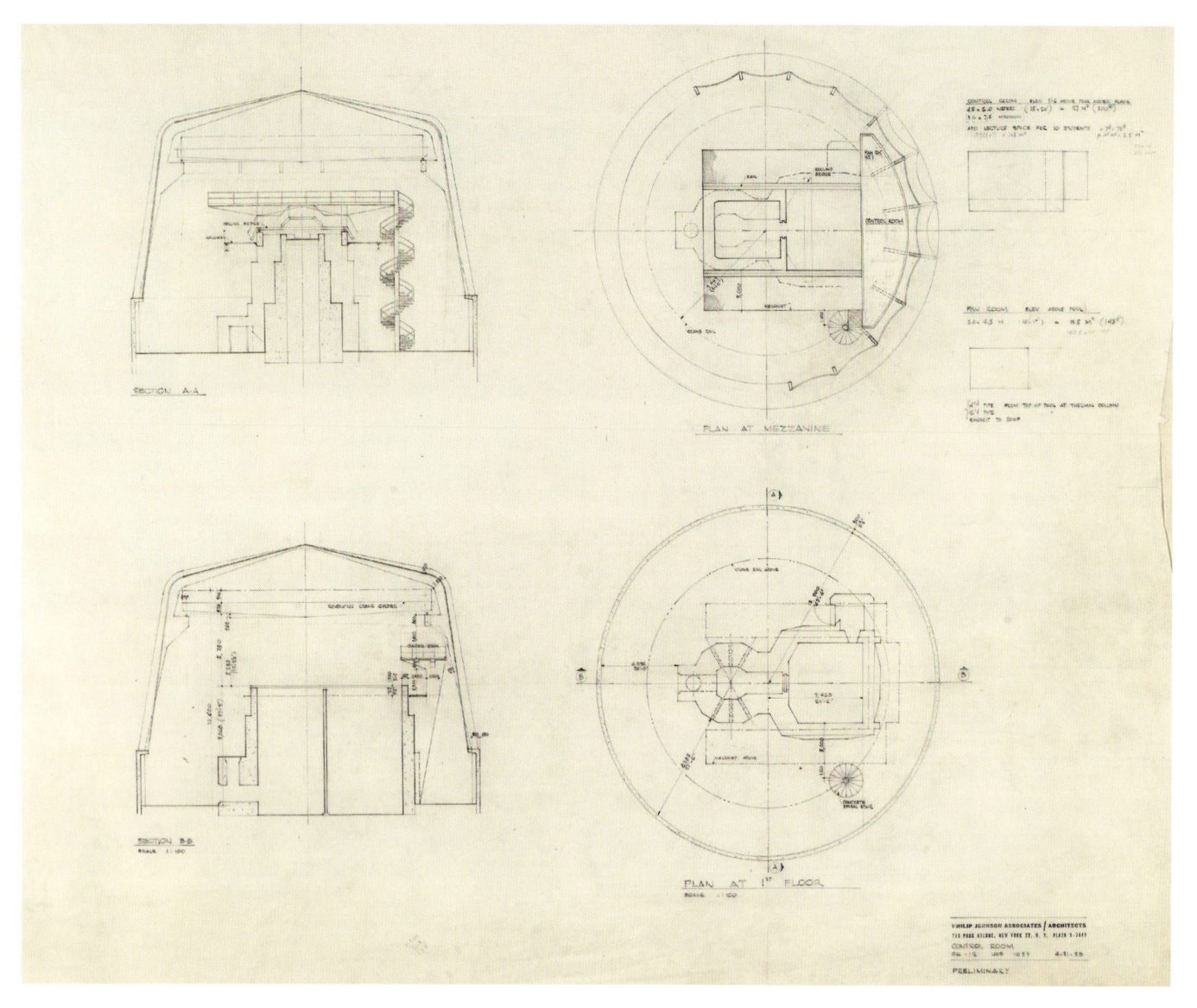

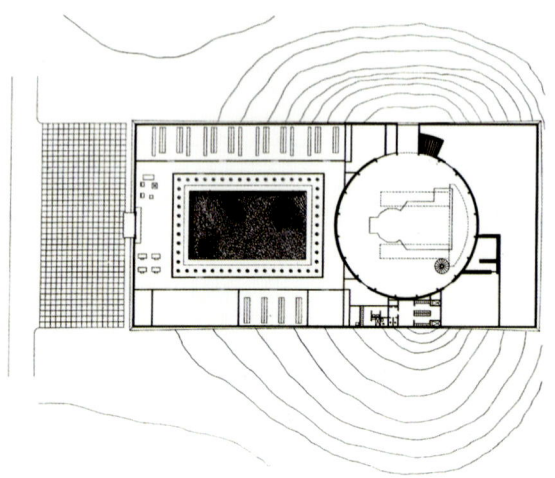

Top: Elevations and plans of the reactor at the Soreq Nuclear Research Center, Rehovot, Israel, 1960. Bottom: Site plan.

Model of the Soreq Nuclear Research Center, Rehovot, Israel, c. 1960.

Perspective drawing of the Soreq Nuclear Research Center, Rehovot, Israel, 1960.

Politician

Perspective drawing of the inner courtyard at the Soreq Nuclear Research Center, Rehovot, Israel, 1960. The reactor appears in the background.

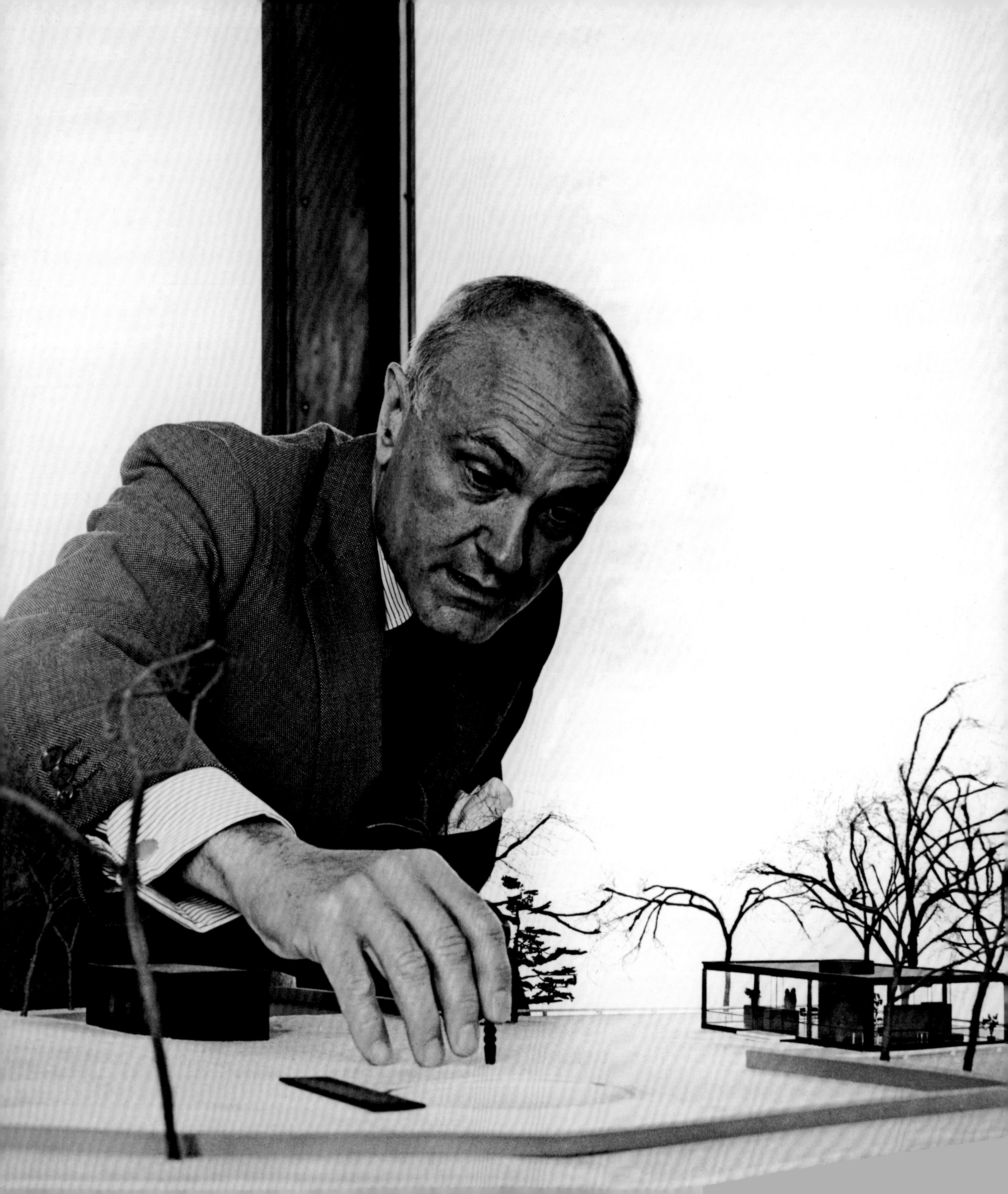

05 Architect

Architect

With America fully involved in World War II, Philip set about reclaiming the cultural perch he had so forcefully renounced a decade earlier. It seems surprising, in retrospect, how easily he was able to do it: slipping back into his old ambit of designers, patrons, and academics, Philip quickly buried his prewar indiscretions beneath a heap of accolades as the East Coast elite's favored architectural tastemaker. With the help of Alfred H. Barr, Jr., he finished his studies at Harvard, resumed his duties at the Museum of Modern Art (MoMA), and launched his own practice in New York—first with his graduate school colleague Landis Gores, later with others—assembling, in the space of a few short years, a portfolio of built work that would point the way to much that would follow.

Returning to Cambridge, Massachusetts marked the first step. Philip arrived at the Harvard Graduate School of Design (GSD) four years into the deanship of Joseph Hudnut. The first to lead the Harvard program into the Modernist camp, Hudnut was rather starstruck by his new student and gave him considerable latitude. Campus politics were thorny (Philip's own past was an open secret, while the presence on the faculty of Walter Gropius, dubbed the "spiritual leader" of the GSD, made for a tense rivalry with Hudnut), but other students were generally impressed by the polish of their much-older classmate, even if he struck some as "too much an aristocratic architect."[1] Surely only an aristocrat could have lighted on Philip's choice of thesis project: a house for himself in Cambridge, the first executed ground-up design of his career. A simple courtyard scheme with a glazed facade facing a discreetly walled garden, 9 Ash Street was an indicator of his subsequent trajectory, if not necessarily a success on its own merits—the all-glass front was hard to see at night, and one visitor crashed through it during a dinner party.

Upon relocating to New York after his stint in the army, Philip teamed up with Gores and promptly began to pluck commissions from well-to-do clients enjoying the postwar economic boom. Many (though by no means all) of the names of Philip's first clients were familiar ones from the East Coast social register and from Philip's particular ambit: Robert Leonhardt, whose wife served on MoMA's junior council, came to the architect for a house on Long Island's North Shore; the Rockefellers came to him for a guest house in Manhattan, subsequently bequeathed to the museum; and MoMA itself commissioned an annex building in 1950, the first of several interventions from its de facto in-house architect. The designs Philip produced for these clients and others were iterations of the highly ordered, glass-and-steel brand of Modernism that Philip had inherited from Ludwig Mies van der Rohe: his very first project, the Booth House in Bedford, New York, was a restatement of Ash Street on a slightly larger scale; the Leonhardt House took the Miesian box and sent it flying over a cliffside; the Wiley House in New Canaan, Connecticut, put it atop a stone plinth and decked it in canvas sunshades.

Mies was never far from Philip's mind at the time, and as the younger architect entered the professional swim, he reasserted his sway at MoMA (never entirely abandoned) to organize a highly influential 1947 retrospective that solidified Mies's reputation as the preeminent European Modernist working in America. The design of the exhibition was Mies's own work; the imperious émigré did not make it easy for Philip, weighing in on matters large and small, right down to criticizing the museum's structural columns. Initial critical reception was mixed (not least from Frank Lloyd Wright, who dismissed it as "much ado about almost nothing"[2]), but the experience did no long-term damage to the relationship between Philip and Mies—allowing Philip to capitalize on it a decade later, when he acted as Mies's architect of record on a new high-rise project, the Seagram Building in Manhattan. Responsible for portions of the interior detailing, as well as the lower-floor restaurants, Philip helped make the building not just the manifest proof of his favorite architect's genius, but also a glamor spot for a generation of New Yorkers.

But nothing that Philip did or said in the heady first years of his career as a designer would rival the building he created for himself—the place that made his reputation and then allowed him to continually remake it for the balance of the century. This was the Glass House, his private estate in New Canaan with its signature jewel box of glass and steel perched at the edge of a bluff. Mies saw it and pronounced himself unimpressed; Wright saw it and only liked parts of it; but most importantly, as Gores said, "every architecture editor in New York"[3] paid a call, and through them the house became known to millions who might otherwise have had no conception of what Modernist architecture could mean for the American landscape, much less that it could be so luxurious and romantic. This was Philip's great coup as an architect, and whatever its functional and aesthetic defects, it was the one work to which almost no one, then or now, could pronounce themselves indifferent. That, after all, was the one reaction Philip never wanted his architecture to produce.

Philip at Harvard Graduate School of Design, Cambridge, Massachusetts, 1940.

The first page of Philip's degree transcript showing his undergraduate studies at Harvard University, Cambridge Massachusetts, 1923–27, including his out-of-course studies until 1930. The transcripts were supplied following his graduation from Harvard Graduate School of Design, 16 June 1942. Philip graduated *cum laude*.

Portrait of Philip, Harvard University, Cambridge, Massachusetts, c. 1930.

"Severe discipline." Though his performance as an undergraduate had been lackluster, Philip had more than just his museum experience as an entrée to the GSD in 1940: he had completed one project, entirely by himself, for a real-life client—a 1934 apartment for his friend Edward Warburg. Stringently gridded, the interior plan was so unforgiving that if "a magazine was not at right angles with the coffee table," Warburg recalled, "you felt that the room hadn't been cleaned up."[4]

"I was thirty-four. All my classmates looked to me like they were fifteen."

—Philip on his late arrival at architecture school

Architect

The Edward M. M. Warburg Apartment, 37 Beekman Place, New York, 1934.

"Few people would be at ease in so disciplined a background for everyday living. But the architect, as we have seen, was not concerned with the requirements of anybody except himself."

—*Architectural Forum*, December 1943, on 9 Ash Street

9 Ash Street. Keen to put his now decade-old obsession with Mies into practice, Philip acquired a lot on the corner of Acacia Street and Ash Street in Cambridge, Massachusetts, and created a quiet homage to the master architect. If the house fell short of his own hopes (and caused some consternation among his neighbors), it was enough to secure him his graduate degree and to rate a mention from *Architectural Forum* as America's "best example" of domestic Modernism. Years later, Philip would say of the Glass House that it was an attempt "to solve the same problem"[5] as Ash Street.

Architect

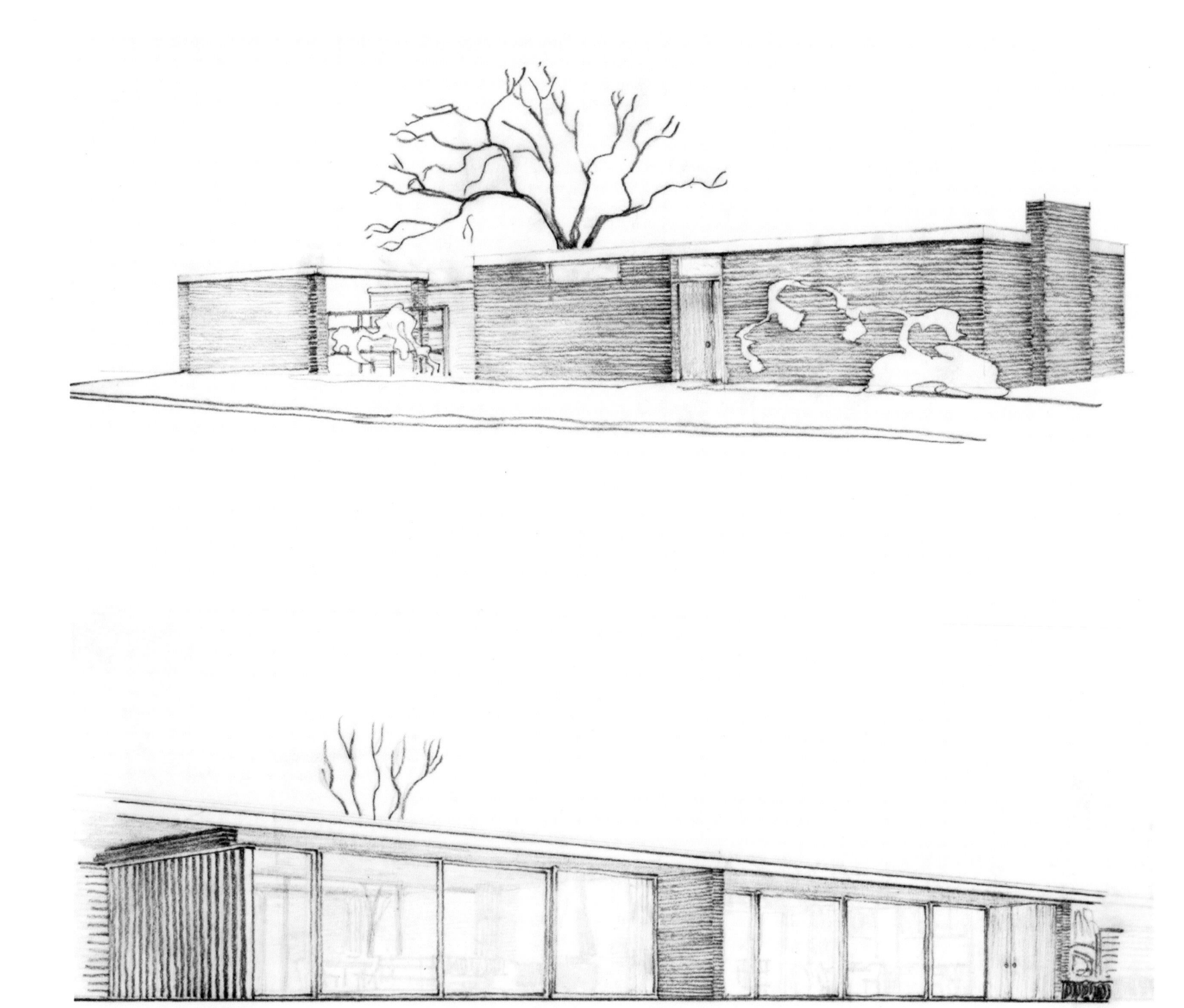

Perspective sketches of a freestanding house and row houses, assignments from Philip's time at Harvard Graduate School of Design, 1941.

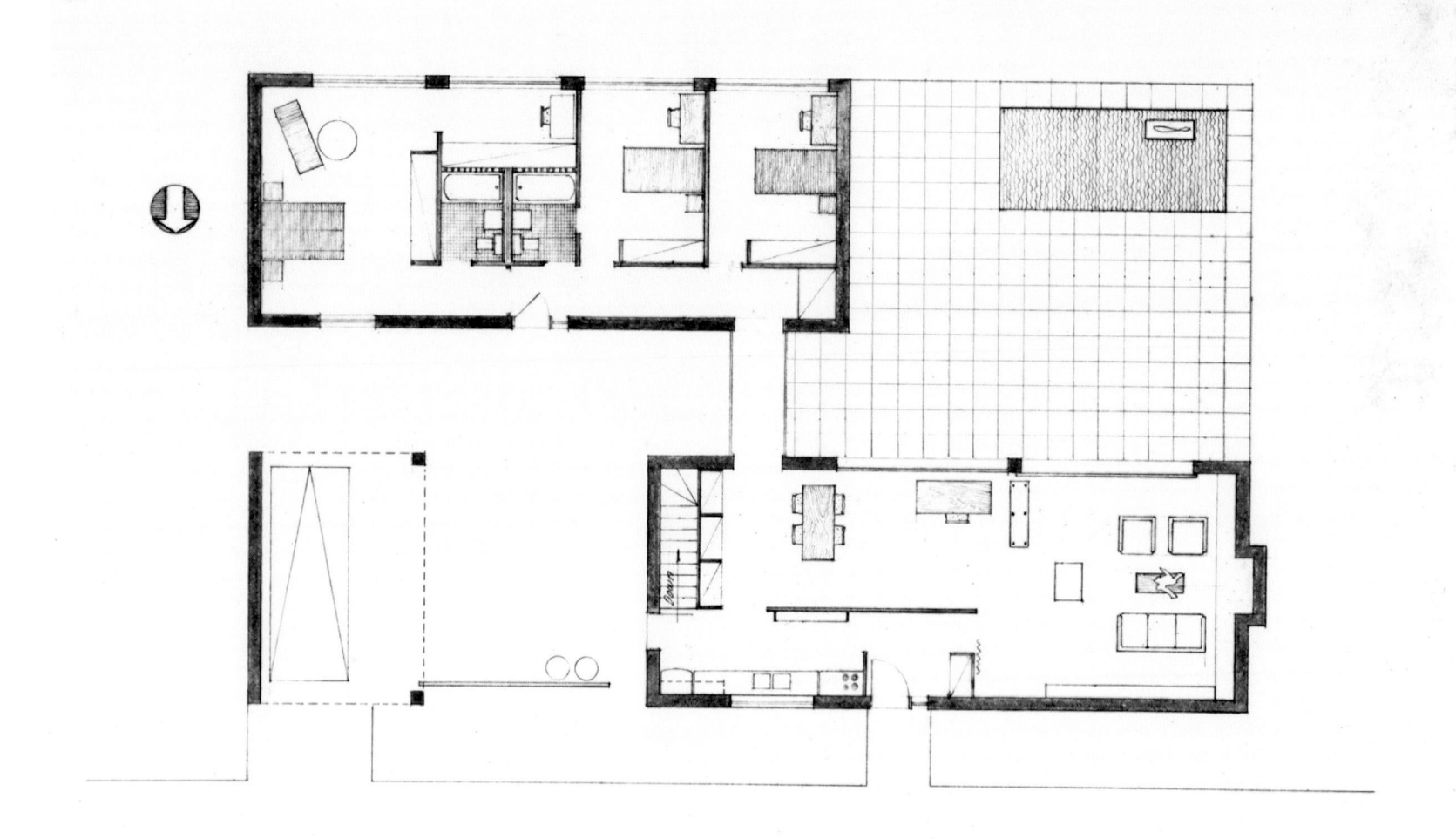

Plan of a freestanding house, an assignment from Philip's time at Harvard Graduate School of Design, 1941. The design shows the influence of Marcel Breuer, who assigned the project, with his concept of the "binuclear" house with separate wings for bedroom and kitchen/dining/living areas connected by a glass walkway.

A BEACH PAVILION

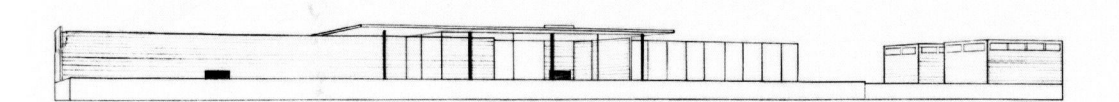

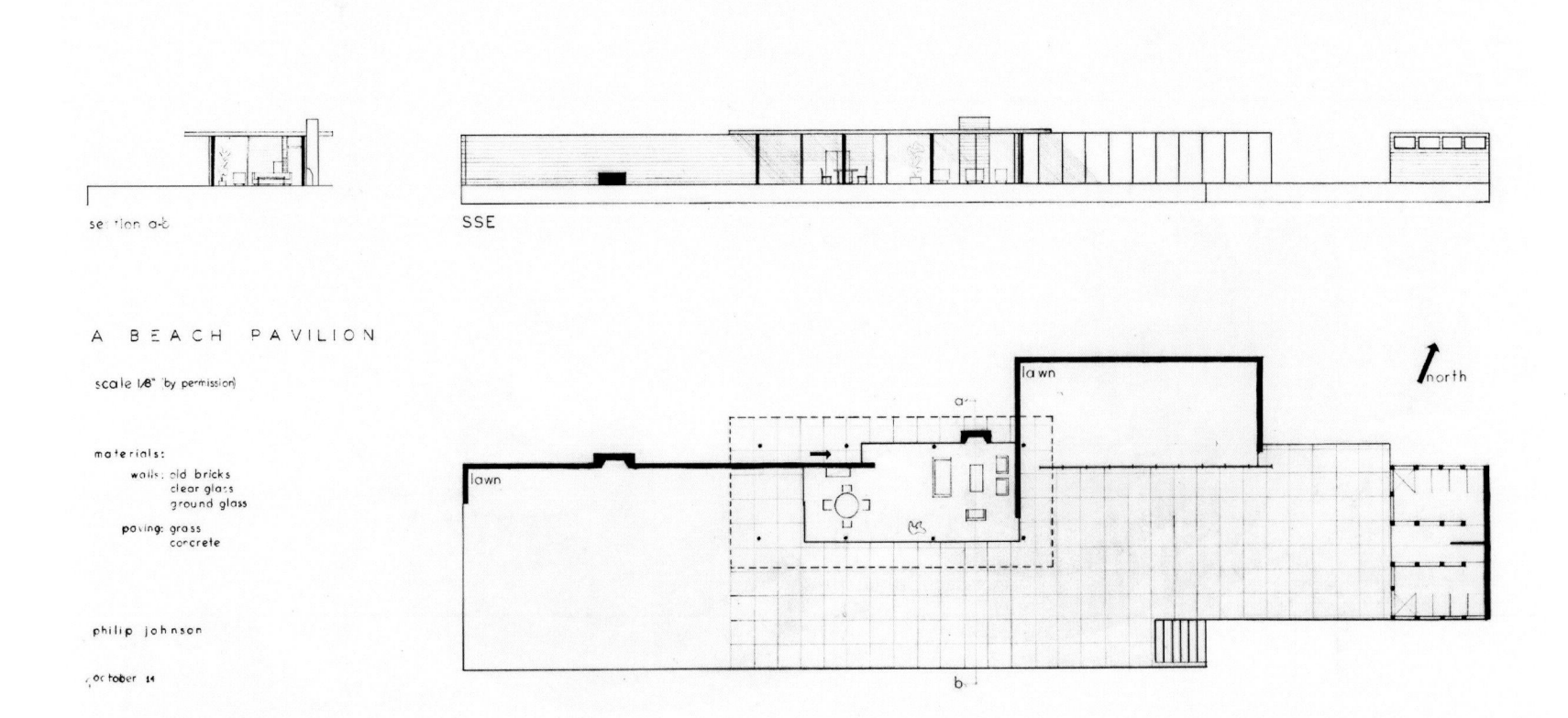

scale 1/8" (by permission)

materials:
    walls: old bricks
        clear glass
        ground glass
    paving: grass
        concrete

philip johnson

october 14

Plan and elevation of a beach pavilion, an early assignment from Philip's time at Harvard Graduate School of Design, 1940. There are a number of hallmarks of the Modern style.

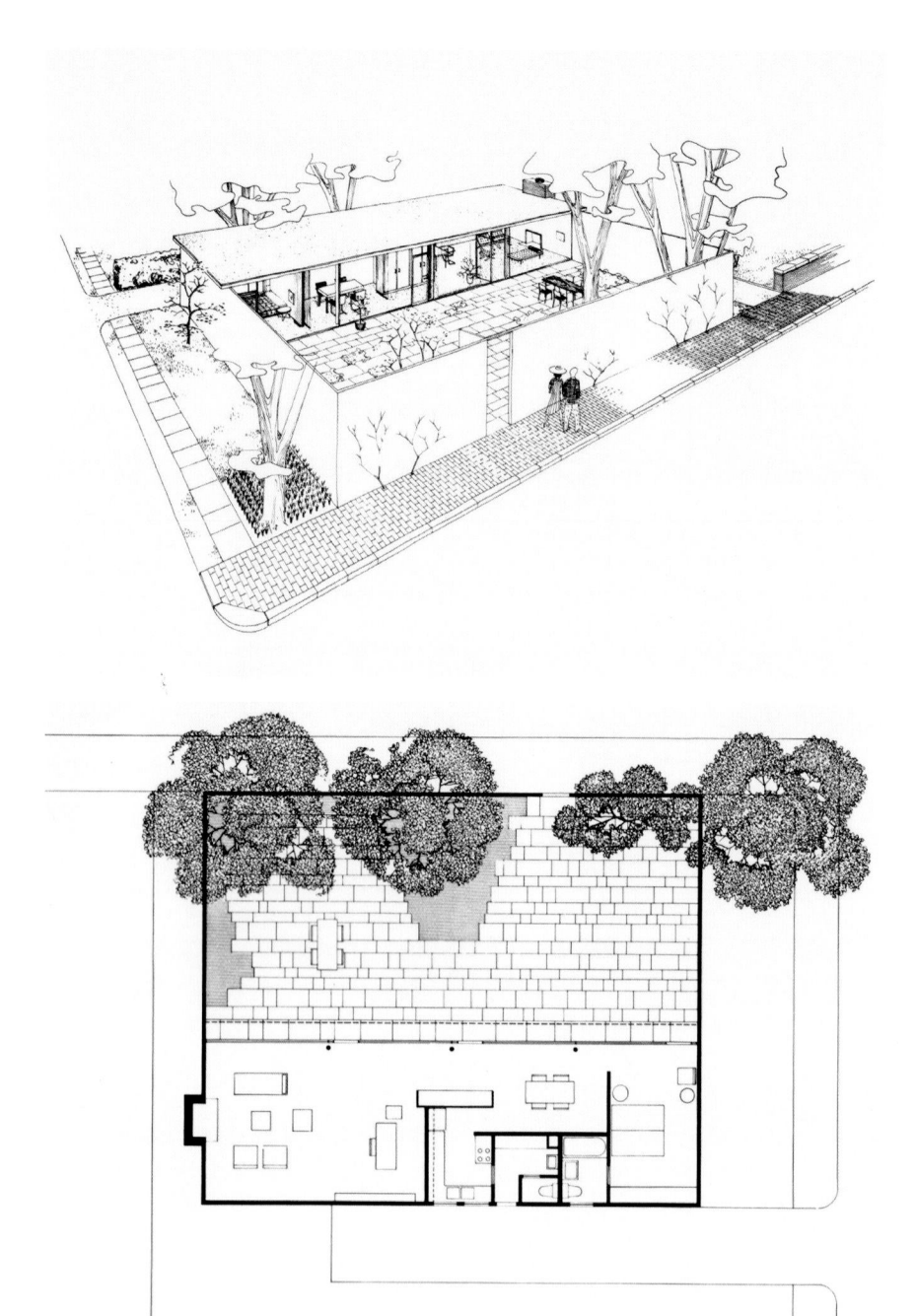

Sketch (top) and plan (bottom) of 9 Ash Street, Cambridge, Massachusetts, 1942.

Architect

130

Night shot of 9 Ash Street, Cambridge, Massachusetts, 1942.

Interior view of the living room, 9 Ash Street, Cambridge, Massachusetts, 1942.

Interior view of the living room, 9 Ash Street, Cambridge, Massachusetts, 1942.

Preliminary elevation of the Glass House, New Canaan, Connecticut, 1947.

Solving the problem. By 1944—out of Cambridge, out of the military, back in New York, and attempting to launch his practice—Philip began casting around for a country residence, a retreat from the city that could serve as a professional calling card. He had considered settling in Washington, D.C., where he'd done his military service, or perhaps in New Haven, until he saw a site in nearby New Canaan, Connecticut: a 47-acre (19-hectare) parcel below Ponus Ridge, adjacent to its eponymous road. Philip bought it almost on sight, enchanted in particular by a rocky plateau in the middle of the property with a sweeping view "almost to New York," as his friend John Stroud declared on his first visit. With the help of Gores, Philip set about dreaming up the kind of home he might build there and what kind of statement he might make with it.

Architect

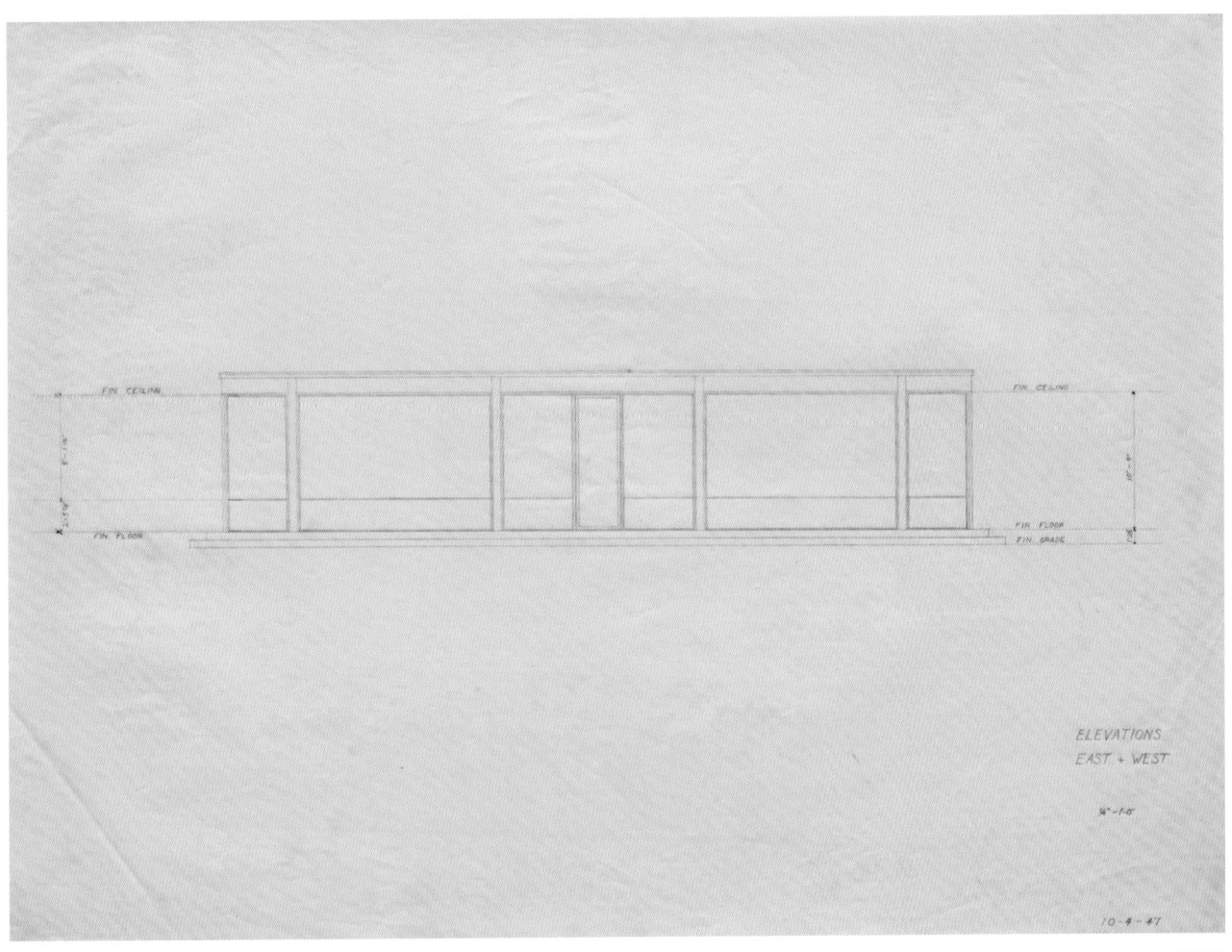

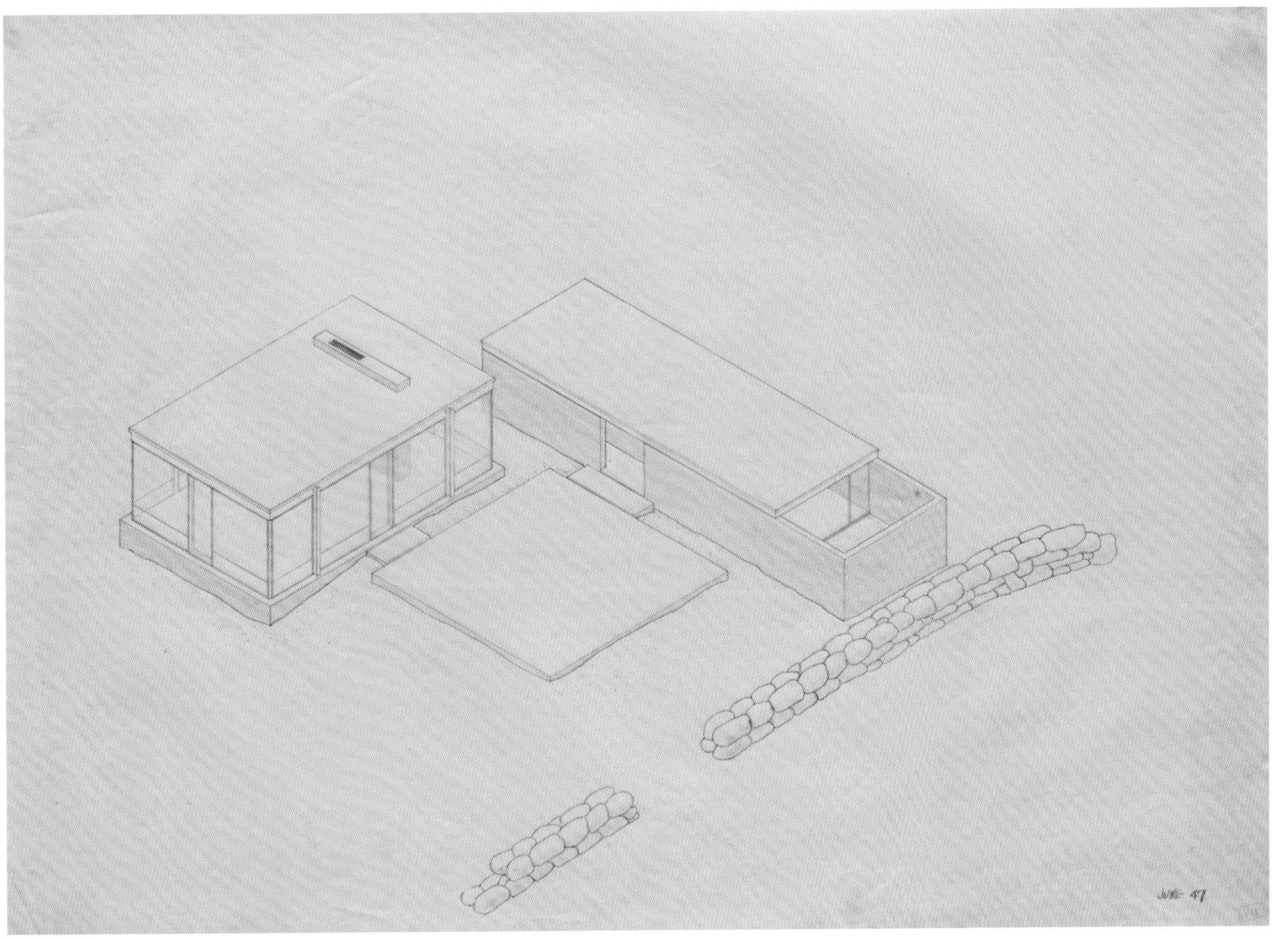

Top: Preliminary elevation of the Glass House, New Canaan, Connecticut, showing the cylindrical core and fireplace, 1947. Bottom: Preliminary perspective drawing of the Glass House and linked terrace, 1947.

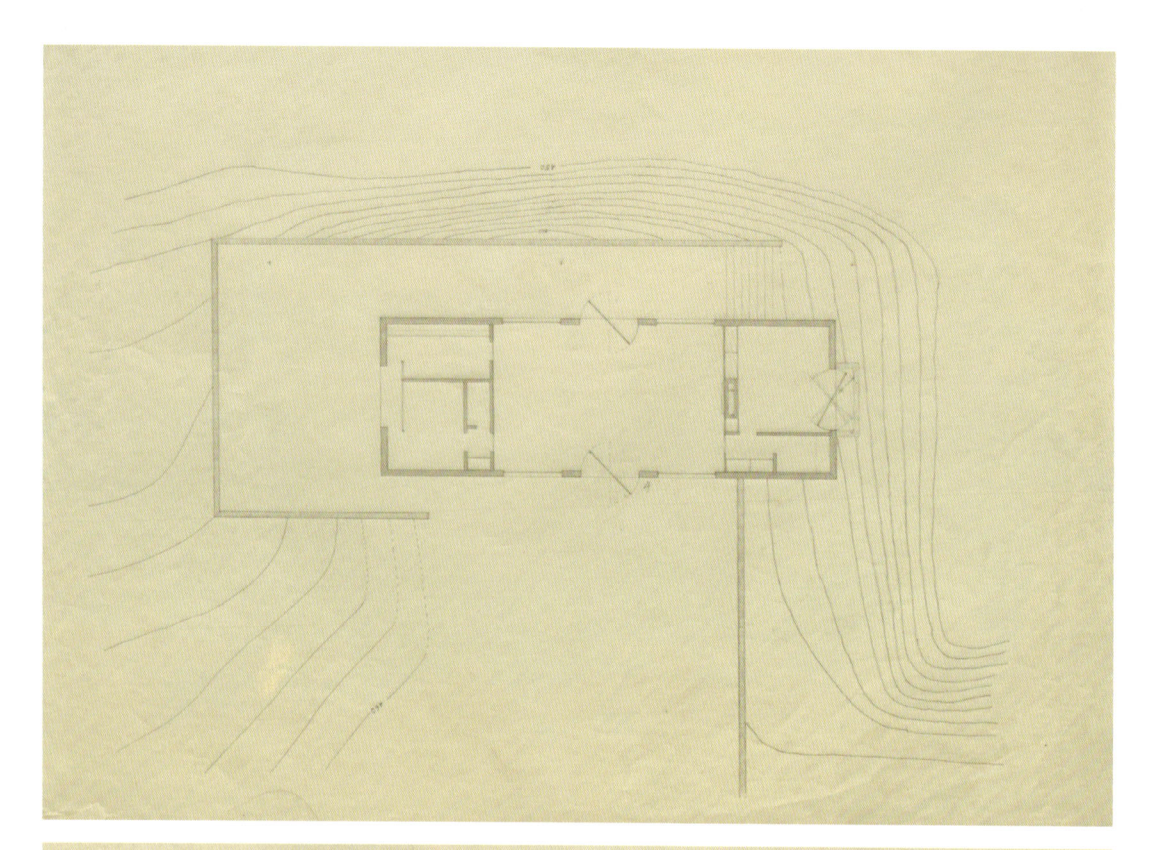

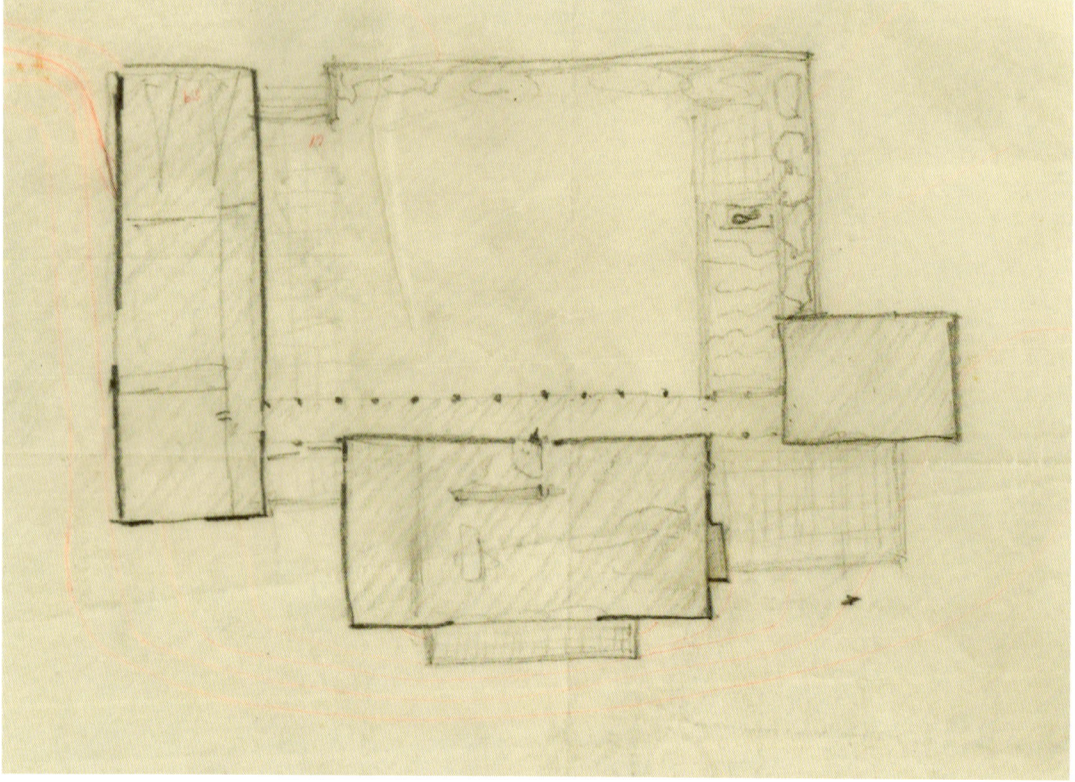

Top: Plan of the Glass House, New Canaan, Connecticut, 1949.
Bottom: Preliminary plan sketch for the Glass House, 1949.

Architect

Final plan, based on Scheme XXVII, of the Glass House, New Canaan, Connecticut, 1949.

View from the south of the Glass House, New Canaan, Connecticut, 1949.

The Glass House, Phase 1. From the man who would declare that architecture is "the art of how to waste space,"[6] the house that Philip built for himself is remarkably economical: just 1,800 square feet (167 m^2), neatly divided into living room, kitchen, bedroom, and bathroom. Though nothing was left to chance, much of its creation was ad hoc: the roof was of simple (and leak-prone) timber, and the corner details do not resolve as neatly as in Mies's projects. Philip's homage to the recently emigrated eminence was not warmly received by Mies—his first visit ended in a drunken rage—nor by Wright, who on entering it for the first time declared that he didn't know whether "to take my hat off or leave it on."[7]

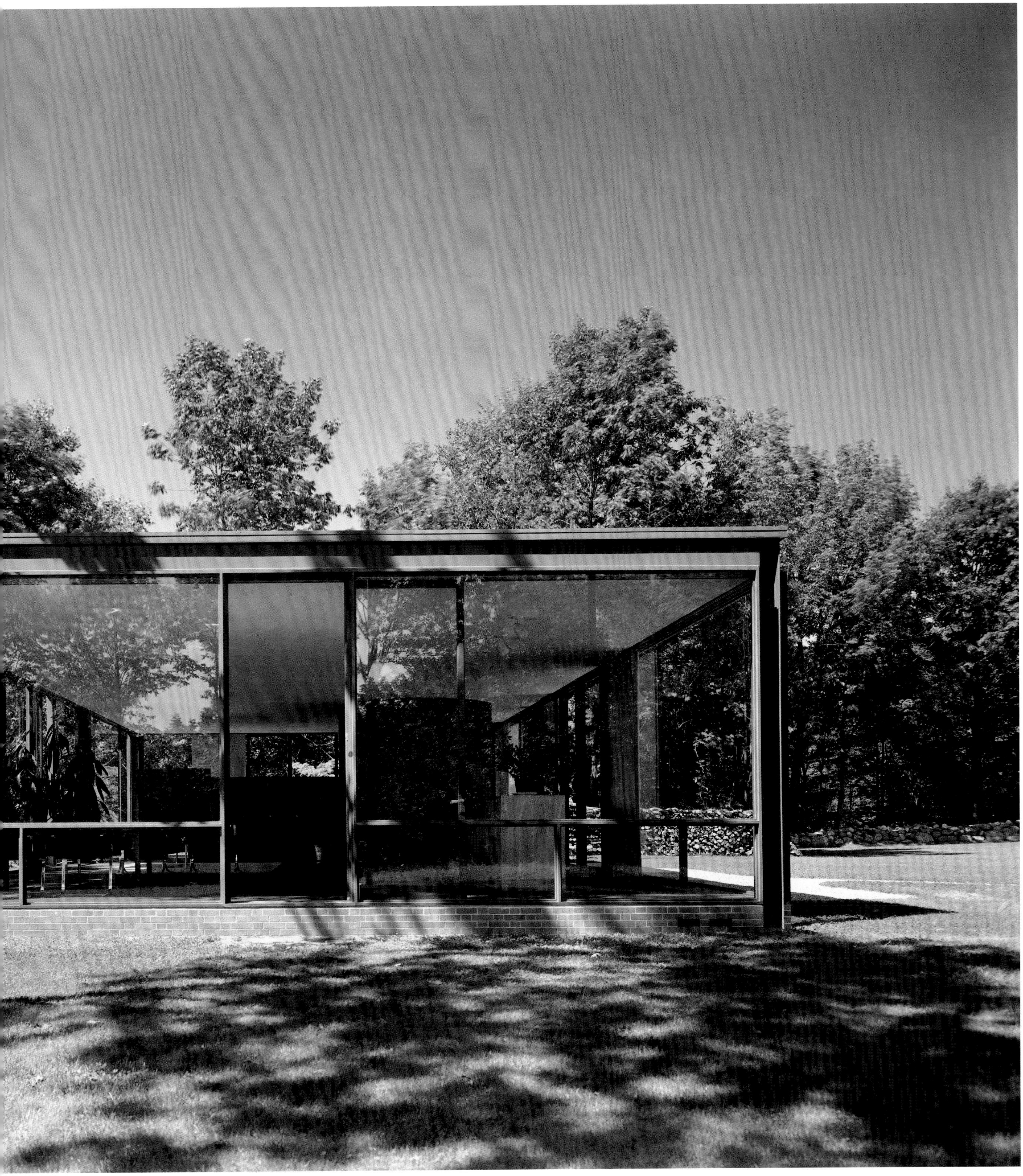

View from the east of the Glass House, New Canaan, Connecticut, 1949.

Architect

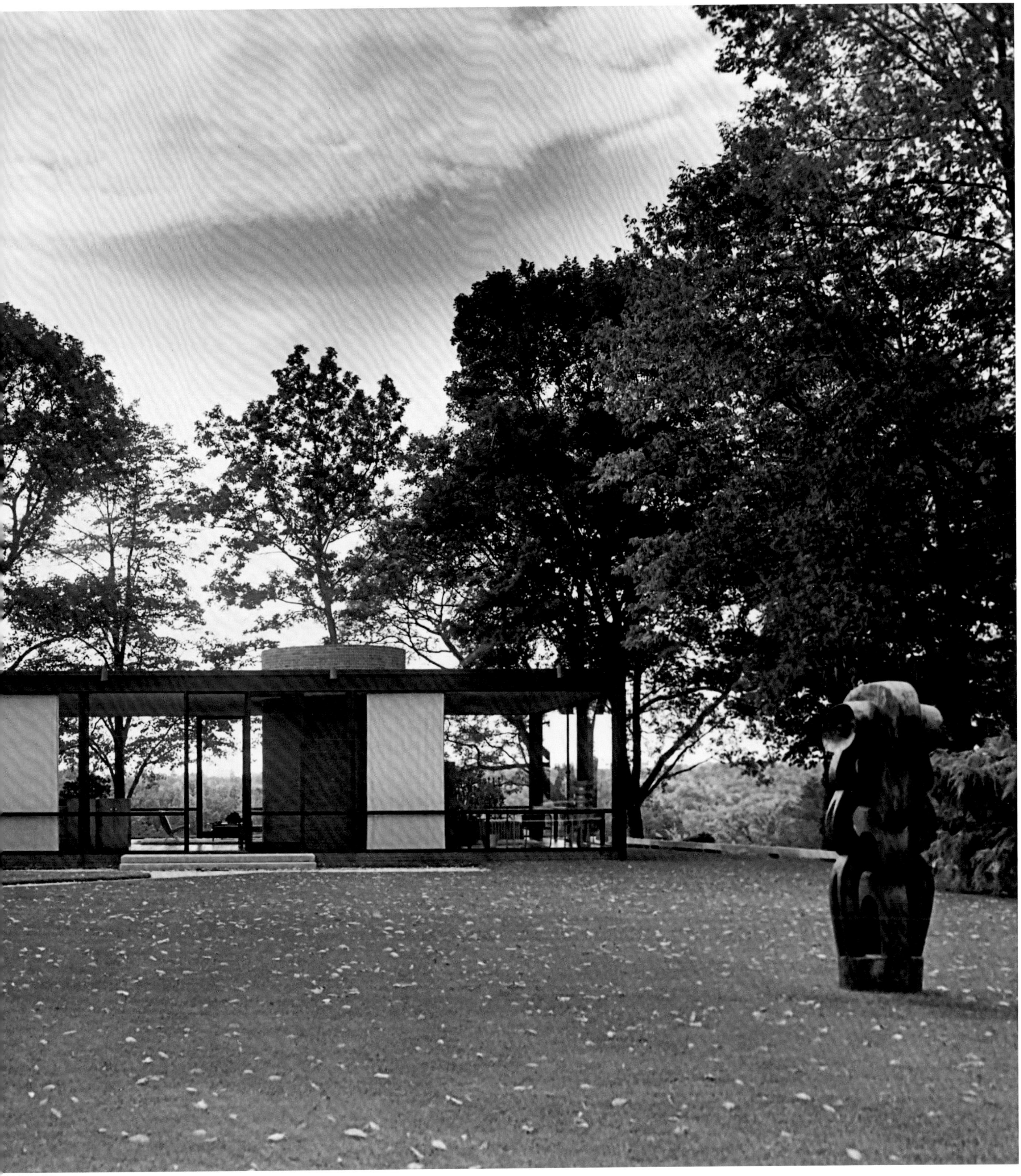

View from the south-east of the Glass House, New Canaan, Connecticut, 1949.

"Don't build a glass house if you're worried about saving money on heating."

—One of Philip's life lessons, aged 92

Architect

View from the south of the Glass House, New Canaan, Connecticut, 1949.

Interior view of the living room, the Glass House, New Canaan, Connecticut, 1949.

Interior view of the living room, the Glass House, New Canaan, Connecticut, 1949.

Interior view of the living room, the Glass House, New Canaan, Connecticut, 1949. A small sculpture by Alberto Giacometti, *Night* (1947), is on the coffee table. Due to deterioration, Philip shipped the sculpture back to Giacometti in the 1960s for repairs. Inspired by this disappearance, the Glass House hosted one-work sculpture shows that brought borrowed works into the house for several months at a time throughout 2015.

Sensation. Never mind Mies and Wright; the rest of the world was obsessed. Early visitors were seized by "awe" and "wonder," the *New York Times* reported, while photographs of the house adorned major architecture publications in America and abroad. Philip, it was said, never considered a project finished until it was published, a principle he first demonstrated with the Glass House. Decked out with artifacts both ancient and modern—an Elie Nadelman statue, a (possibly misattributed) Poussin painting, Mies and Reich's Barcelona furniture—the house was made to be looked at.

Architect

146

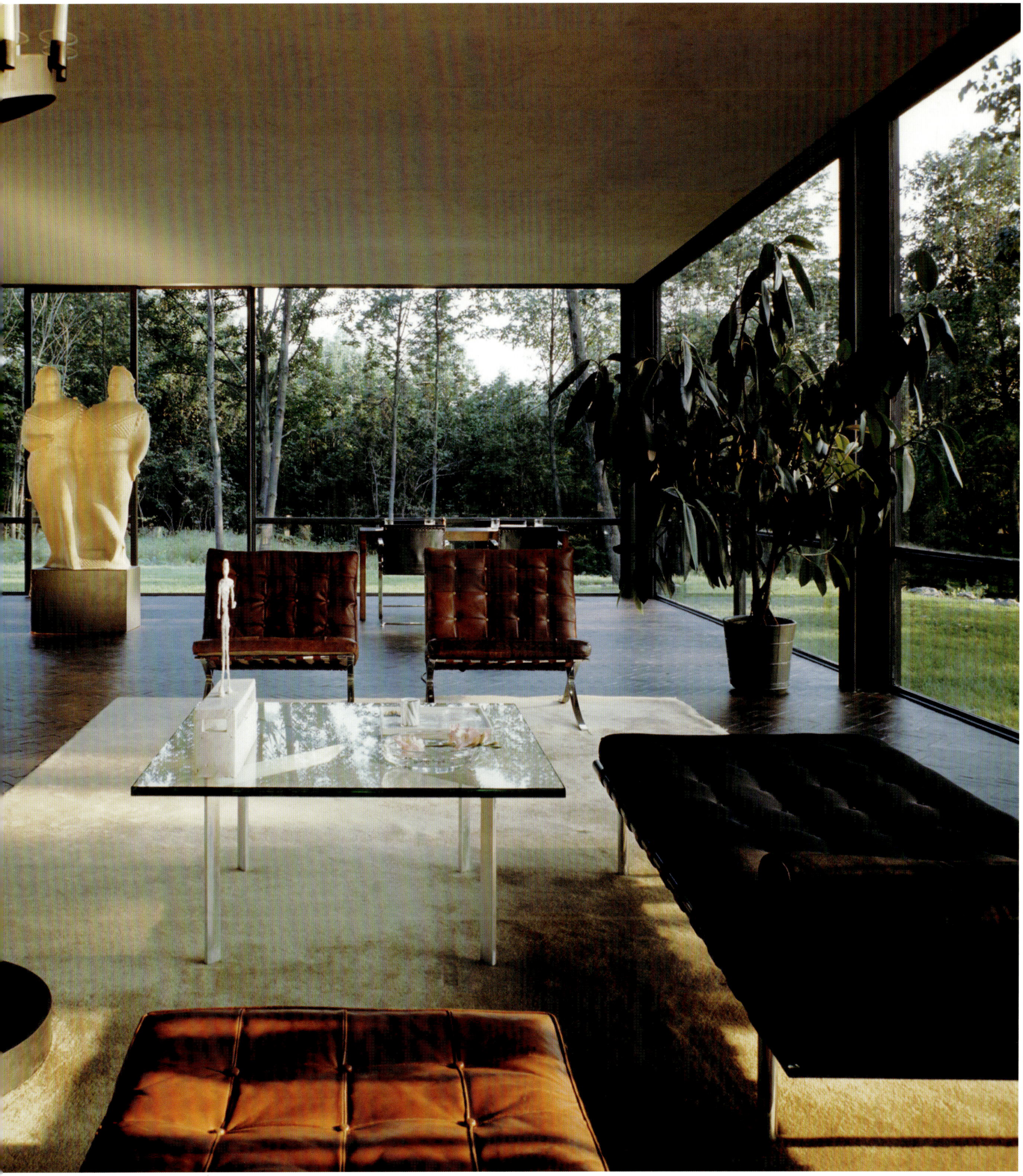

Philip adjusting logs in the fireplace at the Glass House, 1966. The spherical volume houses the bathroom.

Top: Philip relaxing in the Glass House bedroom section, which is separated from the kitchen by cabinets, 1966. Bottom: Philip seated on one of the Barcelona chairs in the Glass House, c. 1959.

149

Philip in his kitchen at the Glass House, 1966.

But was it livable? While Philip would often spend nights in the older, conventional house on the property, he did indeed use the Glass House as a regular residence and made adjustments to the bathroom, lighting scheme, and other particulars in order to render it more hospitable, protected from the elements and the insects of rural Connecticut. Then again, accommodation was never his primary concern. As he wrote in 1954, "I would rather sleep in Chartres Cathedral with the nearest toilet two blocks away than in a Harvard house with back-to-back bathrooms."[8]

Architect

Philip lounging in front of the Glass House, surveying the beautiful Fairfield County vista, 1966.

The Glass House and the Brick House from the north-east.

The Brick House. As part of Philip's original conception for the New Canaan compound, the Glass House was to be accompanied by a guest house that was everything its counterpart was not: completed in 1949, the Brick House was a near-solid box with a romantic interior draped in fabric. Whereas the Glass House had departed only marginally from the Miesian model, the Brick House took greater liberties, with dramatic lighting, lush drapery, and canopies reminiscent of the work of John Soane.

Top: Philip in the Brick House, 1966. A welded metal sculpture hangs over the bed. Bottom: Interior view of the bedroom in the Brick House, New Canaan, Connecticut, 1949.

This page and opposite: Photographer James Welling used colored filters to produce interpretations of the Glass House. The series of large-scale prints was shown at David Zwirner gallery, New York, in 2010. Top: James Welling, *0158*, 2006. Bottom: James Welling, *0696*, 2006.

Architect

Top: James Welling, *0865*, 2006. Bottom: James Welling, *0806*, 2006.

View of the Lake Pavilion pond, featuring Japanese artist Yayoi Kusama's installation, *Narcissus Garden*, 2016. The work, which consists of 1,300 floating steel balls, was originally created for the 1966 Venice Biennale.

Reverberations. Completed two years before Farnsworth House, Philip's Modernist getaway beat Mies to the punch and became a cultural phenomenon—a pilgrimage site, the object of satire and homage, and more recently the subject of artist interventions, sponsored by the Glass House Conservancy, which now maintains the property. Yet, familiar as it is, the Glass House is still a peculiar work, one that hides unsettling secrets in plain sight. The cylindrical brick volume, breaking the simplicity of the steel box, was once likened by Philip to a ruined village he had seen years before; he meant, of course, a place he'd seen in Poland during his fascist period. As historian Anthony Vidler once wrote, the Glass House could then be read as "a Polish farmhouse 'purified' by the fire of war of everything but its architectural 'essence'": an uncanny echo of a dark past, lurking within the familiar icon of American glamor.

Architect

Each of the 1,300 balls drifting on the pond has a diameter of approximately twelve inches (thirty centimeters).

Glass House
New Canaan, CT 1949

As Philip Johnson once observed, "purpose is not necessary to make a building beautiful." He designed his famous house of steel and glass more to be seen than to be lived in. Serene proportion, balance, and overall symmetry distinguish this landmark.

Top: Bill Griffith, *Zippy the Pinhead*, "*Manimalism*", 22 June 2010. The cartoon quips about the perceived masculinity in the lack of embellishment in Philip's architectural style. Above: A 37-cent commemorative stamp depicting the Glass House. This stamp, designed by Margaret Bauer, is one of twelve in a series titled "Masterworks of Modern American Architecture," issued 19 May 2005.

Roz Chast, *A Visit From The Relatives*, 2013. The cartoon points out the absurdity of Philip's Modernist style when overlaid by a domestic scene.

Architect

Grant Snider, *Iconic Houses*, 25 January 2012. The cartoon plays on the phrase "people who live in glass houses shouldn't throw stones."

"My place in New Canaan is a kind of 'diary of an eccentric architect.' I have kept this diary for almost fifty years starting with the purchase of the land in 1946."

Philip Johnson in *Philip Johnson: The Glass House* by David Whitney and Jeffrey Kipnis (New York: Pantheon Books, 1993)

"From the beginning of his career, Philip Johnson's best client has always been Philip Johnson, and his best-known work is still the glass house that he built for himself in 1949, on a green hillside in New Canaan."

Calvin Tomkins, *New Yorker*, 23 May 1977

"In order to live successfully in Philip Johnson's new house one would have to be Philip Johnson, or at least a reasonable facsimile."

Arthur Drexler, *Interiors and Industrial Design*, October 1949

"The Glass House is on a promontory, a peninsula, to make a 'cup' of the experience of entering. A dead end so you know you have arrived: there is no further to go. Within the house there is more procession, however. The 'entrance hall' (the pushing together of the chimney and kitchen cabinet) forces you (gently, to be sure) between them into the living room, where you climb onto the 'raft' of white rug which is the ultimate arrival point, the sitting group which floats in its separate sea of dark brick. I purposely exaggerate the processional aspects, which in reality are not so obvious to the casual visitor. But then what is obvious to a visitor about the quality of architecture?"

Philip Johnson, *Show* magazine, June 1963

"Every grown up child should have his version of a playhouse, and this pavilion in a pond is mine. I designed and built the pavilion for two reasons: one, the place needed a gazebo and, secondly, I wanted deliberately to fly in the face of the 'Modern' tradition of functionalist architecture by trying to hold on to an older, nobler tradition of garden architecture."

Philip Johnson, *Show* magazine, June 1963

"The cylinder, made from the same brick as the platform from which it springs, forming the main motif of the house, was not derived from Mies, but rather from a burnt wooden village I saw once … Over the chimney I slipped a steel cage with a glass skin."

Philip Johnson, *Architectural Review*, September 1950

"A Poussin painting on a metal easel, near the cluster of chairs, is set just where the conventional might have placed an abstraction. By a fortunate arrangement between the architect and the landscape, the trees outside now resemble those in the painting, where they look like feathers stuck in the ground."

Arthur Drexler, *Interiors and Industrial Design*, October 1949

"Throughout his career, the otherwise mercurial Philip Johnson has remained steadfastly faithful to one principle alone: that architecture is first, foremost, and finally a visual art."

Jeffrey Kipnis in *Philip Johnson: The Glass House* by David Whitney and Jeffrey Kipnis (New York: Pantheon Books, 1993)

"In a traditional sense both Pennzoil Place and the Glass House are a-spatial; the latter is a void, and the former is a solid. But both lack the traditional energies—tension, compression, and so forth—that mark architectural space. They represent the beginning and the end of Modern architecture … In a more general context, the Glass House prefigures for me the parallel anxiety of post-World War II architecture. It remains the last pure form, the final gesture of a belief in a humanism so debilitated by the events of 1945."

Peter Eisenman in *Philip Johnson Writings* (New York: Oxford University Press, 1979)

"Taken together, the buildings on his estate at New Canaan are a remarkable group; far more than the ultimate expression of one man's personal taste, they represent an attempt to come to grips, over time, with a variety of notions of what architecture is. They are the result of an agile mind probing, refining, rethinking, from the Glass House's explorations within Miesian vocabulary and ironic interplay of inside and outside, to the art and sculpture galleries' newer, more striking forms and use of space."

Paul Goldberger, *Smithsonian* magazine, September 1975

Interior view of the Rockefeller Guest House, New York, 1950. Blanchette Ferry Hooker Rockefeller, who commissioned Philip to design the Guest House, is sitting in the living room and the sculpture on the right is Alberto Giacometti's *Man Pointing* (1947).

Little house in midtown. Since he first embarked on architecture, Philip had dreamed of a commission from the Rockefellers; now, finally, following his triumph at the Glass House, he got one. Against the objections of her husband, John D. Rockefeller III, Blanchette Rockefeller commissioned the two-story guest house on 52nd Street in 1949. Completed at a cost of $64,000, it was so small that it qualified as an "alteration." Philip lived there himself in the 1970s; in 2000 it was sold to an unknown party for over $11 million, the highest price per square foot for any New York property to that date.

Architect

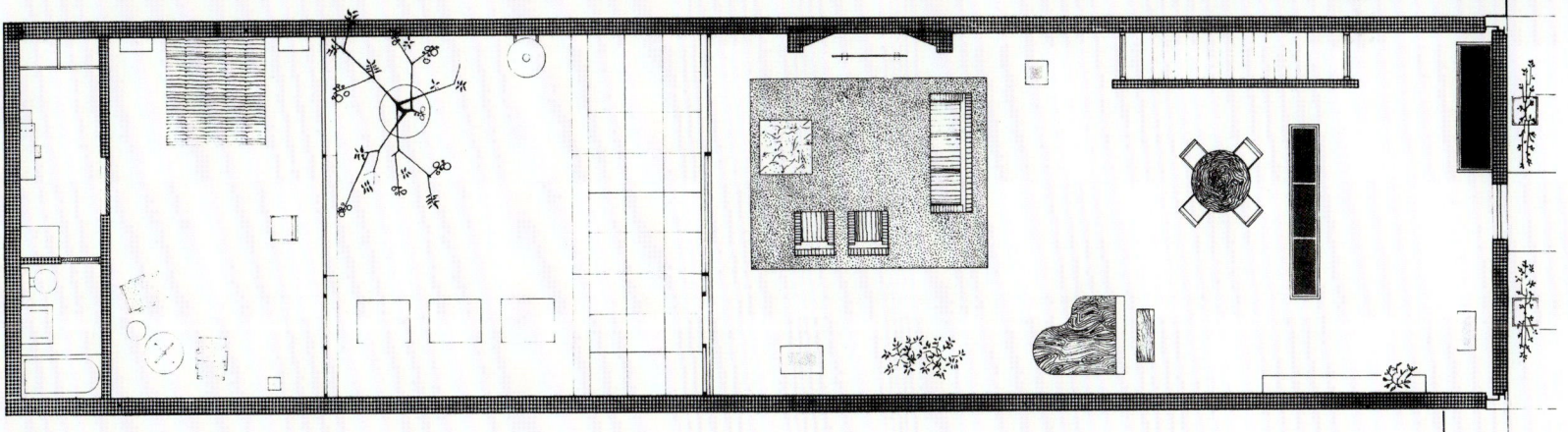

Top: Street facade of the Rockefeller Guest House, New York, 1950.
Bottom: Plan of the Rockefeller Guest House.

163

Installation view, *Mies van der Rohe*, Museum of Modern Art, New York, 16 September 1947–25 January 1948. The display on the left is an image of a lost model of a glass skyscraper project, 1922.

Portrait of Ludwig Mies van der Rohe, 1948.

The master at the museum. In another long-deferred dream come true, in 1947 Philip succeeded in staging a retrospective of Mies at MoMA (to whose good graces Philip had lately been restored). Allowing his subject to design the exhibition himself, Philip sat back and arranged the social and institutional logistics, furnishing a suitable platform for the man who, he claimed (in his catalog essay for the show), surpassed all his contemporaries: "None," Philip wrote, "equalled the breadth and depth of Mies van der Rohe's pioneer work; none of them explored so far." Mies was pleased, if only just.

Architect

Top: Philip and Mies in the galleries of the exhibition *Mies van der Rohe*, Museum of Modern Art, New York, 16 September 1947–25 January 1948. On the left is a collage interior perspective of a concert hall by Mies that was never built, 1942. Bottom: Installation view of the exhibit. On the left is an image of Mies's Monument to the November Revolution, Berlin, 1926, which was destroyed by Nazis in 1935.

Phyllis Lambert working on plans of the Seagram Building.

The tower. A more substantive collaboration between Philip and his favorite architect would begin taking shape seven years after the MoMA exhibition. Canadian architect Phyllis Lambert was the daughter of Samuel Bronfman, the business tycoon behind the Seagram liquor conglomerate; when the company set out to build a new Manhattan headquarters, Lambert took the helm and brought Philip in as her primary consultant. The two embarked on a nationwide search to find an architect to design the proposed tower. In truth, for Philip at least, the choice was a forgone conclusion.

"I consider I was born when I built this building."

—Phyllis Lambert on the Seagram Building

Architect

166

Philip (standing), Lambert, and Mies examine a working model of a fountain in a laboratory at the Massachusetts Institute of Technology, Cambridge, Massachusetts, October 1956. A full-size version of the fountain was intended for the plaza of the trio's Seagram Building, completed two years later.

Philip, Ludwig Mies van der Rohe, and Phyllis Lambert in front of a photograph of a model of the Seagram Building, 1955.

Portrait of Philip and Mies with a model of the Seagram Building, 1955.

"Alfred Barr turned Phyllis Lambert over to me. She came and said, 'How do I find an architect?' I said, 'I'll drive you around the country, and we'll find one.' Then I sort of inched her over until she liked Mies the best. I didn't say, 'You've gotta pick Mies,' but I was influential. That's power, huh?"

—Philip on maneuvering taste

Architect

Model of the Seagram Building showing a view of the plaza, 1956.

East view of the Seagram Building under construction, New York, 1958.

East view of the Seagram Building under construction, New York, 1958.

The plaza at the Seagram Building by Philip Johnson and Ludwig Mies van der Rohe, New York, 1958.

Architect

Seagram Building by Philip Johnson and Ludwig Mies van der Rohe, New York, 1958.

View of the plaza and entrance to the Seagram Building by Philip Johnson
and Ludwig Mies van der Rohe, at night, New York, 1958.

Stairs at the entrance to the Seagram Building by Philip Johnson
and Ludwig Mies van der Rohe, New York, 1958.

The lobby of the Seagram Building by Philip Johnson and Ludwig Mies van der Rohe, New York, 1958.

Mecca. What architecture critic Herbert Muschamp would call "the millennium's most important building" was indeed as influential as any constructed in living memory. The City of New York altered its zoning ordinances to encourage other architects to copy Mies's ample plaza, and soon all of Park Avenue was dotted with similar structures, to say nothing of the countless lookalikes that sprang up all across the country. As the de facto epicenter of American architecture, Seagram was a natural place for Philip to set up shop—especially given his intense personal connection to its design, which he'd overseen after Mies ran into licensing difficulty. Along with many of the interior details, Philip was chiefly responsible for the famed Four Seasons restaurant downstairs: his favored spot for lunches, dinners, and gossipy tête-à-têtes, it became as much a headquarters to him as his office upstairs.

Architect

Interior view of an office in the Seagram Building by Philip Johnson and
Ludwig Mies van der Rohe, New York, 1958.

Interior view of the Seagram Building by Philip Johnson and Ludwig Mies van der Rohe, New York, 1958.

Interior view of the Seagram Building by Philip Johnson and Ludwig Mies van der Rohe, New York, 1958.

Interior view of Philip's office in the Seagram Building by Philip Johnson and Ludwig Mies van der Rohe, New York, 1958. The Queensboro Bridge and River House can be seen from the window.

Architect

Interior view of an office in the Seagram Building by Philip Johnson and Ludwig Mies van der Rohe, New York, 1958.

Portrait of Philip at his desk in his office in the Seagram Building, 1982.

Architect

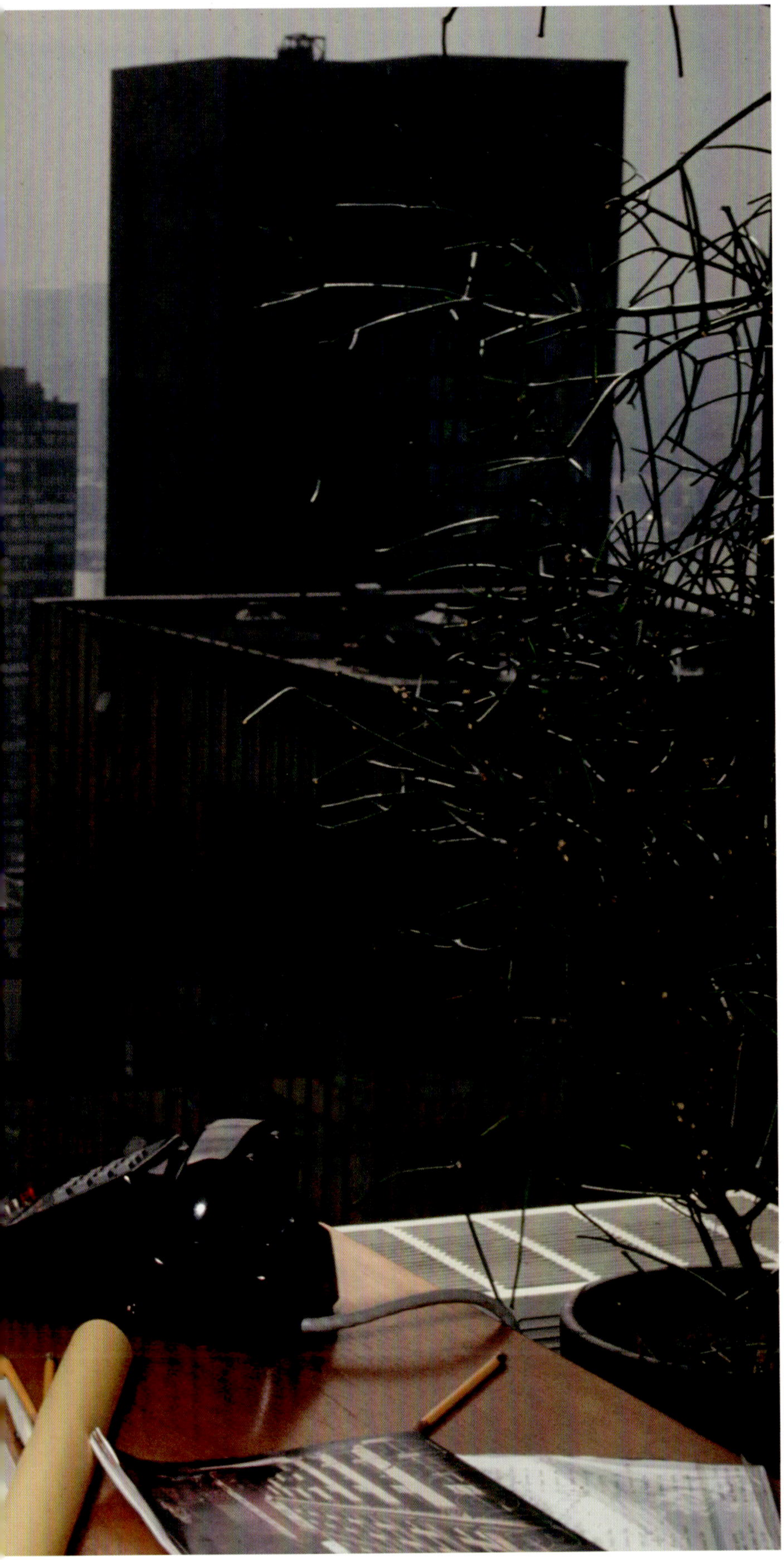

Interior view of the Pool Room in the Four Seasons restaurant in the Seagram Building. The potted trees were changed in tandem with the seasons.

Interior view of the Pool Room in the Four Seasons restaurant in the Seagram Building.

Portrait of the original creative team of the Grill Room at the Four Seasons restaurant in the Seagram Building. The group includes Philip (front right) and Phyllis Lambert (front left).

Architect

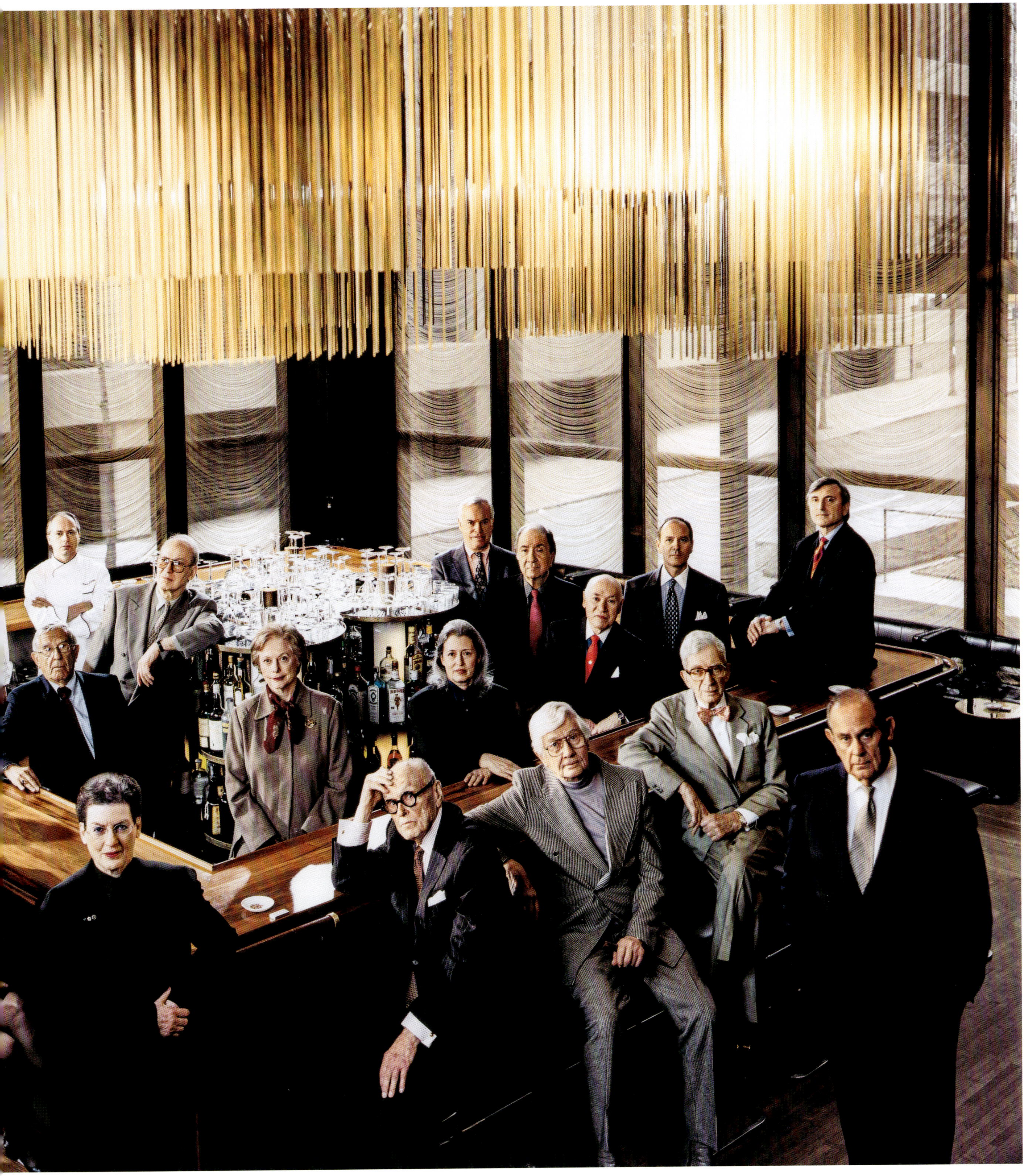

"Interior planting was considered from the early design stages as an integral part of the design ... The clean, elegant articulation of the architecture and its superb refinement are complemented by the majestic specimen trees as living sculptures, plantings with visual and physical strength in the architectural space and volume."

Karl Linn, "The Four Seasons: Collaboration for Elegance." *Progressive Architecture*, December 1959

"The Seagram Building is one of the architectural masterpieces of the 20th century, and arguably the most significant Modern building in New York City. At its center is the Four Seasons, perhaps America's most famous restaurant and an architectural gem itself, having won landmark protection in 1989 ... Mr. Johnson's interior—dominated by two nearly square spaces, the Grill Room and the Pool Room—echoes Mies's exterior through its intense focus on material and details that not only look good, but also shape the ambience of the space."

Phyllis Lambert, "Save New York's Four Seasons." *New York Times*, 15 May 2015

"The problem was unusual: to transform their new ideas for food and service into a distinctive, identifiable line of accessories and equipment in keeping with the sophisticated elegance of the restaurant interiors."

Ada Louise and Garth Huxtable, "The Four Seasons: Collaboration for Elegance." *Progressive Architecture*, December 1959

"America's most powerful lunch is eaten in the Grill, or the Bar Room, of the Four Seasons restaurant, on the ground floor of the Seagram Building, East Fifty-Second Street, in Manhattan."

Lee Eisenberg, "America's Most Powerful Lunch," *Esquire*, October 1979

Architect

"More than a name, it is the restaurant's idea. Four trees, pink for spring, green for summer, red for fall, and brown for winter form the constant graphic motif, but each color establishes the palette for its own season. Each of the four colors appears in its turn on waiters' jackets, menus and matchbooks, while other changing colors, those of the flowers for example, harmonize with it … The sculptures over the bar and mezzanine, made of thousands of gold dipped brass rods by Richard Lippold, quiver almost imperceptibly in the light, creating gently changing patterns. According to Philip Johnson this movement is caused by the 'shock of New York'; specifically perhaps by the trains roaring under Park Avenue toward Grand Central."

"More Elegance at the House of Seagram," *Architectural Record*, November 1959

"My only determined effort was to create a kind of heart for this building of my affections and to translate its beauties into a work of art that would enhance without distraction, repeat without redundancy the virtues of the architecture, and so make an inseparable entity of the two. It is not for me to imply that the building would suffer through lack of the sculpture, but I would like to state that I feel the sculpture would surely lose most of its meaning without the building. Unless this is so, I have not succeeded."

Richard Lippold, "The Four Seasons: Collaboration for Elegance," *Progressive Architecture*, December 1959

"By his own account, Philip Johnson's eyes filled with tears when Mies van der Rohe offered him a partnership as coarchitect of the Seagram Building: 'Shall we make it an der Rohe and Johnson?'"

Phyllis Lambert, "*Stimmung* at Seagram: Philip Johnson Counters Mies van der Rohe," *Grey Room* 20, Summer 2005

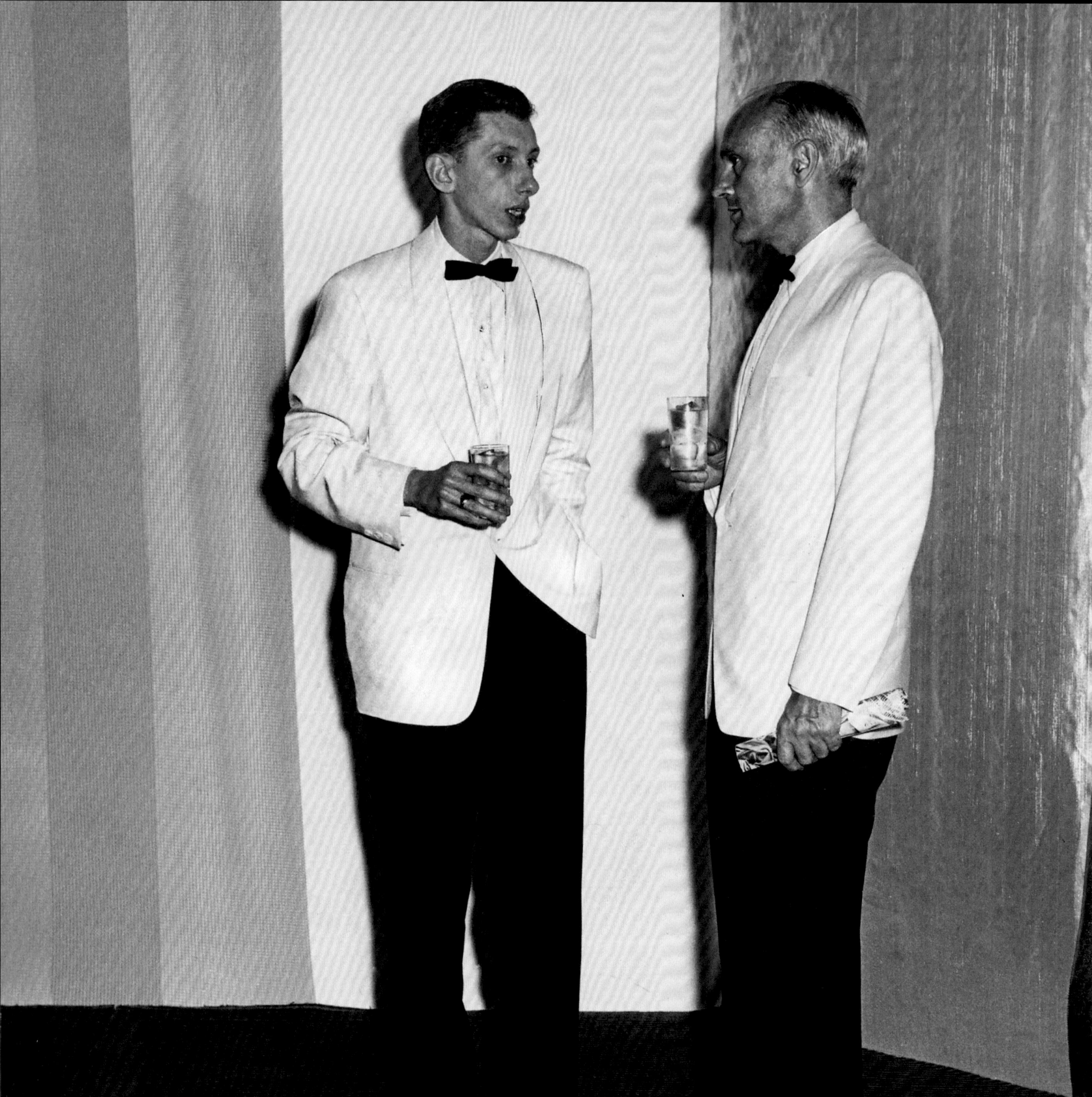

06 Socialite

Socialite

Tying together Philip's life and career was a genius for friendship that ranks among the greatest of the twentieth century. His wit and charm helped him maintain both a stable of devoted clients and a network of influence that went well beyond the world of architecture. Certainly his immense wealth was a factor, allowing him to leave some of the finer points of his practice to various associates while moving easily and comfortably through high society; likewise, his sexuality, though typically a liability at the time, proved in Philip's case to be something of an asset, allowing him to carry on years-long relationships with well-placed women without the complications of romantic involvement. "I seem to have a sort of charisma that I don't understand at all," Philip once remarked. "It isn't due to ability."[1] It could be said that he sold himself short: his charisma *was* an ability, one he parlayed brilliantly into a role as one of America's foremost tastemakers.

His debut among the famous and fabulous was perfectly timed: the coinage of the very term *socialite* dates to the late 1920s, invented by the editors of *Time* magazine (on whose cover Philip would eventually appear, the last architect to do so). While analogous figures had existed for eons, the debut of the neologism signaled a new potential for a certain kind of public actor—the confluence of modern media, modern economics, and an (at least somewhat) more liberal and meritocratic pecking order allowed someone of precisely Philip's flair, affluence, and talent to assume an outsize prominence. And so it was at the tail end of the Jazz Age that Philip first began to ply the waters of the beau monde, dating the café singer Jimmie Daniels, befriending the composer Virgil Thomson—for whom Philip helped stage his most famous opera, *Four Saints in Three Acts*, with its Gertrude Stein libretto—and generally hobnobbing with a smart set that included Edward Warburg, Lincoln Kirstein, and Rockefellers and Whitneys of varying descriptions.

In the postwar years, the sphere that Philip inhabited would dilate dramatically. Especially beginning in the 1960s, with Philip's reputation as an architect firmly established, the locus of his fame shifted from the society pages (already rather outmoded) to the front pages of glossy magazines. In addition to the old-money, art-collecting crowd with whom he'd long mingled, Philip could now count Jacqueline Kennedy Onassis, New York mayor John Lindsay, and author Arthur M. Schlesinger among his regular associates. A whole new realm of acquaintanceship opened up to him through his last and longest romantic partner, David Whitney: while no relation to the museum of the same name, Whitney moved in the most rarified circles of contemporary art, and through him the emerging New York avant-garde suddenly had a conduit to the now nearly sixty-year-old architect. Andy Warhol, Lou Reed, John Cage, and Merce Cunningham all became intimates, at least by proxy, and various of their collaborators and hangers-on would put in at least cameo appearances at the Glass House.

The distinct nature of Philip's celebrity was (and remains) unique among American architects. "His fame as a designer," noted Mark Lamster, his second biographer, "rested largely on his own house."[2] For all of the work accumulated over seven decades in the field, no Philip building—save perhaps for the little cube in New Canaan, Connecticut—was half as famous as the architect himself. Even the Glass House paled, for general recognition, in comparison to the bespectacled face of the guru-like figure who lived there, the nightlife gadabout always ready with pithy quotes like "I am a whore" and "Architecture is the art of how to waste space." Many (Lamster among them) have seen Philip as prefiguring the twenty-first-century "starchitect," the bold-name designer whose presence adds sizzle to big-money developments; and yet, unlike with most of the practitioners who would later assume that title, Philip's success did not rest on creating a singular, iconic, and instantly identifiable aesthetic that could then be commodified and replicated the world over. What Philip sold, at all events, was Philip.

In that regard, his was a kind of "pure" fame, the variety best exemplified by his friend Warhol: Philip was famous for being famous, for keeping company with famous people—people like Warhol himself, who also embodied this new kind of social agent, living his life to the rhythm of flashbulbs. It was joked about the artist that he would "attend the opening of an envelope"—and so might Philip, if only the name on the envelope were interesting enough. In what must be a credit to the architect's capacious intellect (if not necessarily his personal discernment), the people he found interesting came in infinite shapes and sizes: Isaiah Berlin, Shimon Peres, Barbara Walters, Kitty Carlisle Hart, Bill Paley—and, yes, Donald Trump. Philip took them all in, seemingly without fear or favor, and they all returned the compliment.

Socialite 192

The Velvet Underground at the Glass House in 1967. The group performed for a Merce Cunningham Dance Company benefit.

A garden party taking place outside the Glass House.

Party central. Nothing else was as much of an asset in Philip's social dealings as the New Canaan, Connecticut, property, a place everybody knew about but only a privileged few were able to visit in person. The events that Philip staged there were the stuff of legend, and the great and the good would flock there to see and be seen—and to see the house, a celebrity in its own right. Its owner was an unfailingly gracious host and a witty one: on entering the Glass House for the first time, one visitor declared that it was "lovely, but I would never want to live here." "Madame," replied Philip, "no one has asked you to."[3]

Socialite

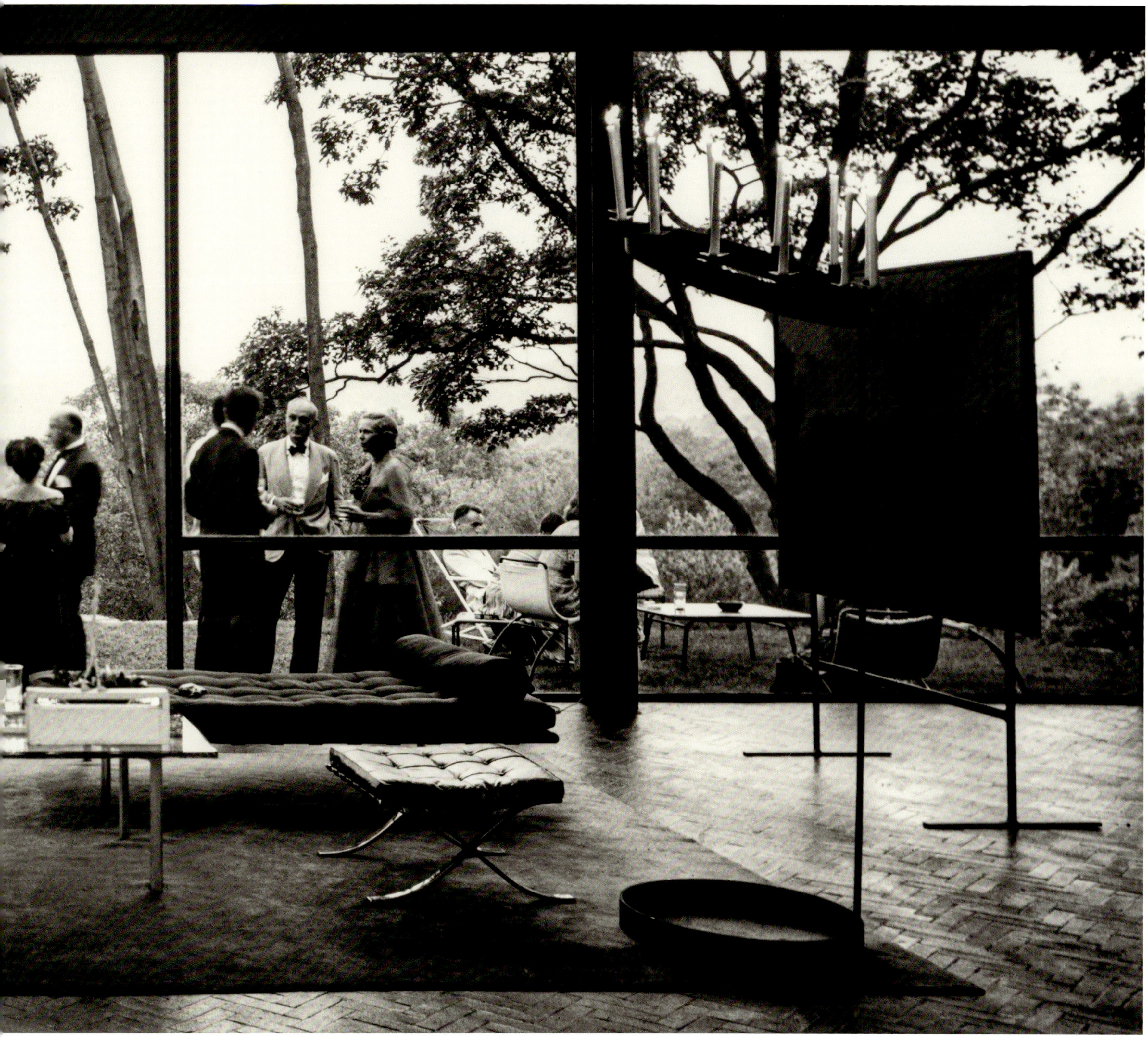

Philip seated halfway up the Monument to Lincoln Kirstein (1985) with the Glass House in the distance.

The enchanted circle. Of the writers, artists, and musicians who formed the core of Philip's social constituency, only one was ever actually enshrined on the Glass House campus itself. Kirstein had met Philip when both were at Harvard, and he became a linchpin connecting Philip to influential figures in New York's dance, literary, and art worlds, just a few of the fields in which Kirstein distinguished himself. The monument Philip built for him in New Canaan has a dedicatory placard at the top with a quote selected by Kirstein—but Philip never disclosed it to nonvisitors. "Each person will have to go for himself and read it," he said. He himself continued to scale the tricky structure even into old age.

Socialite

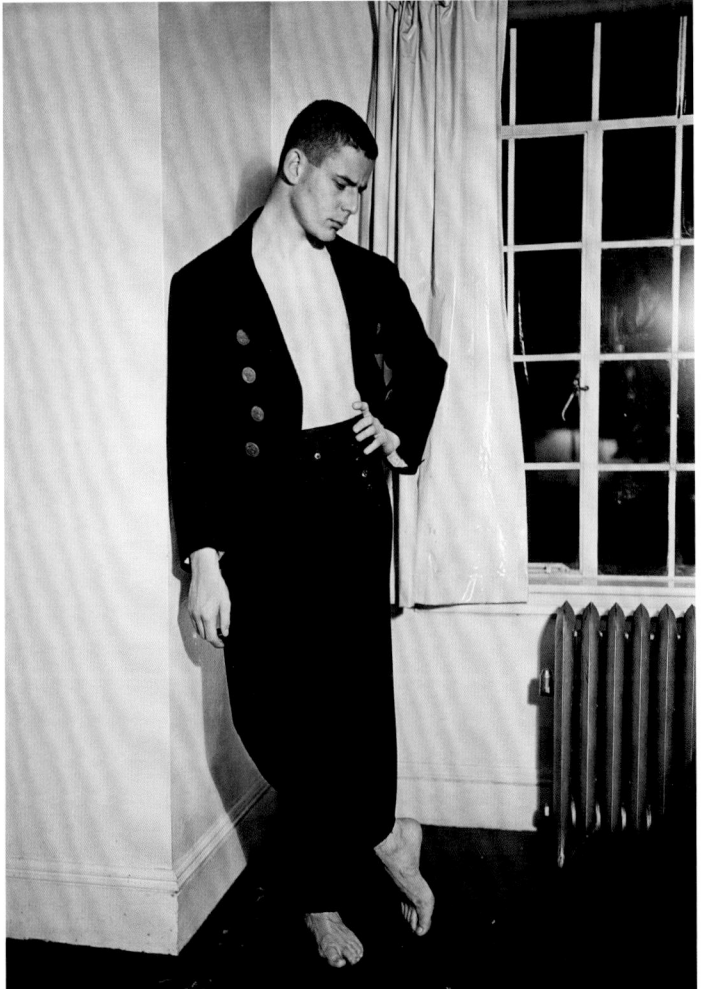

Top: Writer and impresario Lincoln Kirstein with American choreographer George Balanchine, cofounder of the Ballet Society (which later was to become the New York City Ballet), New York. Bottom: Portrait of Lincoln Kirstein, New York, c. 1931.

Top: George Balanchine poses aboard the liner *America*, 26 February 1947. Bottom: Composer Virgil Thomson with writer Gertrude Stein, around the time they collaborated on the opera *Four Saints in Three Acts*, 1927–34.

Above, left: Jacqueline Kennedy Onassis and Philip talk to reporters, voicing their concern for the preservation of Lever House (1952). They joined the New York Landmarks Conservancy to urge the city to uphold the landmarks designation that the building received in 1982. Above, center: Invitation to the opening of *Philip Johnson, Architect: The First Forty Years*, 4 December 1983. Above, right: A clipping of an interview of Philip by Italian journalist Livia Manera, published in *Panorama*, 30 July 1985. It opens, "He loves scandal. Being called a whore does not upset him." The photograph shows Philip with Jacqueline Kennedy Onassis.

Politics. What Philip wanted, from the 1960s onward, was to find what his friend and sometime client Gerald D. Hines called "the Medici of today"—a patron with sufficient power and vision to create great architecture for its own sake. In the postwar years, that meant government projects, and to pursue them Philip ingratiated himself with the governing class, putting himself in the orbit of governors (Nelson Rockefeller especially, who spurned his advances) and mayors (John Lindsay, who did the same), as well as presidents and first ladies. If he never quite found his Lorenzo, he did secure some very high-profile commissions and made a few very high-profile friends.

Socialite 198

Top: Philip, Jacqueline Kennedy Onassis, Bess Myerson, and Ed Koch, New York, January 1975. The picture was taken after a news conference for the Committee to Save Grand Central Station. Bottom: Philip with Jacqueline Kennedy Onassis, New York, December 1983.

Philip with a model of his memorial to John F. Kennedy, December 1965.

Philip holding his design for the John F. Kennedy Memorial, 1965.

JFK. What might have been Philip's most important public commission —a memorial for John F. Kennedy near the site of his assassination— proved to be among his least successful endeavors. Despite his personal friendship with the president's widow, Jackie never visited.

Socialite

Philip kneeling by a plaque at the John F. Kennedy Memorial, Dallas, Texas, 1970.

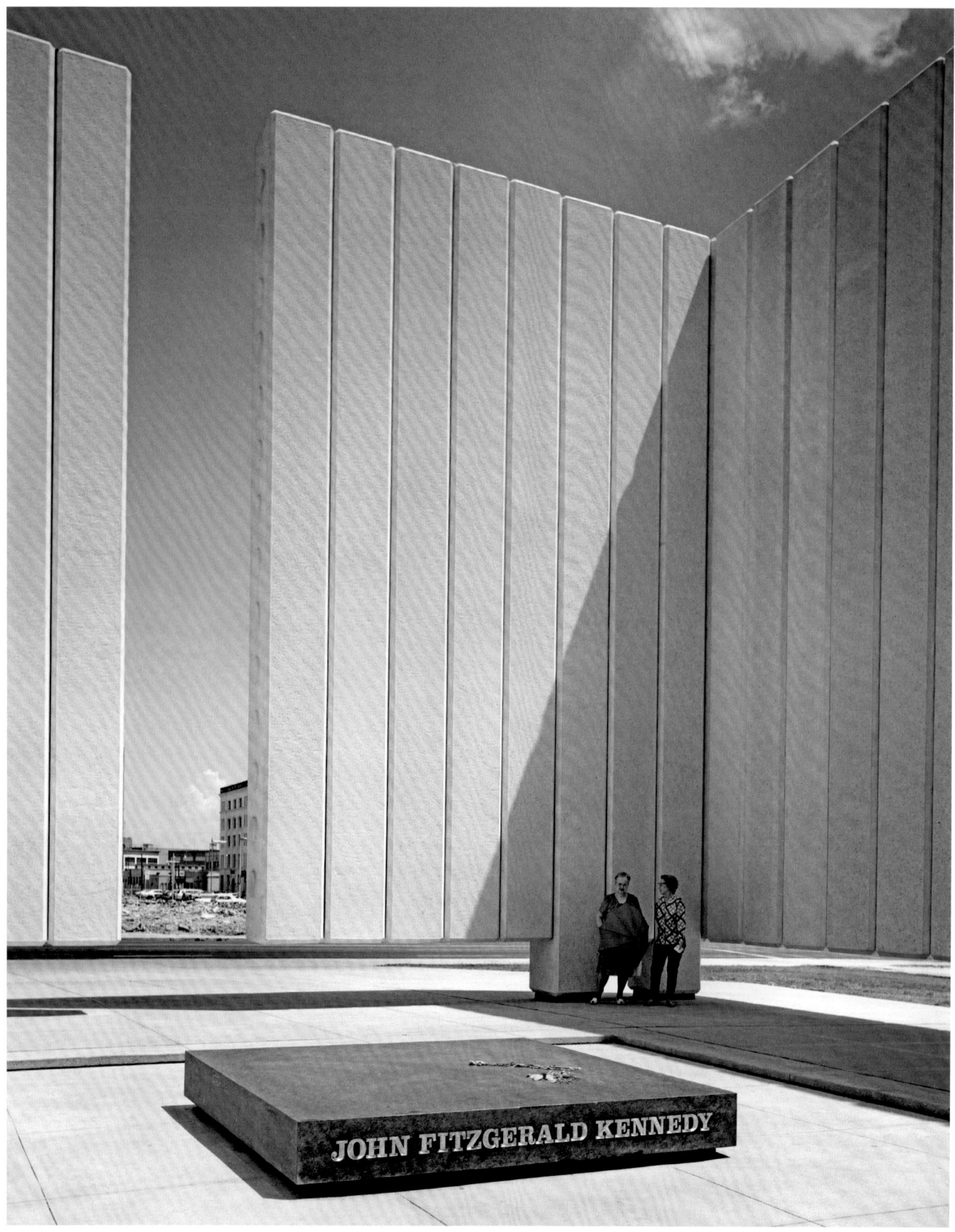

John F. Kennedy Memorial, Dallas, Texas, 1970.

John F. Kennedy Memorial, Dallas, Texas, 1970.

Aerial view of the John F. Kennedy Memorial, Dallas, Texas, 1970.

Socialite

204

John F. Kennedy Memorial, Dallas, Texas, 1970.

Philip talking to Eliza Bliss Parkinson Cobb, a trustee of the Museum of Modern Art, New York.

Socialite

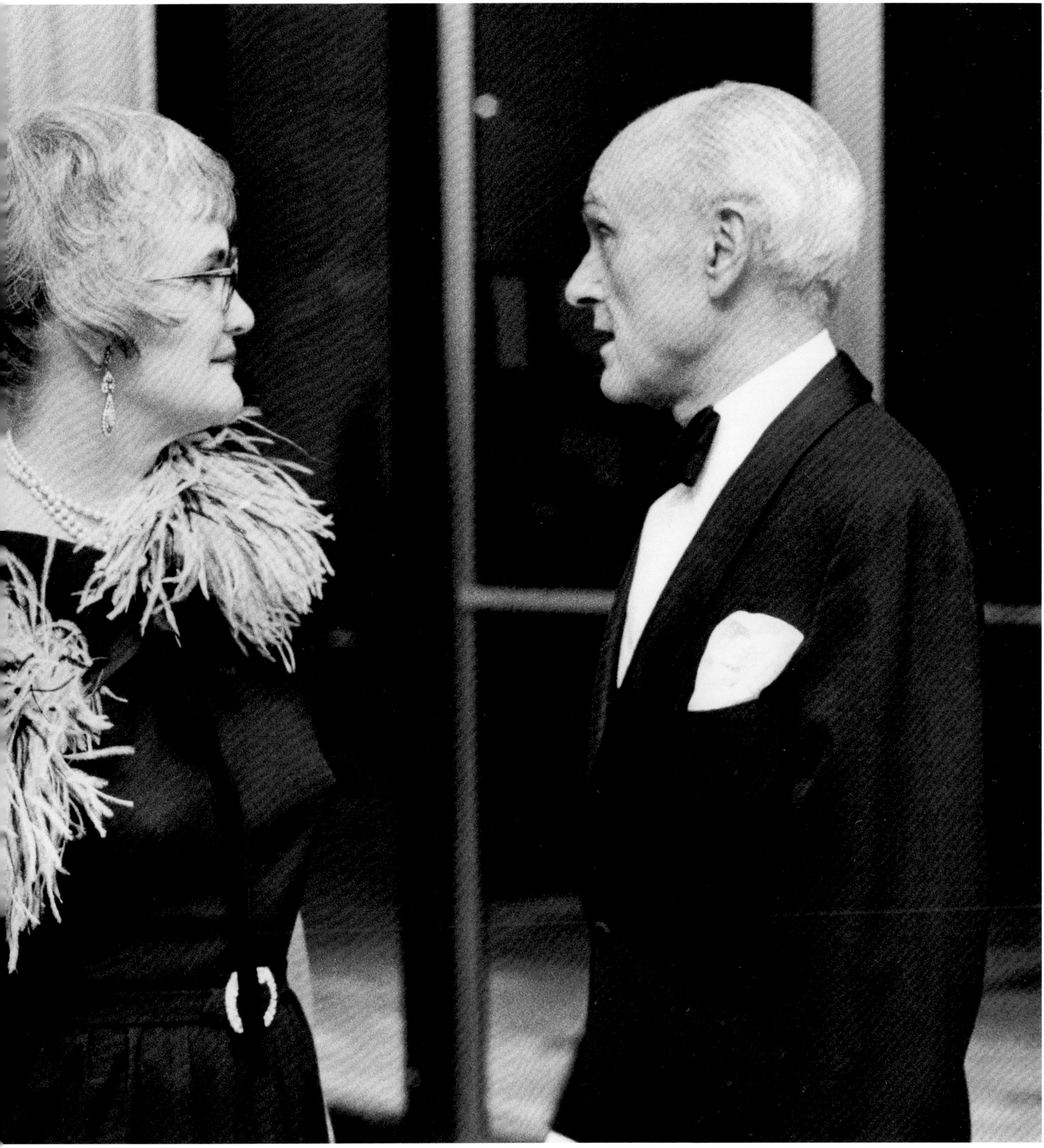

Mayor John Lindsay and Governor Nelson Rockefeller study a model of a housing and industrial development planned for Lower Manhattan, 13 May 1966.

Governor Nelson Rockefeller, Mayor John Lindsay, and Philip, c. 1965.

Socialite

Philip and real estate developer Gerald D. Hines, c. 1985.

President Ronald Reagan and First Lady Nancy Reagan congratulate Philip after presenting him with a certificate honoring him for his work. The presentation was made at the White House following a luncheon for the President's Committee on the Arts and Humanities, 17 May 1983.

Socialite

Philip in the Oval Office for the 1979 Pritzker Architecture Prize ceremony.
From left to right: Carlton Smith, César Pelli, Philip, Cindy Pritzker,
President Jimmy Carter, Jay Pritzker, and First Lady Rosalynn Carter.

200, 180, and 160 Riverside Boulevard by Philip Johnson/Alan Ritchie Architects and Costas Kondylis & Partners, developed by Donald Trump, New York, 1999–2001.

Commercial break. By the late 1970s, Philip's office turned away from the public realm toward large-scale corporate work. This was part of a broad shift in architectural practice at the time, and indeed of the American economy; but few architects proved quite so adept at handling wealthy and ambitious developers as Philip, who seemed to possess a special appeal for such figures. Besides the Dallas-based Hines, one real estate mogul in particular—a brash New Yorker and tabloid fixture with a penchant for what his memoir referred to as "truthful hyperbole"— found Philip fairly irresistible. Together, they did a series of projects, none terribly successful either aesthetically or financially (the largest, on Manhattan's West Side, had to be completed by a different client). But it was enough to forever link Philip's name with that famous 1980s playboy and future president.

Socialite

September 2, 1992

Mr. Philip Johnson
Philip Johnson Architects
885 Third Avenue
Suite 1220
New York, NY 10022

Dear Philip:

From your standpoint, I loved the article in THE WALL STREET JOURNAL.

Four years ago, when I wanted to use you, I spent more time arguing over allowing your name to be prominently displayed than I was able to spend on the project itself. It was ridiculous.

Now that you are "free," ==I have a very exciting project for you in Atlantic City==. I will be ==redoing the front boardwalk facade== and the ==main porte cochere entrance at the Taj Mahal Hotel and Casino==.

As you have probably heard, the Taj has become the most successful hotel and casino anywhere in the world. In July and August of 1992, the Taj won in excess of $80 million dollars, the largest two month win in the history of gaming.

In our front entrance and porte cochere design, we are looking to create a feeling of opulence, coupled with rich materials --- marbles, granite, etc. We do not want to change the entrance locations. The new design will, hopefully, create far more glass for retail and commercial space. (Atlantic City boardwalk retail space is very much in demand.) The finished product will be reviewed and seen around the world, as the Taj Mahal has become the most photographed hotel in the world.

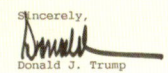

==Please call me== as soon as you and your group have a chance to think about this. It has always been one of my great ambitions to work with Philip Johnson, the legend.

Sincerely,

Donald J. Trump

THE TRUMP ORGANIZATION
725 FIFTH AVENUE · NEW YORK, N.Y. 10022 · 212-832-2000 · TELEX 427715

Top left: Donald Trump to Philip, 2 September 1992. He writes requesting Philip consider taking on a project with him. Top right: Philip, Donald Trump, and Bobby Short at the Landmarks Preservation Foundation Honors Philip Johnson event, the Plaza Hotel, New York, 20 October 1994. Bottom: Groundbreaking ceremony for the Trump International Hotel and Tower at Columbus Circle, New York, 21 June 1995. Lieutenant Governor Betsy McCaughey, Mayor Rudy Giuliani, Donald Trump, and Philip are all shown holding electric jackhammers.

Philip's diary from February 1993, revealing his busy schedule including meetings with biographers, curators, producers, photographers, and scholars of his life and work including Franz Schulze, John O'Connor, Hilary Lewis, Sharon Maguire, Michael Moran, and Ujjval Vyas.

> "Architects are pretty much high-class whores. We can turn down projects the way they can turn down some clients, but we've both got to say yes to someone if we want to stay in business."

—Philip on his work ethic

Socialite

GOTHAM

THE SCENE

All the Trimmings

Photographs by Patrick McMullan

THE SUBTERRANEAN LAIR SERENA'S WAS AWASH WITH ANIMAL prints and pretty young things when the CFDA hosted a party for accessory designers on November 1. Seventh Avenue royalty like Nicole Miller and Kenneth Cole—who wore a pair of his own black leather lace-ups—popped in, and Cynthia Rowley, clutching one of her own pastel handbags, chatted with the CFDA's executive director and fashion's den mother, Fern Mallis. But tonight's stars were the unsung heroes of fashion, the people who outfit swanlike necks, delicate wrists, and coiffed crowns with their baubles, belts, and bags. Despite their bright-red name tags, though, it was still a guessing game for some: One guest well-versed in Calvin and Ralph (Lauren himself was once a struggling tie designer) confided, "I'm not sure who people are. I recognized Colette Malouf [known for her architectural hair jewelry], but I confused Tony Valentine [shoes] with Rafe Totengco [handbags]." There was one accessories designer, at least, who was unmistakable. Arriving late, with her husband, Andy, in tow, she had her name emblazoned right there on her own oversize leather tote, just in case there was any doubt: KATE SPADE. — MAURA EGAN

1. Janis Savitt and Kenneth Cole at the CFDA party. **2.** Philip Johnson and Anna Wintour at the Dia Center for the Arts annual fall gala. **3.** Tyra Banks and Miss Universe, Mpule Kwelagobe, at the Absolut Africa benefit at the Puck Building. **4.** Elton John and Moby at *Interview*'s thirtieth-anniversary party at Canteen. **5.** Tommy Hilfiger and Martha Stewart at the New York Council for the Humanities benefit dinner honoring Stewart. **6.** Lou Reed and Ana Condo at *The Class of Click* book-release party at Broadway City. **7.** Virginia Madsen and Azzedine Alaïa at the Assouline Publishing new-books party at the Madison Avenue Bookshop. **8.** Robert F. Kennedy Jr. and Mitsuko Akimaru at the opening of the Stream store in SoHo. **9.** Barbara Smith and Florence Henderson at the launch of *B. Smith* magazine at Smith's restaurant Three-Twenty.

18 NEW YORK NOVEMBER 15, 1999

A page from *Gotham* magazine featuring Philip with Anna Wintour at the Dia Center for the Arts Annual Fall Gala, New York, 15 November 1999.

From BBC producer Ruth Rosenthal to Philip, 6 December 1993. Ruth thanks Philip for his input into the 1994 television series *Building Sights*.

Letter from Ruth Carter Stevenson, for whom Philip designed the Amon Carter Museum of American Art, Fort Worth, Texas, 1961.

Lights, camera, Johnson. "Never turn down an opportunity to have sex or go on television," Gore Vidal famously advised, and Philip scrupulously followed the second half of the dictum (and often the first). He also rarely turned down a gala invitation, a lunch appointment, or a photo opportunity (indeed, Vidal may be one of the few celebrities he did not have his picture taken with). Had he but lived to see the age of the selfie, it is not hard to imagine the images that would have filled the Instagram profile of @philipjohnson.

Socialite

Philip being interviewed by Barbaralee Diamonstein-Spielvogel for the television program *American Architecture Now*, c. 1984.

For Philip, with admiration and affection from Brendan
July 8th 1981

A DIALOGUE AT AN EXCEPTIONALLY HIGH LEVEL

[Before Philip Johnson was born, God decided to have an eyeball-to-eyeball confrontation with him. God and the agitated little foetus proceeded to hold the following conversation]

GOD: Philip!

PHILIP: Oh, God! Not Philip!

GOD: Wait till you hear the last name: Johnson.

PHILIP: Philip Johnson? But, God, I want to be a great poet and—

GOD: My dear boy, I have it in mind that you should be an architect.

PHILIP: An architect? Ugh!!

GOD: It will serve to keep you out of the gutter. Or just barely. I happen to think "Philip Johnson" is a very good name for an architect.

PHILIP: But, God—

GOD: Not another word. Take your time about launching your career. I assure you that you will have plenty of time.

PHILIP: But, God—

GOD: Not only plenty of time, but you will go, as we say in the Bible, from strength to strength. You should try reading the Bible now and then.

PHILIP: I don't read books, I write them.

Excerpt from a scrapbook entitled "For Philip, from his friends on his 75th." This page, "A Dialogue at an Exceptionally High Level," includes an imagined conversation between God and the fetus of Philip. A handwritten note says, "For Philip, with admiration and affection from Brendan, July 8th 1981." This was likely written by Brendan Gill, Philip's friend and a writer for the *New Yorker*.

In the company of architects. For all his mingling among the beau monde, it was in his own small professional niche that Philip's friendships were the most important. Nowhere is this more evident than in the birthday scrapbooks—visual Festschrifts replete with sketches and poems—prepared for him by younger architects and thinkers who, in his old age in particular, regarded him as a mentor and guiding light of the profession. Several such books were assembled over the years and were duly presented to Philip over dinner at the Four Seasons, always the scene of his greatest social triumphs.

Socialite

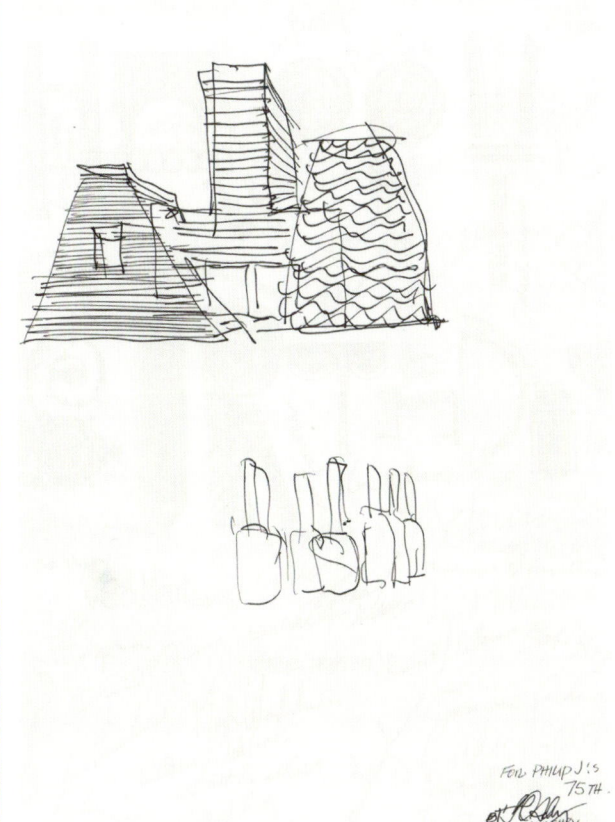

Top: A sketch of Philip by architect César Pelli and his wife Diana Balmori, given to Philip for his seventy-fifth birthday, New York, 8 July 1981. The inscription reads: "HAPPY BIRTHDAY PHILIP— CESAR AND DIANA." Bottom: A sketch by Charles Gwathmey, architect and member of the New York Five, given to Philip for his seventy-fifth birthday. The inscription reads: "An [sic] continuing inspiration."

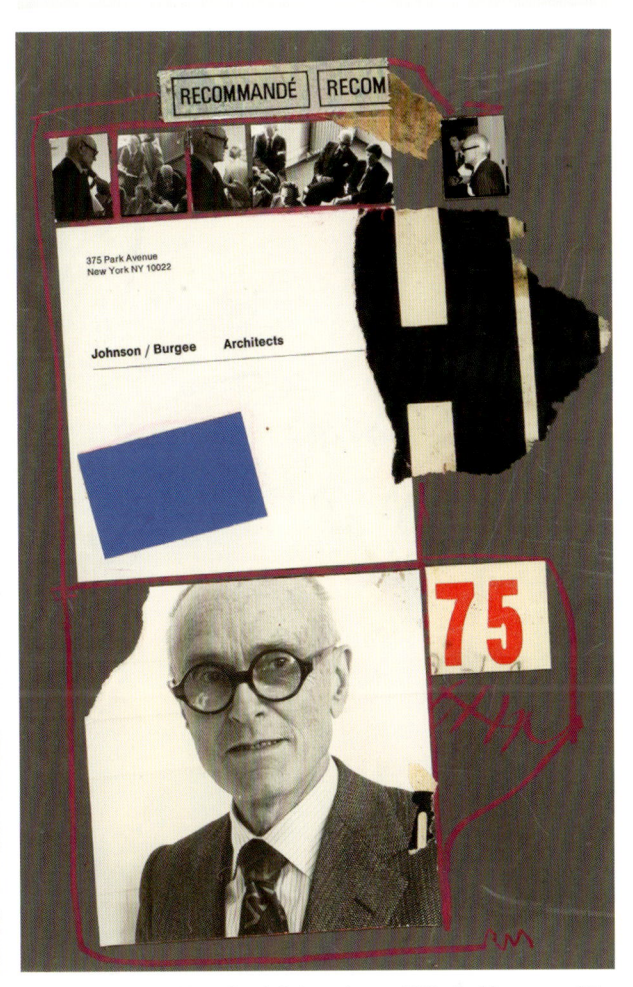

Top: A sketch by architect Frank Gehry, given to Philip for his seventy-fifth birthday. Bottom: A page of a scrapbook for Philip's seventy-fifth birthday, perhaps given by John Burgee.

219

You are most cordially invited to help celebrate

Philip Johnson's 80th Birthday

Tuesday, July 8, 1986

2 until 5 o'clock

The Glass House

New Canaan, Connecticut

Invitation to celebrate Philip's eightieth birthday at the Glass House in 1986.

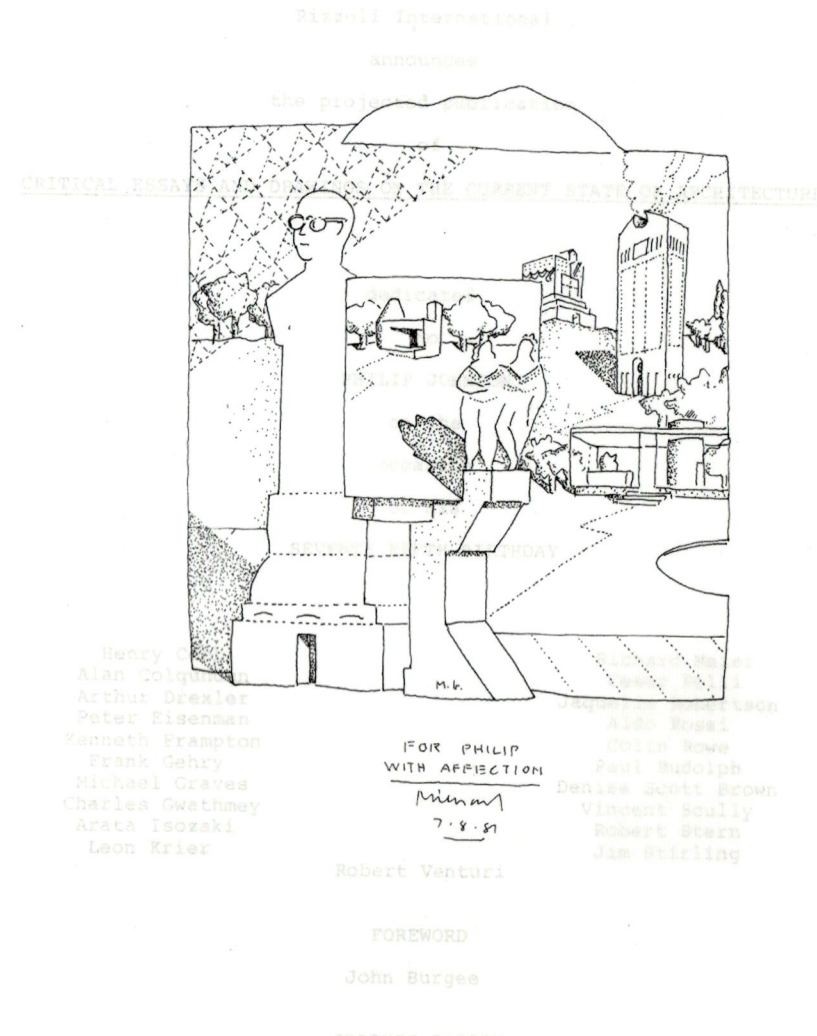

A sketch by Michael Graves, architect and member of the New York Five, given to Philip for his seventy-fifth birthday, New York, 8 July 1981. The sketch features Philip's architecture, including the AT&T Building, the Glass House, and the Wiley House. The inscription reads: "For Philip with Affection."

Socialite

A sketch by Michael Graves given to Philip for his eighty-fifth birthday, New York, 8 July 1991. The sketch, drawn on Four Seasons restaurant paper, features the Glass House from the west with the Brick House in the background. The inscription reads: "The *best* peice [sic] of Glass in America!"

Original sketches by Italian designer Massimo Vignelli for the book *Philip Johnson/John Burgee Architecture 1979–1985*. The sketches were given to Philip by the designer on the occasion of Philip's eightieth birthday in 1986.

Socialite

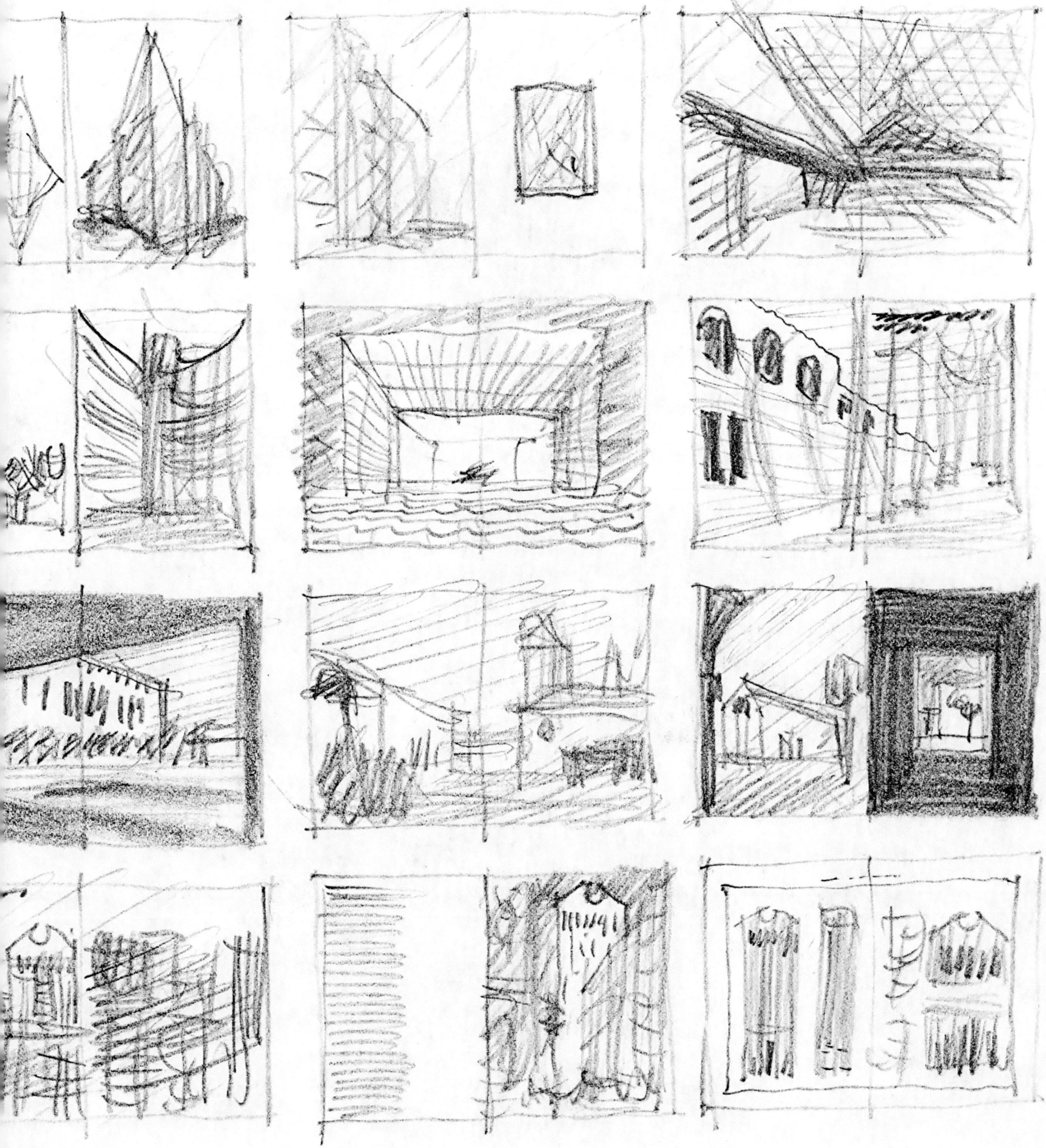

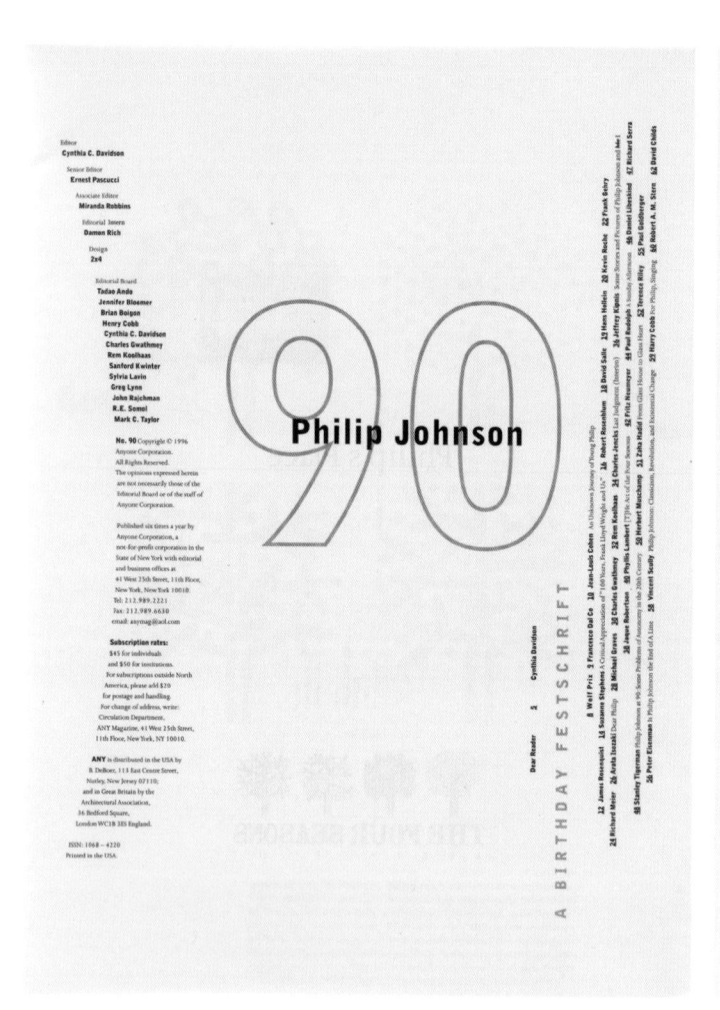

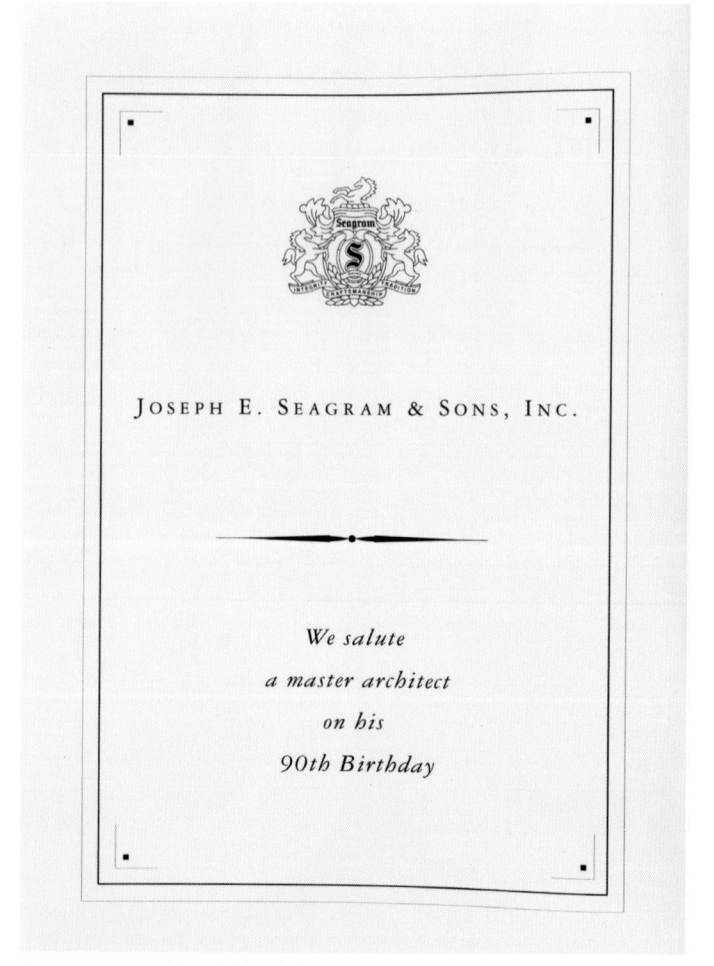

Pages from an article titled "Philip Johnson 90: A Birthday Festschrift," *ANY* magazine, New York, July 1996.

Socialite

Philip celebrating his ninety-fifth birthday at the Four Seasons restaurant, New York, 2001.

Philip celebrating his birthday with a cake, New York.

Philip's ninetieth birthday celebration at the Four Seasons restaurant, New York, 9 July 1996.

Socialite

Philip celebrating his ninetieth birthday at the Four Seasons with a number of architecture's luminaries, New York, 9 July 1996. The guest list included Frank Gehry, Zaha Hadid, Arata Isozaki, Jeffrey Kipnis, Rem Koolhaas, Phyllis Lambert, and Robert A. M. Stern.

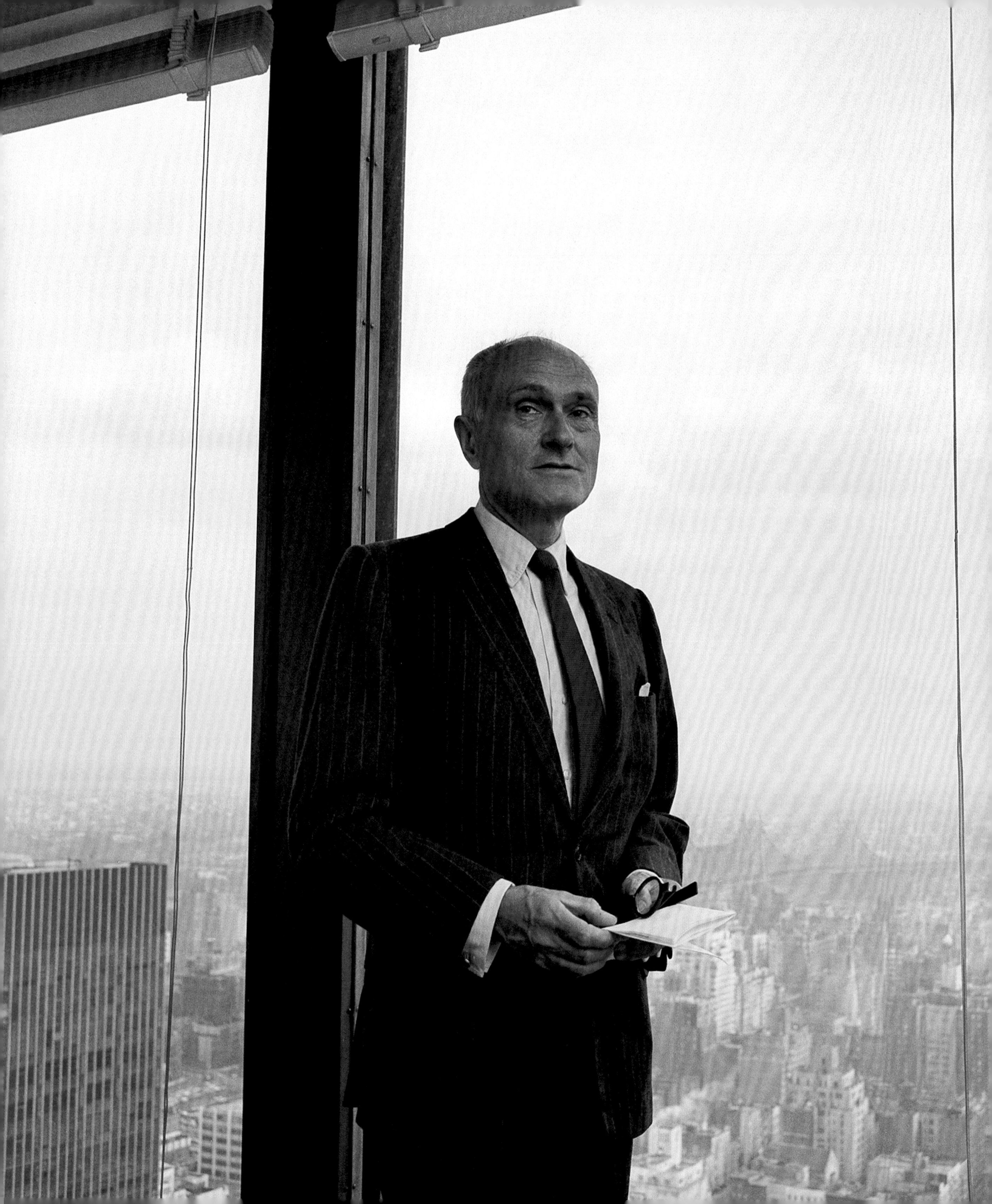

07 Transformer

Transformer

In the 1960s and 1970s, even as Philip's stature as a cultural authority continued to grow, his architectural practice took a number of curious turns. One moment he was still the good pupil of Ludwig Mies van der Rohe, producing brick-lined, glass-fronted boxes; the next he was turning out Modernist homages to Renaissance palazzos; the next he was peddling Futurist-inflected megastructures. Spurning Mies's dictum that one should not be "interesting" but "good," Philip would say that he "wouldn't know how to be good"[1]—and so he determined, instead, to be interesting. The results were often mixed (and not always well received), but Philip's signature aversion to dogma allowed him to remain more open to new ideas than most architects over sixty.

His increasing heterodoxy was actually evident far earlier. Even in the Glass House, Philip's insertion of the brick cylindrical volume that contained the building's fireplace and bathroom represented a subtle break with the rectilinear simplicity of the Miesian mode. (The Brick House, with its Liberace-esque interior, was an even more explicit departure, though well hidden within its modest envelope.) At the Yale School of Architecture in 1954, Philip delivered a lecture entitled "The Seven Crutches of Modern Architecture," a teasing inquiry into some of the bad habits he felt that his contemporaries, and he himself, had lately slipped into; in particular, his critiques of "the Crutch of Utility" and "the Crutch of Structure" took dead aim at Modernist moralizing over function and purity of form. The speaker ended by exhorting the future architects in the audience to "not be afraid [to] wander into some little bypath" and to abjure an architecture "where nothing can possibly evolve."

Evolution would shortly become the order of the day, and not just for Philip. By the early 1960s, Eero Saarinen, Edward Durell Stone, and Charles Luckman were just a few of the major figures whose buildings were veering sharply toward the theatrical. A thousand sub-Modernist flowers bloomed—Googie, Space Age, Ballet School—some of them wildly abstract and gestural, others formal, nostalgic, even classical. In the main, Philip's preference was for the latter: in 1962, in the latest addition to the Glass House grounds, he installed a small pavilion on the pond, a reinforced-concrete folly too small for a human being to actually stand up in but suggesting, from a distance, a tiny Renaissance palazzo. Its designer called it "an amusing attempt,"[2] a mere exercise; yet its arched bays and slender beveled piers shortly found their way into larger-scale work, such as the Sheldon Memorial Art Gallery (1963) and Beck House (1964), which exuded a distinctly old-world stateliness. This tendency would find its fullest expression with the opening of the Lincoln Center's State Theater, its marble, colonnaded porch a perfect complement to the equally grandiose plaza in front of it, which Philip also co-designed.

The transformation did not stop there. Over the next decade, yet more strains of architecture appeared on the American scene: Louis Kahn's hard-edged poetics, Paul Rudolph's structural romance, and concrete-loving Brutalists of various persuasions would set the pace, and for the most part, Philip moved with the rhythm. From his Kline Biology Tower at Yale (1965) to his Boston Public Library (1972), Philip mined a monumental vein that occasionally manifested "a great arrogance,"[3] as critic Paul Goldberger wrote. Just as quickly, the architect could pivot in the opposite direction—especially after forming a successful partnership with John Burgee in 1967, with the duo espousing an approachable brand of corporate pop in projects like the 1972 IDS Center in Minneapolis.

That project, with its glassy indoor courtyard, was a clear nod to Kevin Roche, just one of many younger designers whose ideas Philip was gleefully, albeit admittedly, cribbing. This process would accelerate as still other, still younger architects entered his orbit—yet even as he absorbed the new thinking of an emerging generation, Philip also became a de facto godfather to many of that generation's leading lights. The Institute for Architecture and Urban Studies (IAUS), launched in New York in 1967, was a hotbed for a highly intellectualized, theory-infused architecture that spread through universities nationwide; its founder, Peter Eisenman, became a sort of Johnsonian protégé, and Philip donated the funds that got the IAUS off the ground. Eisenman subsequently created a book chronicling his own work alongside that of four of his friends; Philip again stepped up, contributing an approving essay to the second edition of *Five Architects* (1975), which helped introduce the world to Richard Meier, Michael Graves, Charles Gwathmey, and John Hejduk, as well as Eisenman himself. A source of everything from client introductions to candid taped interviews to casual dinners at the Glass House, Philip was a good friend for a junior architect to have.

The transformations in Modern architecture—that being the title, as it happens, of a 1979 Museum of Modern Art (MoMA) show that included Philip's work—taking place after the 1950s were the products of a host of forces, chief among them a broadly felt dissatisfaction with the limitations of the International Style. The co-inventor of the term, alive as always to the climate at large, sensed this as early as anyone and tacked with the prevailing winds; at the same time, he succeeded in helping those winds along, becoming not just the object of change but also its agent. "I love the give and the take and the prophesying what's happening and catching onto the next," Philip said years later. "History's in the making …. To be in on it is my biggest pleasure."[4]

Portrait of Philip and John Burgee.

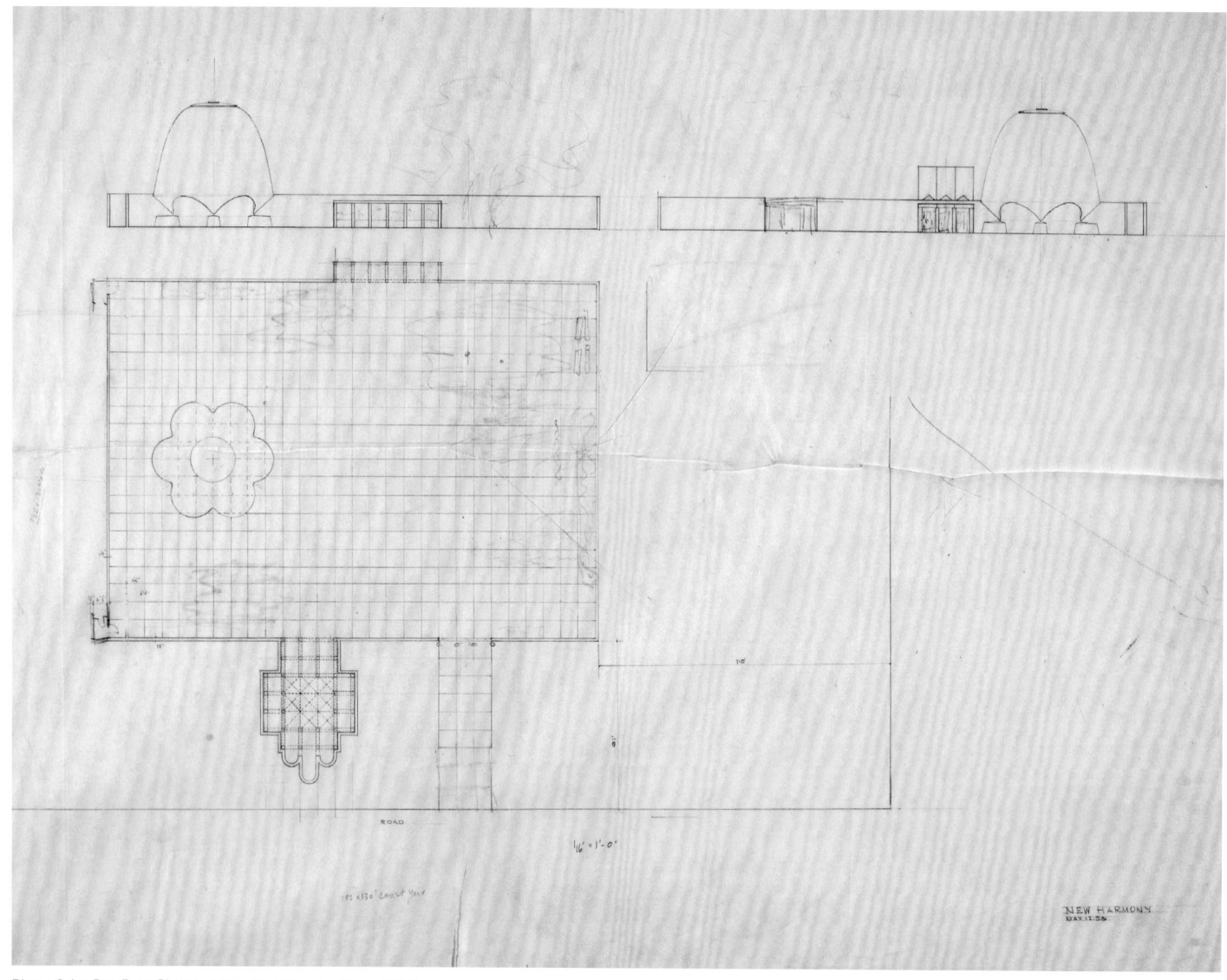

Plan of the Roofless Church, New Harmony, Indiana, 1960.

Throwing a curve. Religious buildings would become a key component of Philip's practice, an opportunity for him to exercise his more grandiose impulses. With the Roofless Church, commissioned by oil baroness Jane Blaffer Owen, Philip cast off right angles and embraced the parabolic and the Baroque, as well as the context of rural Indiana. The design expressed "the softness of our countryside," his client remarked. Sheltering a Jacques Lipchitz sculpture, the slate-clad baldachin riffed on exactly the kind of "ballet-classicism," as British critic Marcus Whiffen termed it, that Philip had previously derided. More in this style would follow.

Transformer

Roofless Church, New Harmony, Indiana, 1960.

The Lake Pavilion, viewed from the west with the Glass House in the background, New Canaan, Connecticut, 1962.

The Lake Pavilion and fountain, viewed from the east, New Canaan, Connecticut, 1962.

Folly. Though mostly functioning as a bit of scenery to be viewed from the Glass House, the Lake Pavilion had to be walked through, sat in, or dined in to be fully understood. Its ceilings were coated in gold leaf, and carved channels divided the floor. For Philip, the greatest thrill was in simply getting to it, which required stepping over an unbridged stretch of pond between the shore and the structure. The hint of danger, he claimed, was literally arousing. "I sometimes get an erection when I jump over that little stretch of water,"[5] he said.

Transformer

Philip sitting in his Lake Pavilion, 1964.

The Lake Pavilion, viewed from the south, New Canaan, Connecticut, 1962.

Transformer

The Lake Pavilion, viewed from the west with the Glass House in the background, New Canaan, Connecticut, 1962.

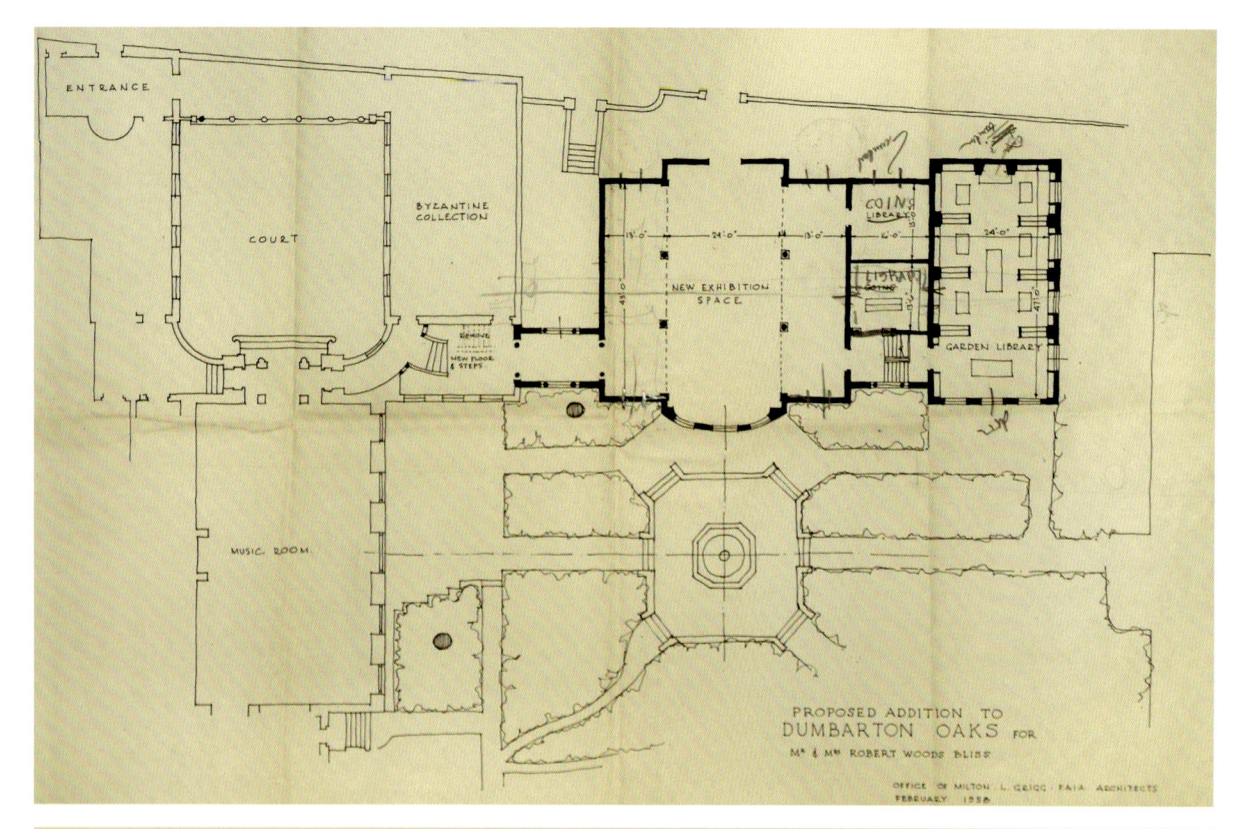

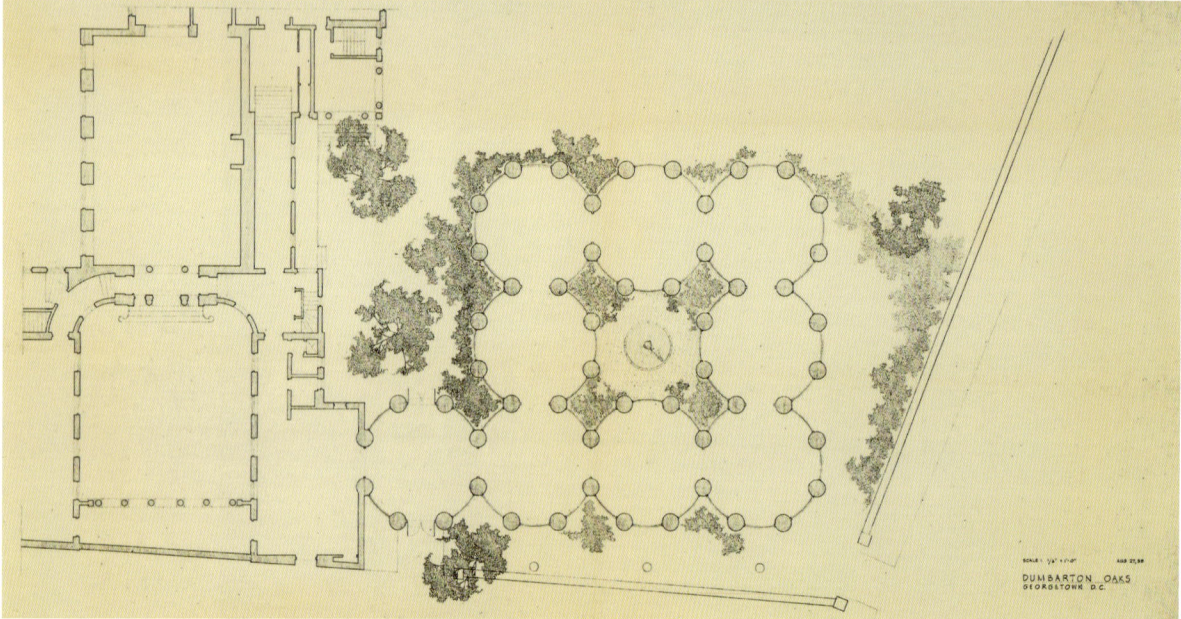

Plans of proposed additions to Dumbarton Oaks, Washington, D.C., 1958.

Tombs and monuments. The Lake Pavilion signaled the direction of Philip's changing attitudes. "Let Bucky Fuller put together the Dymaxion dwellings of the people," he declared (referring to the engineer-visionary Buckminster Fuller), "so long as we architects can design their tombs and monuments." With his next brace of major public commissions, his formal preoccupations—curved arches, thickened poché, colonnades, and lofty domes—would all betray his monumental intent.

Transformer

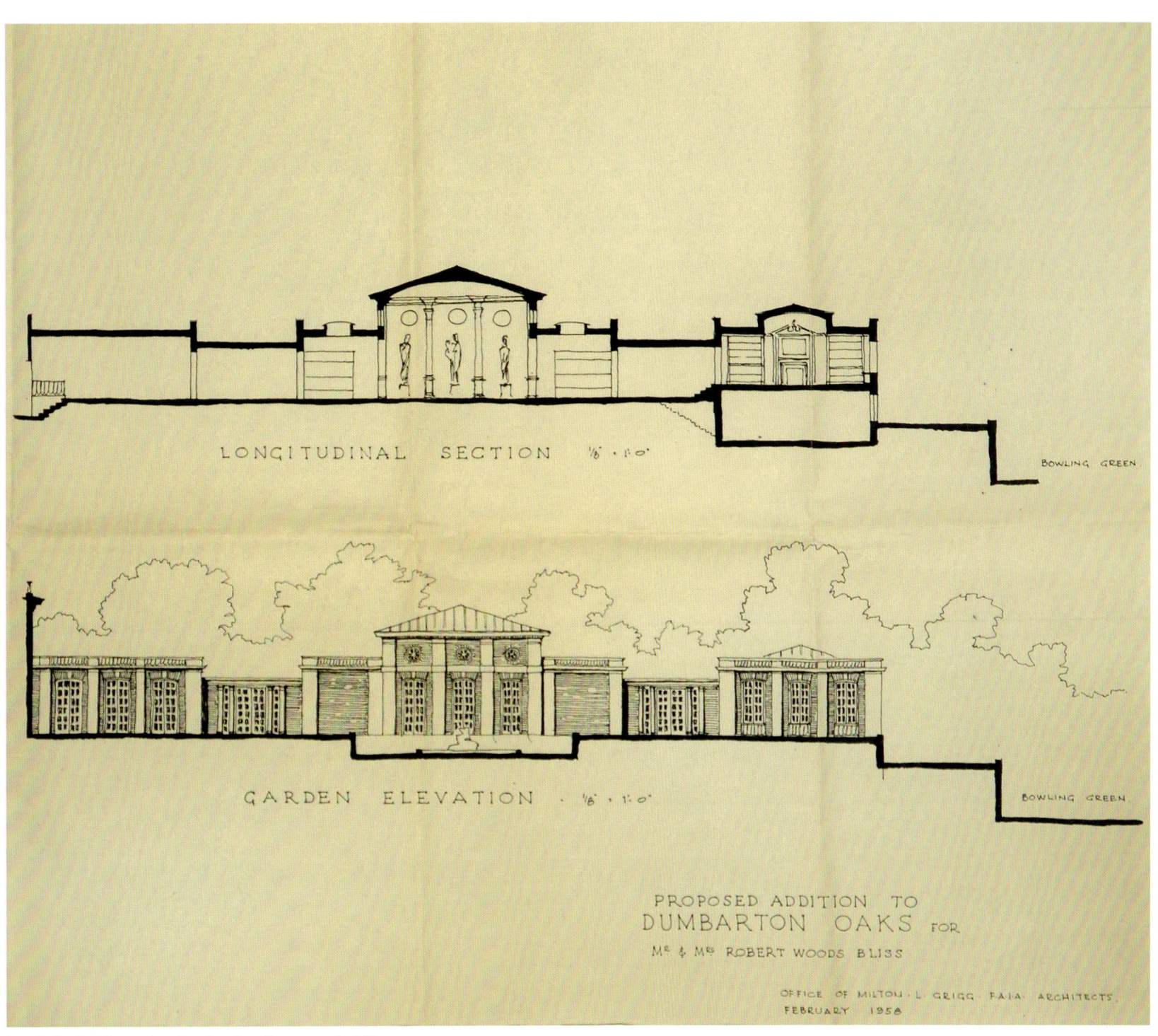

Longitudinal section and garden elevation of a proposed addition to Dumbarton Oaks, Washington, D.C., 1958.

Project drawing by Helmut Jacoby for the Pre-Columbian Pavilion,
Dumbarton Oaks, Washington, D.C., c. 1960.

Model for the Pre-Columbian Pavilion, Dumbarton Oaks, Washington, D.C., 1959.

Exterior views of the Pre-Columbian Pavilion, Dumbarton Oaks,
Washington D.C., 1963.

Installation view of the Robert Woods Bliss Collection of Pre-Columbian Art, with Elizabeth P. Benson and James Mayo inside the Pre-Columbian Pavilion, Dumbarton Oaks, Washington, D.C., 1963.

Philip with a model of Kreeger House (now the Kreeger Museum), 1963.

View from the west (top) and east (bottom) of Kreeger House (now the Kreeger Museum) by Philip Johnson and Richard Foster, Washington, D.C., 1963.

Interior view looking east through the main hall of Kreeger House (now the Kreeger Museum) by Philip Johnson and Richard Foster, Washington, D.C., 1963. The sculpture through the window is Aristide Maillol's *Pomona* (1910), which is part of the collection of David Lloyd Kreeger and Carmen Kreeger.

View from the north-east of the terrace of Kreeger House (now the Kreeger Museum) by Philip Johnson and Richard Foster, Washington, D.C., 1963. The sculptures are part of the collection of David Lloyd Kreeger and Carmen Kreeger. From left to right, the sculptures are by Henry Moore, Jacques Lipchitz, Francesco Somaini, and Hans (Jean) Arp.

View from the north-east of the terrace of Kreeger House (now the Kreeger Museum) by Philip Johnson and Richard Foster, Washington, D.C., 1963. The sculptures are part of the collection of David Lloyd Kreeger and Carmen Kreeger. From left to right, the sculptures are by Aristide Maillol, two from Hans (Jean) Arp, Jacques Lipchitz, and Henry Moore.

View from the south-east (top) and looking south from the terrace (bottom), Kreeger House (now the Kreeger Museum) by Philip Johnson and Richard Foster, Washington, D.C., 1963.

Perspective drawing by Helmut Jacoby of an arcade at the Lincoln Center Plaza that was not constructed, 1964.

Center stage. To create a new performing arts complex for New York, the Rockefeller family assembled a veritable dream team of twentieth-century architects: Pietro Belluschi, Wallace Harrison, Eero Saarinen—and Philip, tasked with designing the project's new dance theater but hoping to do much more. In the end, Philip prevailed on his colleagues to adopt his favored plaza-with-flanking-structures arrangement, though not without considerable acrimony. "You cannot do a job as big as Lincoln Center, I suppose, without this kind of recrimination and backbiting," said Philip. Collaboration was never his strong suit.

Transformer

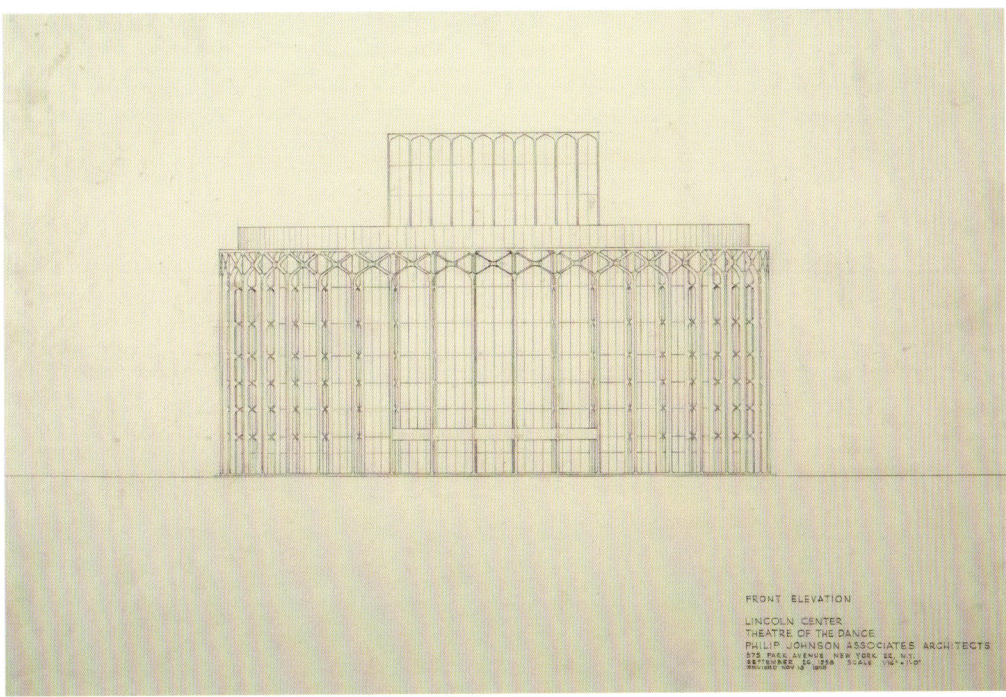

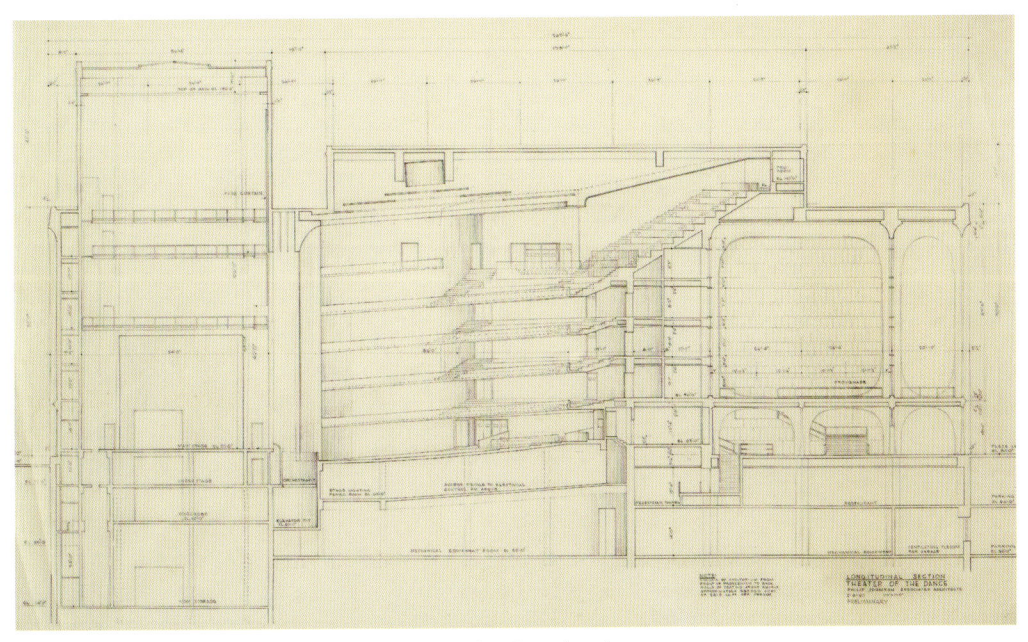

Top to bottom: A preliminary drawing of the north elevation, front elevation, and cross-section of the New York State Theater (now David H. Koch Theater) by Johnson/Burgee Architects, New York, 1964.

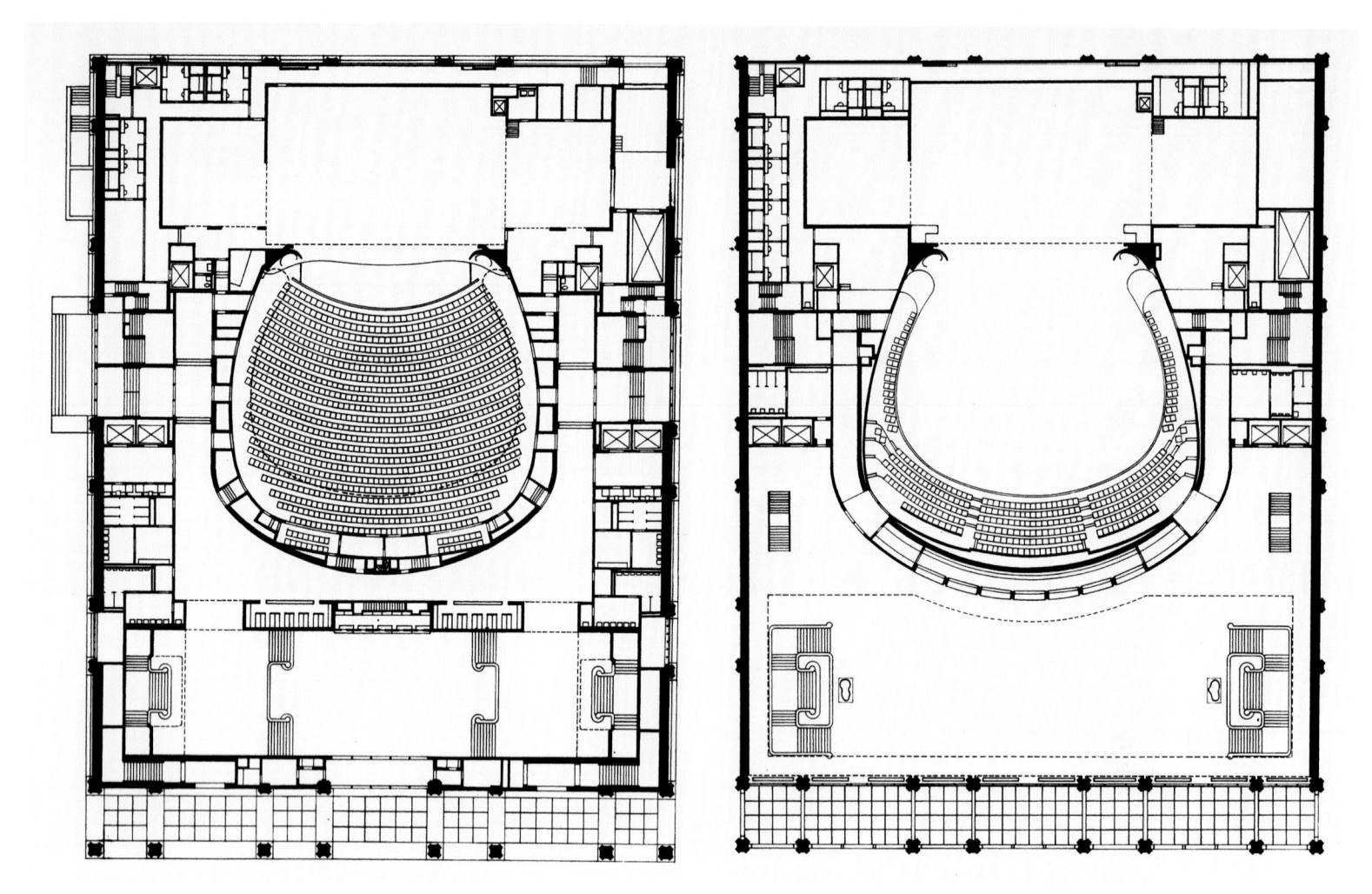

Plans of the New York State Theater (now David H. Koch Theater) at balcony and stalls levels by Johnson/Burgee Architects, New York, 1964.

Philip points out some of the features of the final plans on a model of the
New York State Theater to be built at the Lincoln Center, New York. The final
plans for the nine-story building were announced on 26 June 1961.

253

West view of the New York State Theater (now David H. Koch Theater) by Johnson/Burgee Architects, New York, 1964.

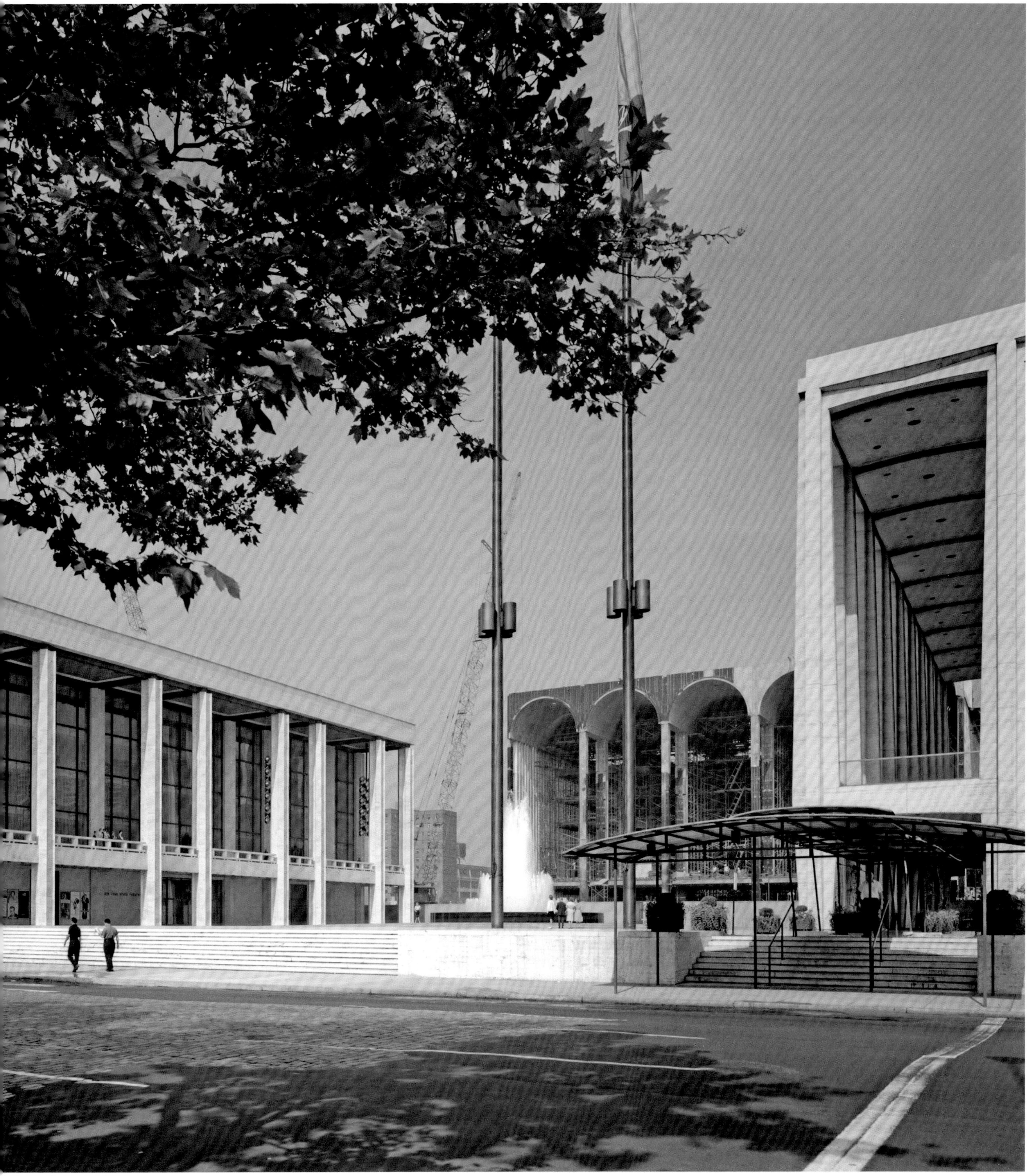

Interior view of the New York State Theater (now David H. Koch Theater)
by Johnson/Burgee Architects, New York, 1964.

Top: Interior view of the promenade inside the New York State Theater (now David H. Koch Theater) by Johnson/Burgee Architects, New York, 1964. The sculptures are by Elie Nadelman: in the foreground, turned away, is *Two Circus Women*, and in the background is *Two Female Nudes*, both 1931.
Bottom: Philip in the lobby of the New York State Theater.

Perspective drawing of the Abby Aldrich Rockefeller Sculpture Garden and the East Wing of the Museum of Modern Art, New York, 1953 and 1964 respectively.

Modern again. Having reasserted his curatorial sway at MoMA, Philip set about doing what he had been unable to do as a cub designer thirty years earlier: score a commission to design a building for the museum. Ultimately, he would oversee two expansions, one to the east and one to the west of the original Philip Goodwin and Edward Durell Stone structure (which Philip loathed), in addition to the famous garden, hailed by architecture critic Ada Louise Huxtable as "fine esthetically and ... as an example of the way expensive midtown land can be 'wasted' by leaving it open for the pleasure of people."[6] It remains one of Philip's most highly regarded projects.

Transformer

South-east view of the Abby Aldrich Rockefeller Sculpture Garden and the East Wing of the Museum of Modern Art, New York, 1953 and 1964 respectively.

North-west view of the Abby Aldrich Rockefeller Sculpture Garden, Museum of Modern Art, New York, 1953.

South-east view of the Abby Aldrich Rockefeller Sculpture Garden and the East Wing of the Museum of Modern Art, New York, 1953 and 1964 respectively.

South-east view of the Abby Aldrich Rockefeller Sculpture Garden, Museum of Modern Art, New York, 1953.

Top: Portrait of Philip on the occasion of his nomination to the Board of Trustees of the Museum of Modern Art, New York, 1957. The photograph was taken in the Abby Aldrich Rockefeller Sculpture Garden. Bottom: Philip with French painter Jean Dubuffet at the Museum of Modern Art, New York, c. 1965.

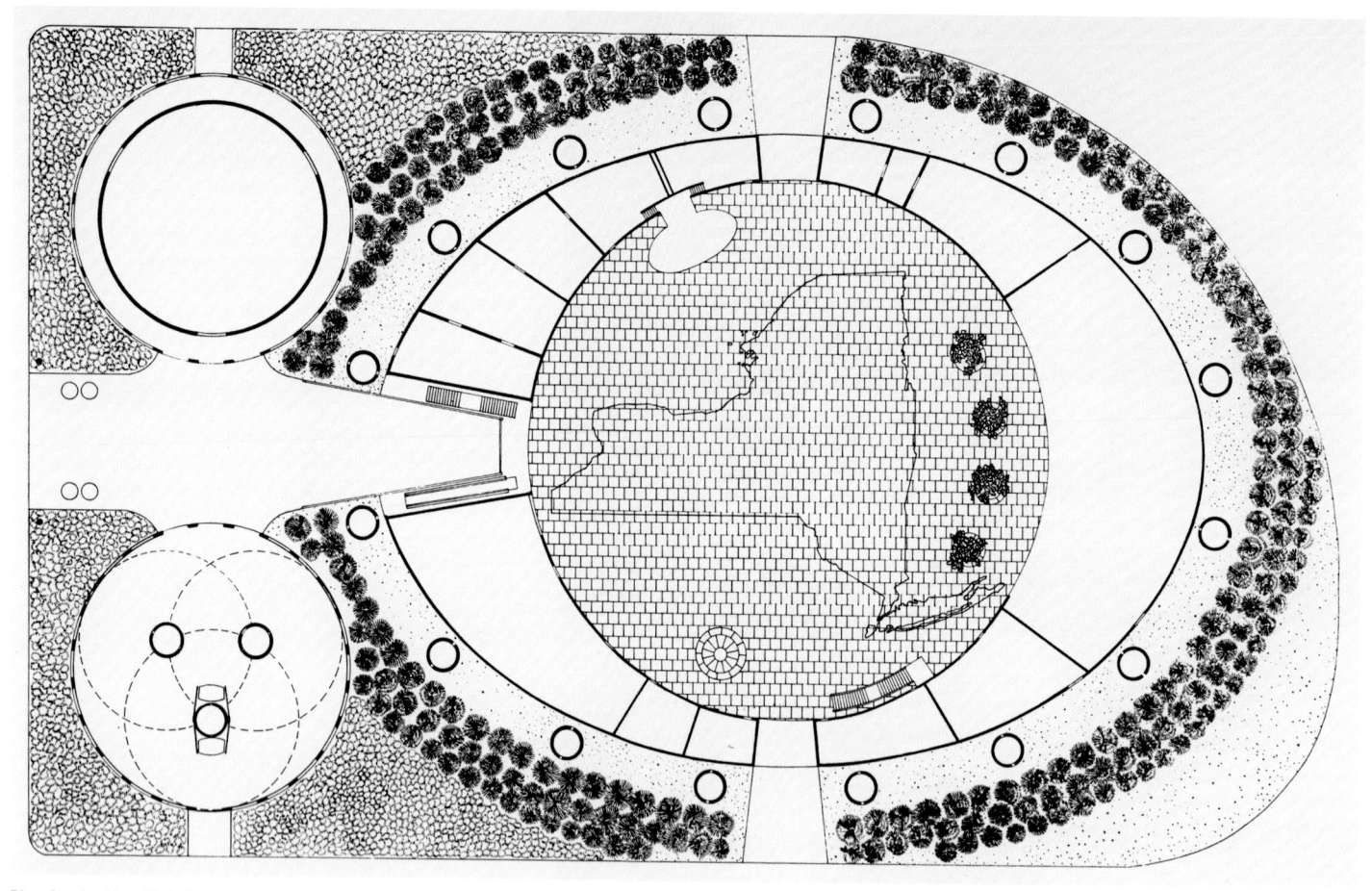

Plan for the New York State Pavilion by Philip Johnson and Richard Foster, showing the outline of a map of New York State set in floor tiles, New York, 1964.

Public palaces. As Philip's cachet continued to rise, he was able to claim at least a modest share of the institutional largesse he craved. For Robert Moses, New York's famed master planner, he designed the New York State Pavilion at the 1964 World's Fair, suitably festive and futuristic; for Yale University and New York University, a suite of somewhat dour academic buildings; and for New York at large, an array of public buildings and master plans—the former sometimes rather too bombastic, the latter only imperfectly realized, if at all. As he continued along "unorthodox Modernist paths" (in the words of architecture historian Frank D. Welch), Philip leaned heavily on his able draftsman John Manley, a staple of his office for five decades.

North view of the New York State Pavilion by Philip Johnson and Richard Foster, New York, 1964, with the observation towers in the foreground. This photo was taken in November 2012 and shows the pavilion in a state of partial disrepair.

South view of the New York State Pavilion by Philip Johnson and Richard Foster, New York, 1964. The observation towers are in the foreground.

Aerial view of the New York State Pavilion by Philip Johnson and Richard Foster, New York, 1964. The Queens Theater is on the upper left and the observation towers to the bottom.

267

View north through the western side of the interior of the New York
State Pavilion by Philip Johnson and Richard Foster, New York, 1964.
The observation towers are visible in the background.

View north through the interior of the New York State Pavilion by Philip Johnson and Richard Foster, New York, 1964. The top of the Unisphere is visible in the background.

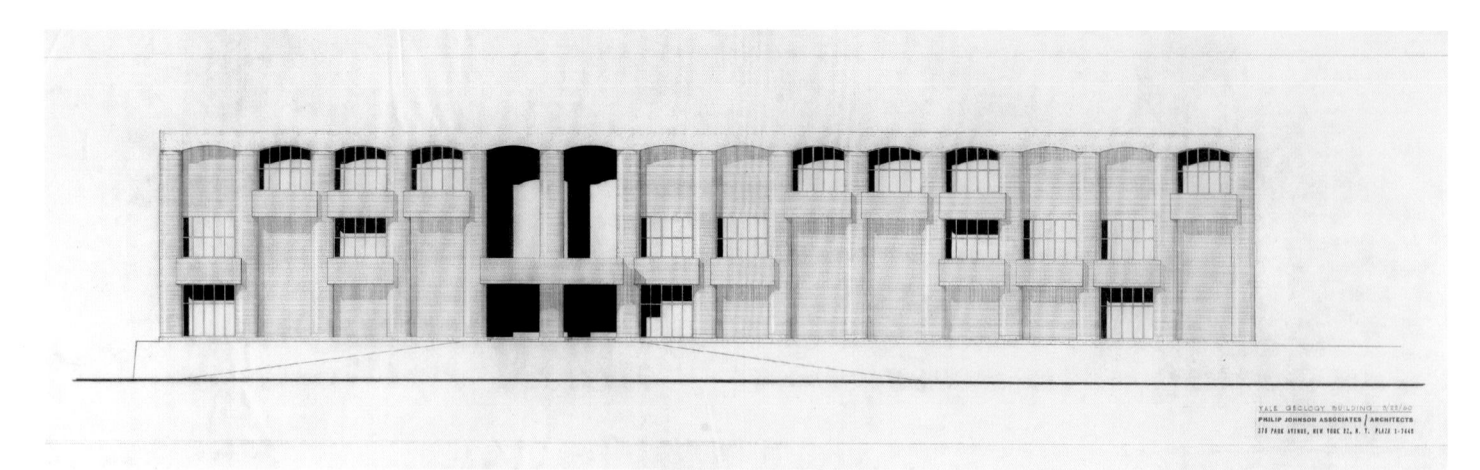

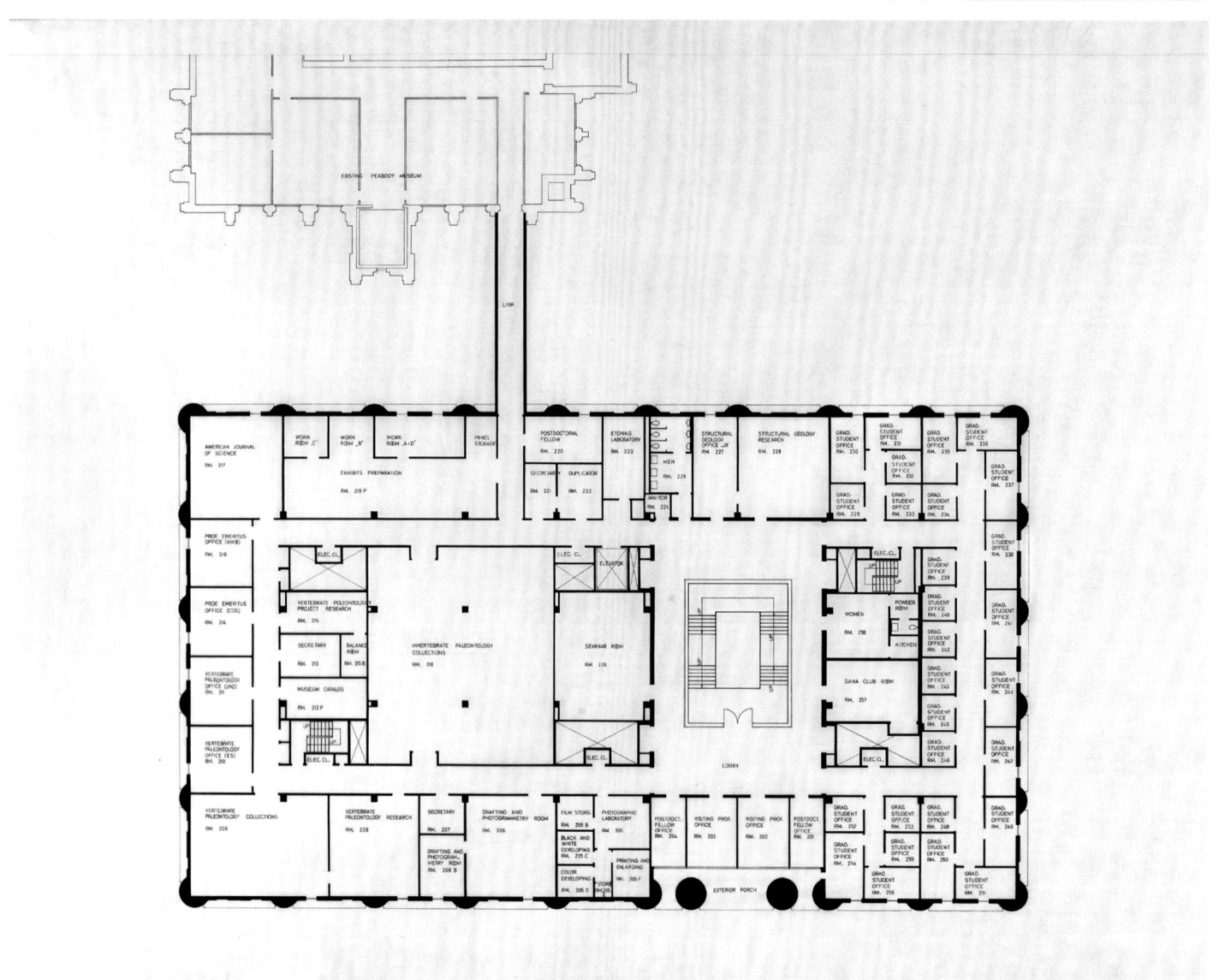

Elevation (top) and plan (bottom) of Kline Geology Laboratory,
Yale University, New Haven, Connecticut, 1963.

View from the north (top) and south-west (bottom) of the Kline Geology Laboratory, Yale University, New Haven, Connecticut, 1963.

Perspective drawing of Kline Biology Tower, Yale University, New Haven, Connecticut, 1966. This drawing was made in 1962.

View from the north-east of the Kline Biology Tower, Yale University,
New Haven, Connecticut, during construction, 1 June 1965.

Philip and writer Jane Jacobs picketing Penn Station to protest the building's demolition, New York, 1963. The placards read: "AGBANY is here" and "Save Penn Station." AGBANY stands for Action Group for Better Architecture in New York.

Amid the tumult of the 1960s, Philip exhibited a vacillating outlook on the urban scene. One moment he was championing the new historic-minded tendency beginning to gain traction among academics and advocates—fighting unsuccessfully to save the old Penn Station in New York, making inroads with young architects dissatisfied with the Modernist status quo, and throwing support (and cash) into MoMA's publication of architect Robert Venturi's *Complexity and Contradiction in Architecture* (1966), a bold treatise that would overturn decades of orthodoxy. The next moment, Philip was tackling enormous urban renewal projects—in Greenwich Village, Harlem, Roosevelt Island, and the Bronx—that seemed like everything the journalist-activist Jane Jacobs and Venturi were fighting against.

Transformer

OCULUS

NEW YORK CHAPTER AMERICAN INSTITUTE OF ARCHITECTS

JULY-AUGUST 1962

PENN PALS: Architects and writers, including many Chapter members, picketed Pennsylvania Station early this month as AGBANY (Action Group for Better Architecture in New York) sought to stop its demolition and replacement by a new Madison Square Garden-hotel-office building complex. Left to right: Attorney Raymond Rubinow, Author Jane Jacobs, Mrs. Eero Saarinen, Architect Philip Johnson. Photo by Walter Daran for Architectural Forum.

to the Statue of Liberty and Staten Island.

The committee voted approval of the project after a presentation by Morris Ketchum, Jr., on May 31. In a letter to Parks Commissioner Newbold Morris the committee said that "even without the mementos of Pennsylvania Station the Mall is a fine idea."

The committee noted that the approaching demolition of Penn Station is a "major tragedy" for the city, but offered the Parks Department their "support, encouragement and best wishes for the successful accomplishment of this exciting proposal."

The plan approved by the Executive Committee is one of several that have been proposed. These include other schemes by the architectural department of Pratt Institute and at least one New York City architect, suggesting use of Penn Station relics in Central Park, Prospect Park, Fort Tyron Park and other locations through the city.

The Parks Department has no present plans to go ahead with the proposed mall. However it is ex-

Press clipping reporting on the AGBANY protest on the front page of *Oculus*, July–August 1962.

Interior views of model for the New York University Bobst Library by Philip
Johnson and Richard Foster, New York, 1973. The library was designed in 1964.

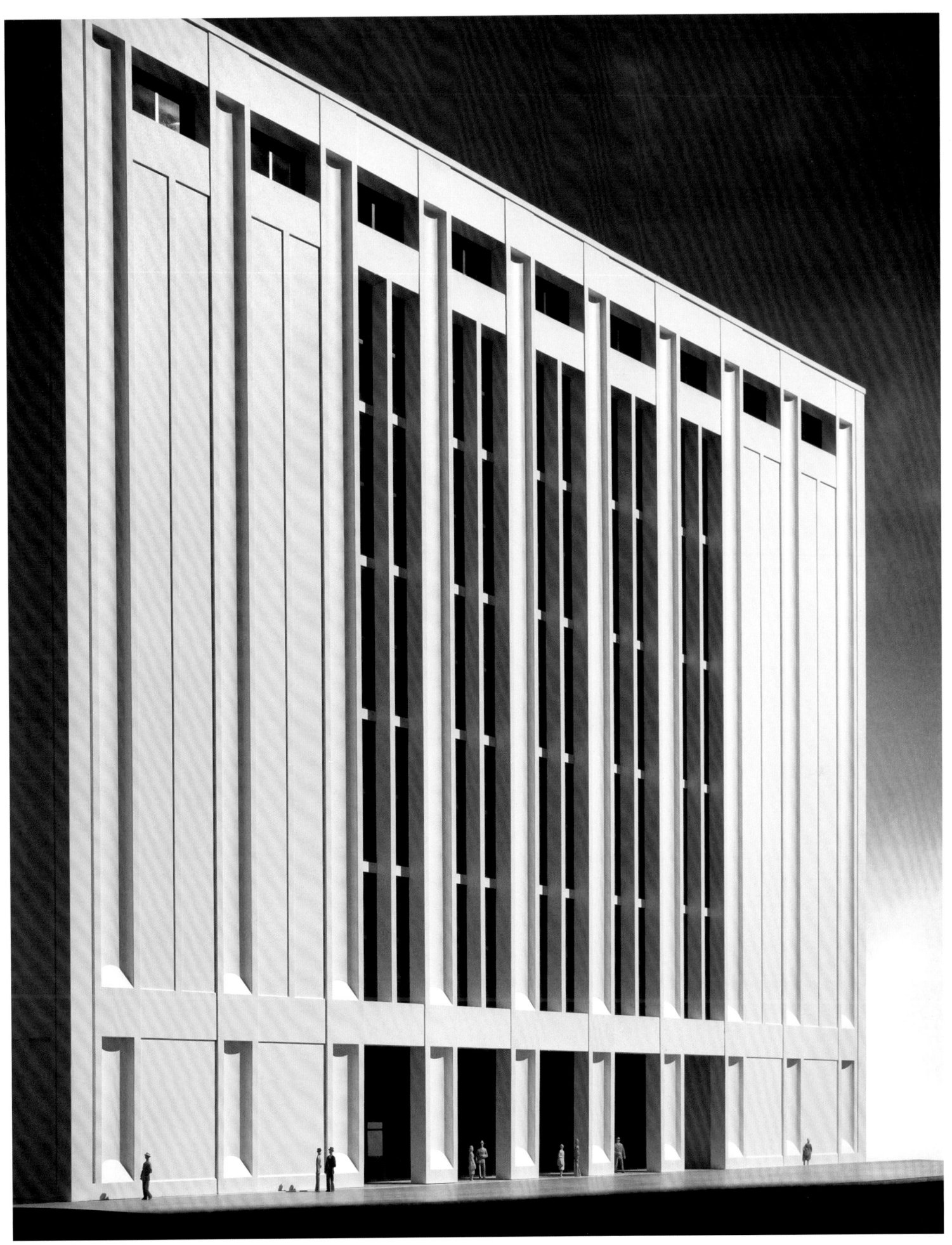

Model for the New York University Bobst Library by Philip Johnson and Richard Foster, New York, 1973. The library was designed in 1964.

View from the west of the Moses Research Tower, New York, 1966.

Transformer

View from the north-west of the Moses Research Tower, New York, 1966.

Drawing of Philip's proposed park atop a sewage plant, New York, 1968. The design, suggesting four fountains and a reflecting pool for the plant's roof, was never constructed in this form, but later became Riverbank State Park, completed in 1993.

Philip poses with a model of his proposed park, New York, 1968.

The program cover for *The Island Nobody Knows* exhibition, which was held at the Metropolitan Museum of Art to announce Philip Johnson and John Burgee's Welfare Island (now Roosevelt Island) master plan, New York, October 1969. Only a fraction of this radical design, which included the exclusion of automobiles, came to fruition.

Drawings of the planned development of Welfare Island (now Roosevelt Island).

JOHNSON-BURGEE

Mockup of cover for the 1977 issue of *a+u Architecture and Urbanism* magazine, Japan, featuring Pennzoil Place.

Top: Change of address notice announcing that John Burgee Architects with Philip Johnson will be moving to 885 Third Avenue, New York on 1 February 1986. Bottom: First page of a text entitled "How We Work Together" by Philip, describing how he came to partner with Burgee.

Burgee. John Burgee joined Philip's firm in 1967. In the years that followed, the energetic young architect from Chicago would rise to become a full partner, leading Philip's practice into a bold new phase full of big-money corporate commissions. "In many ways the antithesis of Johnson," as the *New Yorker* once described him, Burgee nonetheless enjoyed a congenial working relationship with Philip for much of their time together—until things fell apart.

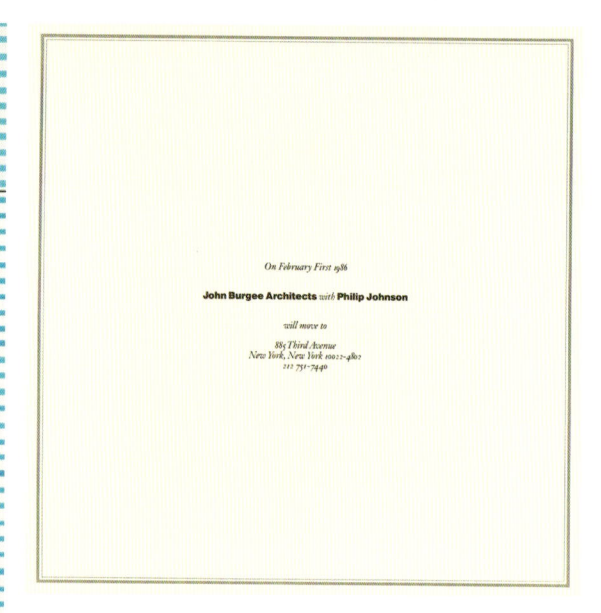

Philip and John Burgee with their models for the proposed 42DP office towers to be built at Times Square, New York, 1984. The towers were never built and the models no longer exist.

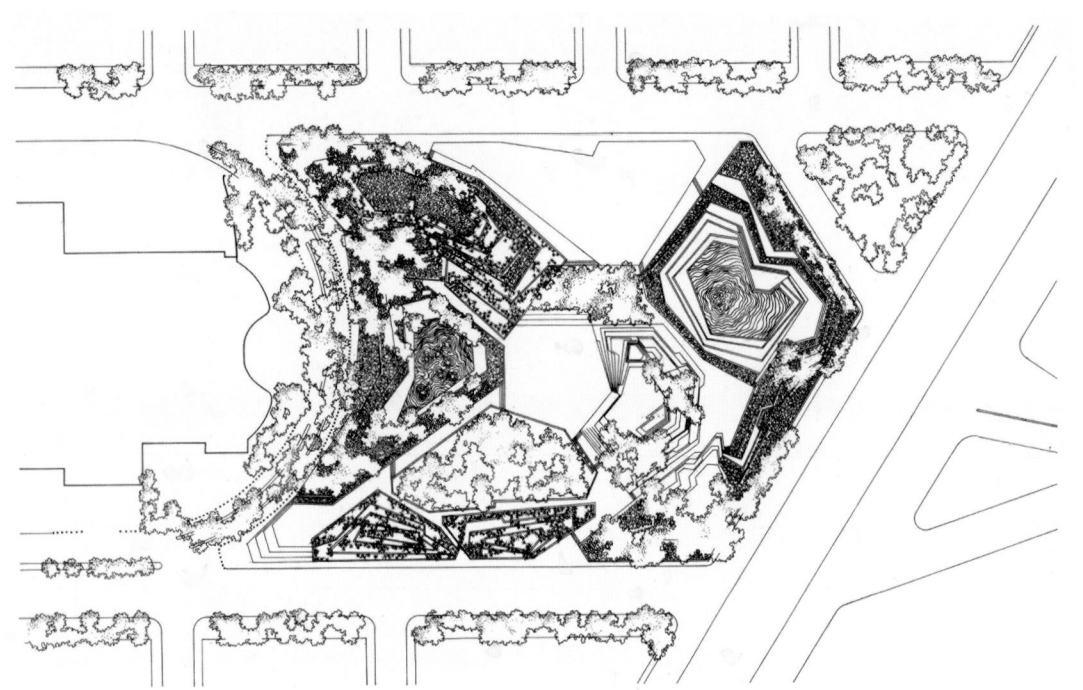

Plan of Fort Worth Water Gardens by Johnson/Burgee Architects, Fort Worth, Texas, 1974.

Philip and Ruth Carter Stevenson inspecting a model of the Fort Worth Water Gardens, 1971.

Texans and towers. Despite a rocky economy in the 1970s, the commissions that Johnson/Burgee secured were not only great in number but also vast in scale—major urban parks, huge commercial towers, and indoor winter gardens all poured out of the office. Much of this was owing to Philip's ongoing love affair with Texas, a relationship dating back to his early residential project for the art-loving de Menil family. With a series of large-scale commercial projects in the 1970s, he firmed up his status as the Lone Star State's go-to out-of-town architect.

Transformer

Fort Worth Water Gardens by Johnson/Burgee Architects, Fort Worth,
Texas, 1974.

IDS Center by Johnson/Burgee Architects, Minneapolis, Minnesota, 1972. The reflective design is carved through vertically by intricate step-backs, termed "zogs" by Philip, which create up to thirty-two corner offices on every floor.

Pennzoil Place by Johnson/Burgee Architects (from a concept by Eli Attia, an architect within their firm), Houston, Texas, 1976. The design is lauded for introducing postmodernism by breaking free from the glass box, a hallmark of the Modernist style.

Philip as president of the International Competition Jury presenting hundreds of construction projects for the redesign of Les Halles, Paris, 24 January 1980.

Power broker. No longer just seeking out powerful patrons, Philip was now one himself. "A king-maker," as critic Gwendolyn Wright called him, Philip was uniquely poised to connect young designers with potentially lucrative clients, as well as dispense sage advice and deliver quotable quips to the press, making him a one-man clearinghouse between the media, institutions, and the profession. Even as part of an all-star commission jury in Paris, Philip could make himself the center of attention.

Transformer

290

Top (from left to right): Renzo Piano, Su Rogers, Richard Rogers, Ted Happold, and Peter Rice in front of a presentation board featuring their design for the Beaubourg site competition, Paris, 1971. Bottom: The competition jury for Beaubourg, which selected Richard Rogers, Renzo Piano, and Gianfranco Franchini's design for the Centre Pompidou. Seated in the front row (from left to right): Oscar Niemeyer, Frank Francis, Jean Prouvé, Émile Aillaud, Philip, and Willem Sandberg (back turned), Paris, 1971.

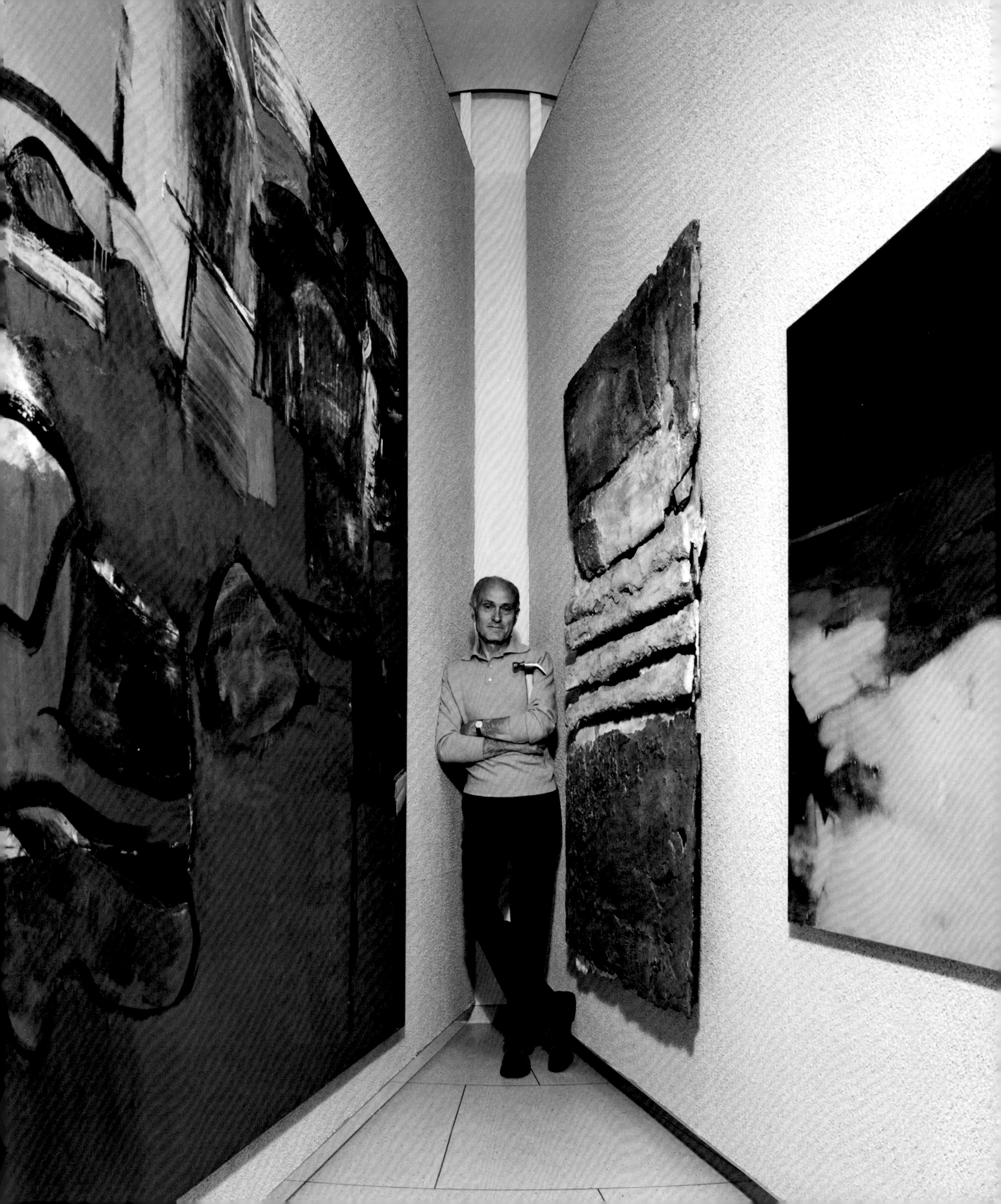

08 Collector

Collector

It began with the Paul Klee painting *Sacred Islands*, which Philip purchased in 1929 for less than a hundred dollars from the artist himself in Berlin. Klee's creation features a network of delicate lines inscribed with vaguely Gothic, ogival forms. Philip praised the painter's "long parallel lines making sections like an onion," in a letter to Alfred H. Barr, Jr. He went on to disparage his own art instincts: "I find my reactions to painting are horribly primitive," he wrote. "I really must learn something about it."

Uninformed as he might have been, there was nothing crude or clumsy about Philip's instincts. The string of acquisitions that immediately followed the first testified to his very keen eye or, at least, a susceptibility to good advice: alongside a few choice pieces of Bauhaus design, Pablo Picassos and Aristide Maillols also came home with Philip from the same German excursion. These would shortly be joined by a Piet Mondrian (in dreadful shape), an Otto Dix (a portrait of a rotund doctor seated before a convex mirror), and an Oskar Schlemmer (the celebrated Bauhaus stairway painting, rescued from Germany), as well as more Picassos, a Joan Miró, and eventually a Nicolas Poussin—albeit of somewhat doubtful attribution—destined to hold pride of place in the Glass House.

Philip always had the taste, as well as the means, to scoop up extraordinary contemporary artworks, and his buying was further abetted by his art-minded friends. More than abetted: Barr in particular encouraged it, using Philip to acquire pieces outside the Museum of Modern Art's (MoMA) budgetary means with a promise of future donation; the Klee, the Schlemmer, the Dix, and much else would later reside in the museum's collection. But it was only after the war that the pace as well as the purpose of Philip's collecting assumed a different character, facilitated by two important factors: the gallery structures on the Glass House campus and the influence of his companion, David Whitney.

Whitney was Andy Warhol's personal confidant ("We were [like] two lonely widows,"[1] he said of the artist, speaking of their shared sense of isolation) and a fairly ubiquitous figure on the New York scene (sometimes a little too ubiquitous: his drinking was a problem). It was he, beginning in the early 1960s, who introduced Philip to the artists, gallerists, and dealers who would make possible what became a treasure trove of Pop and Minimalist art, most of it squirreled away in New Canaan, Connecticut. To see it all in a suitable setting, Philip added the so-called *Kunstbunker*—a puzzling mini museum half-buried into Ponus Ridge, the paintings mounted on panels that could be spun around like giant lazy Susans—and later the Sculpture Gallery—descending the hill via brick stairs, topped with a greenhouse roof that made for unbeatable natural light, if sometimes unendurable heat. A part of any personal tour of the Glass House compound, the exhibition spaces added to the social and cultural allure that drew many collector-clients to his doorstep.

Whether it was the de Menils, his first major clients in Texas, or the Arizona- and New York-based Tremaine family, the people behind some of Philip's most successful projects were themselves major lovers of Modern art. It could be said that Philip got along better with them than he did with artists: shortly into a collaboration with Mark Rothko on what would become the de Menils' famed chapel, the artist tutted that he and the architect "might come to an impasse"[2]—as indeed they did, with Philip coming out the loser. (Artists, in any case, were unlikely to commission a building themselves.) But while he was among the country's most established collectors, Philip was not necessarily of them.

For many famous art hoarders, collecting serves as the sincerest form of autobiography, their intellectual and psychological preoccupations reliably playing out across the assembled canvases. Not so for Philip, or at least not in the same way. Between the John Chamberlains that huddle menacingly in the sculpture gallery and the cheeky Roy Lichtensteins hiding in the bunker, the thematic through line seems hard to follow. Indeed, if anything holds together Philip's collection, it is only how eclectic, how general the body of work really is: how exactly like a museum, in fact, a sort of greatest-hits assortment representing a certain period in American art. (And never representative in a broader sense, being almost entirely the work of white men, most of them well-known entities in the international market.)

What the paintings and sculptures do suggest is that for Philip, collecting was yet another field for his tireless search for self: an endless series of mirrors, always changing with the passage of time, reflecting his own always-changing attitudes.

By 1964, when Philip curated a small (and ultimately highly controversial) exhibition for the World's Fair, he had finally come to appreciate his own powers of perception. "I frankly love my choices," he said, and with a group that included Robert Rauschenberg and Ellsworth Kelly, it would have been hard to disagree. In later life, a falling-out with MoMA would lead to an almost full halt to his donations there; at issue had been the museum's failure to tap Philip for its late 1970s expansion—yet further proof of the overlap between his architectural and artistic pursuits. Yet the change in outlook would only amplify the importance of his collection: portions would go instead to museums as far-flung as California and Nebraska. Most of it remains in Connecticut. If what's there resembles a fairly conventional American museum, that is partly because of how thoroughly Philip's own collecting influenced museums all across the country. Surely that must be reckoned one of the more estimable aspects of his legacy.

Portrait of Philip at his worktable in the Sculpture Gallery at the Glass House, 1978.

Above, left: Philip at the exhibition *Modern Painting and Sculpture*, MoMA, New York, 1 January–31 March 1950.
Above: Interior view of living room, Philip Johnson Apartment by Ludwig Mies van der Rohe and Lilly Reich, New York, 1931. This photograph, c. 1934, shows Oskar Schlemmer's *Bauhaus Stairway* (see p. 103; 1932). Philip gave the painting to MoMA in 1942.

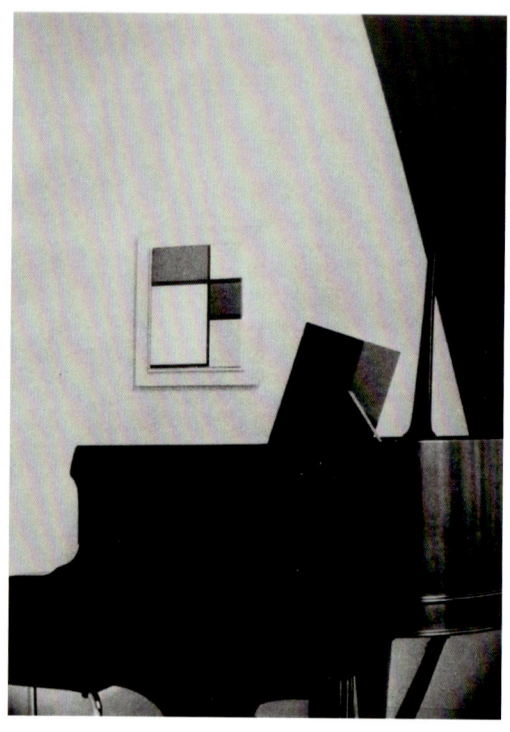

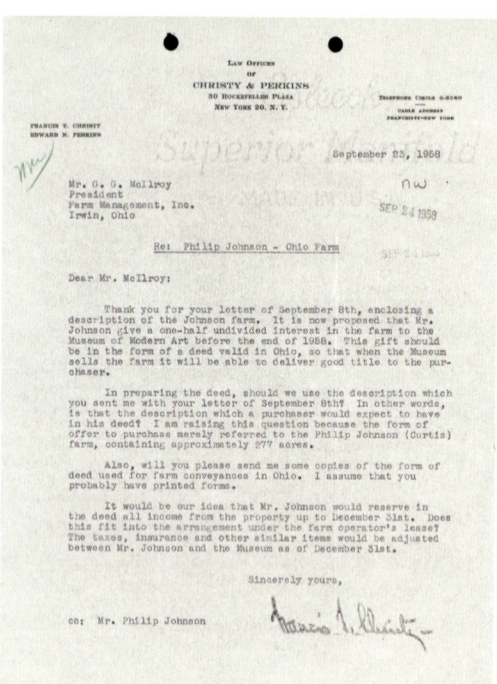

Interior view of living room, Philip Johnson Apartment. This photograph, c. 1934, shows Piet Mondrian's *Composition No. II, with Red and Blue* (1929), above the piano. Johnson gave the painting to MoMA in 1941.

Bottom: Letter from Philip's lawyer, Francis Christy, to Glen McIlroy at Farm Management Inc., 23 September 1958. He writes to request that half of the Philip Johnson farm be gifted to MoMA, New York.

Acquisitions. Art was always on Philip's mind—and if he didn't know where to find it at first, he knew just whom to ask. J. J. P. Oud helped him buy his first Mondrian (a bad one, as it turned out), while the Berlin gallerist Alfred Flechtheim introduced him to Klee. Following his visit to Dessau, Germany, in 1927, Philip began adding works from the Bauhaus circle to his collection; only three years later, he had already become a donor of sorts, lending works to a pioneering Bauhaus show at the Harvard Society for Contemporary Art. Philip would develop personal relationships with several Bauhaus artists, helping Josef and Anni Albers flee Nazi Germany to the United States. Decades later, he remained close friends with Sibyl Moholy-Nagy—widow of the acclaimed Bauhausian László Moholy-Nagy—despite her strident criticism of everything Ludwig Mies van der Rohe had done in Germany and after.

Collector

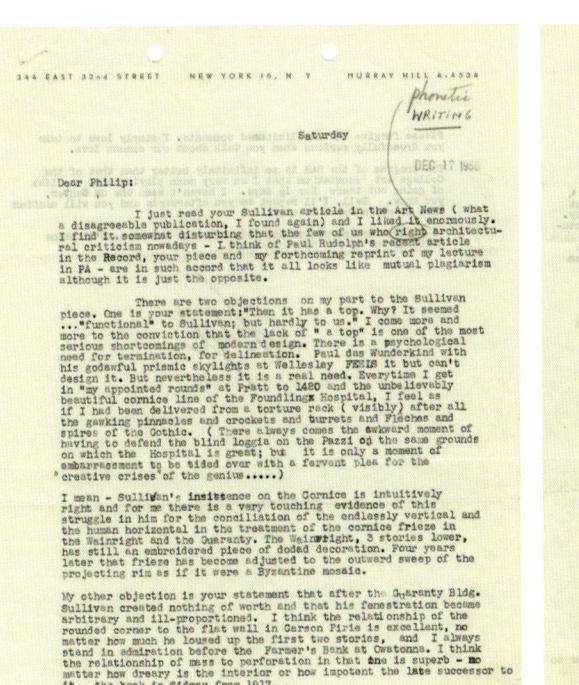

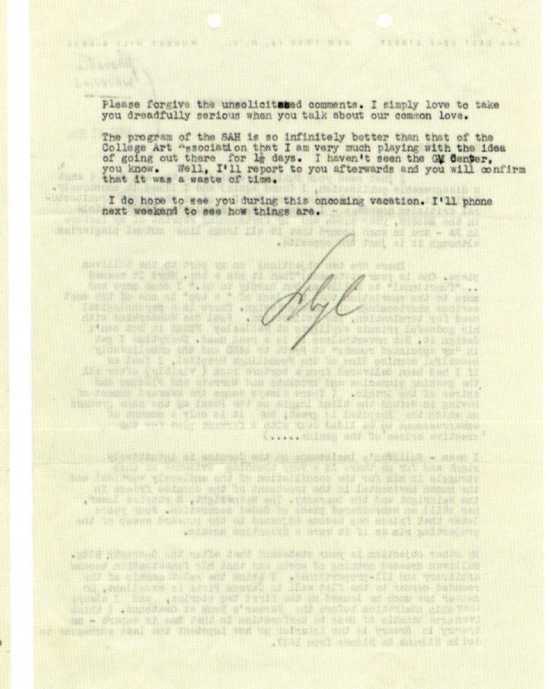

Top row: Two pages of a letter from Sibyl Moholy-Nagy to Philip. New York, 17 December 1956. The letter is primarily a defense of aspects of Louis Sullivan's style: a building's "top" is necessary—"there is a psychological need for termination, for delineation." Bottom row, left: From Philip to Sibyl Moholy-Nagy, 19 December 1956. This letter is a continuation of a debate over building "tops" and Louis Sullivan. Bottom row, center: From Philip to Sibyl Moholy-Nagy, 12 May 1959, in which Philip justifies his style of architecture for "ordinary buildings": "You cannot walk on hyperbolic paraboloids." Bottom row, right: Letter from Sibyl Moholy-Nagy to Philip, 15 May 1959.

DAVID operates the David Whitney Gallery in downtown New York. He specializes in the new "lyrical abstractions," like those here (from left) by Showell, Wofford, Landfield.

David Whitney's Gallery on East 19th Street favors romantic expressionism.

Top and bottom: Portraits of David Whitney in the David Whitney Gallery, New York, 1970.

David Whitney looking at *Monogram* (1955–59) by Robert Rauschenberg.

David. In 1960, after a lecture at Brown University, a young Whitney (then a student at the Rhode Island School of Design) approached Philip and asked what had drawn him to the work of Jasper Johns. The two became an item, and they remained that way until the end. The path never did run smooth: Whitney's attempt to run his own gallery faltered; of his drinking, Warhol would recall that a martini-fueled Whitney would sometimes loudly discuss what he would do "when Pops pops off." And yet as an intellectual helpmeet, Whitney was invaluable, connecting Philip with a whole new constellation of artists—Warhol foremost among them.

Collector

Top: "8 Gamblers on Young Artists: Art Dealers in New York," *Vogue*, 1 February 1970. The photo shows David Whitney (left) among seven other up-and-coming New York art dealers. Bottom: Lunch at Da Silvano, New York, May 1985. Back row, left to right: Cy Twombly, Jasper Johns, Maxine Groffsky, Bill Katz, Paula Cooper, Mark Lancaster, Aldo Crommelynck, Roberta Bernstein, Julian Lethbridge, Vija Celmins. Front row, left to right: Hiroshi Kawanishi, Lois Long, Joni Weil, David Whitney, Sidney Felsen.

Portrait of Philip and David Whitney, likely by Andy Warhol.

Andy Warhol, *Philip Johnson and David Whitney*, 1984.

Collector

Andy Warhol, *David Whitney*, 1980.

Andy Warhol, *David Whitney*, 1980.

Andy Warhol, David Whitney, Philip, Dr. John Dalton, and Robert A. M. Stern at the Glass House, c. 1964-65.

Andy Warhol kissing Philip, New York, 1979.

"People always ask me, 'How does he go to the bathroom in that place?'"

—Andy Warhol on the Glass House

Andy Warhol, *13 Most Wanted Men*, 1964, on the facade of the New York State Pavilion.

Controversy. In tandem with his New York State Pavilion project for the 1964 World's Fair, Philip was responsible for wrangling pieces from a slew of contemporary artists to adorn it—a tricky proposition, only grudgingly accepted at the last minute by fair organizer Robert Moses. The most contentious submission ended up being Warhol's *13 Most Wanted Men*, a silvery montage of assorted criminals then wanted by the New York Police Department. "It just had something to do with New York and they paid me just enough to have it silk screened," Warhol said. The authorities cried foul, obviously concerned it would tarnish the state's image; the work was painted over (in silver paint, no less) before the fair opened.

Collector

Andy Warhol, *Philip Johnson*, 1972.

Philip in the Glass House, 18 June 1966. The sculpture is *Two Circus Women* by Elie Nadelman. It is a small version of a marble sculpture that is in the lobby of the New York State Theater.

Meanwhile, in New Canaan, Connecticut… The works that had adorned the Glass House proper were impressive, but the space was hardly large enough to accommodate Philip's expanding collection, which would instead be housed on land he had acquired to the east and north. The first dedicated arts structure, the Painting Gallery, had an entrance faintly reminiscent of an Egyptian mastaba or the Mycenaean Lion Gate; the second, the Sculpture Gallery, featured stepped terraces that make it feel almost like an Italian town. If the Glass House complex was Philip's "fifty-year diary," as he once called it, the two entries for art found Philip in a distinctly escapist mood.

Collector

Interior view of the living room with a freestanding painting room screen. The painting is a version of Nicolas Poussin's *The Funeral of Phocion* (1648).

Philip looking at an art display by Jasper Johns in the Brick House, New Canaan, Connecticut, 1949.

Entrance to the Painting Gallery at the Glass House, 1965.

"There's only one reason for my whole life, and that's art. Nothing else counts; nothing else gives me pleasure; nothing else gives me satisfaction."

—Philip on the importance of art

Interior view of the Painting Gallery, New Canaan, Connecticut, 1965.

Collector

Interior view of the Sculpture Gallery, New Canaan, Connecticut, 1970.
The works on display are by Donald Judd, Barnett Newman, and Frank Stella.

Art: from I.R.T. to A R T

Keith Haring

with Halston & Philip Johnson

In the progression of artistic movements from Expressionism through Pop, the figurative work of Keith Haring stands out as an exceptional step forward. Incorporating the simplicity, frivolity and humor of Pop, Haring has gone further to invent an original vocabulary of symbols at once recognizable and evocative—the crawling baby, barking dog, portable pyramid, zapping spaceship—sometimes done on canvas, more often chalk-drawn on subway station ad boards, buildings or sidewalks. Free of specific cultural references, the drawings speak with equal clarity to sophisticated viewers and mere passersby, in a deeply human voice.

Raised in Kutztown, Pennsylvania, Haring came to New York in the late '70s and attended the School of Visual Arts. Soon discovering that the "most beautiful paintings in the city were being shown on wheels (by the graffitists)," Haring began his subway drawings as a lark, and became a celebrity underground and above, with his first gallery exhibition in 1981. In spite of the proliferation of international showings and press since then, including the recently published photographic study "Art in Transit" (Harmony Books), the artist and his work have maintained their charming innocence.

These two interviews, the first with designer Halston and Andy Warhol at a weekend house in Montauk, the second with Philip Johnson at the architect's home in Connecticut, offer a stereoscopic view into Haring's special world.

HALSTON: When did you start drawing?
KEITH HARING: When I was four years old. Everybody draws when they are little.
ANDY WARHOL: I drew flies.
HALSTON: You drew flies?
AW: Doesn't everybody draw flies?
HALSTON: Do you do work for TV?
KH: I got asked one time to do the graphics for the Pan-Am Games.
HALSTON: You should do them.
KH: I wish I had done something for these Olympics. It would have been great to have done a huge running man on top of the Coliseum or something.
HALSTON: You should do a comic strip, too. Did you ever do a comic strip?
KH: No, not really. I've been drawing cartoons since I was little but....
HALSTON: Walt Disney could use a new character.
KH: I've always wanted to work for Walt Disney. That's what I thought I was going to do when I grew up.
AW: The crawling baby could really be a good daily comic strip.
KH: Except I think that would ruin it. I think when you turn things into serials like that it ruins it.
HALSTON: What if you make a movie out of it?
KH: When they put Snoopy and Peanuts on television it just ruined it.
HALSTON: Well, then you could go into crawling teenagers and dolls and things. And then women and old people.
KH: Speaking of old people, I did a thing for a medicine company in Germany to advertise a heart medicine.
HALSTON: A heart medicine? What kind?
KH: It's a new heart medicine, I forget what it's called. It's for cardiac arrest.
HALSTON: I like it just called "heart medicine."
KH: They used some of my drawings to promote their product in medical journals and things. It's funny, I get the weirdest offers.
HALSTON: What's the weirdest offer you ever had?
KH: I had a call from a firm that represents the polyester industry. It had to do with a big media event to try to get polyester back on the map.
HALSTON: I never thought it left the map. You've done a book already?
KH: I've published one book with Tony Shafrazi. It was sort of like a catalog, not really a book. I have a book coming out now that I did with Harmony Books of photographs by Tseng Kwong Chi of the subway drawings from the last three years with a foreword by Henry Geldzahler. Actually, I have a great picture of me with Mayor Koch, as I present him this book and he makes this really horrible face, like, "Who is this guy and how did he get in my office?"
HALSTON: I saw him on TV the other day saying that he hated graffiti. But you don't consider yourself a graffiti artist.
KH: Mayor Koch hates it a lot. What I call it doesn't matter because the media calls it graffiti.
HALSTON: What would you prefer calling it?
KH: I call it drawing. It was ironic that I got to meet the mayor because of that litter pig thing. The Sanitation Department has a new anti-litter campaign for the city called "Don't Be a Litter Pig" and they asked me to design the pig for it. I had to do this press conference with him for the anti-litter campaign, so I took the opportunity to give him the book and sort of confront him with it. He had to accept it and shake my hand because I was there to do something free for the city.

HALSTON: It costs ten million dollars a year to remove graffiti, doesn't it?
KH: Yes, but it's really a waste of money because they're not going to wipe it out anyway. They can't stop it. All they do is chase the good artists off the trains.
AW: What's the difference?
KH: The trains in 1978 and 1979 were incredible. That's when an artist would spend eight hours on one car. No one does that anymore. Every now and then you see a piece, but now they have these huge buffing machines with a chemical wash that they run the trains through. No one will spend the eight hours if they're going to have their piece ruined in two days.
HALSTON: Where did you grow up?
KH: I grew up in Pennsylvania in a small town. Real small, like one high school and one movie theater. Well, there was a state college there, that was the only good thing about it.
AW: When I came to New York I had one dish, one spoon, one fork. It's actually more fun to have one school, one post office.
KH: It made everything simpler, except that everybody knew you and everybody knew everything you were doing. And for me that wasn't good because I started my childhood being a really good little kid: churchgoer, straight-A student, little league team. And then by the time I was fifteen and wanted to be a hippie....
AW: What made you want that?
KH: I guess being a little bit progressive by myself and just reading Life magazine and seeing Woodstock and the Democratic convention in Chicago on TV, things like that. It got to the point where I wanted to smoke pot so bad I bought tea. When I was thirteen or fourteen, I tried to smoke tea hoping that would do something. I had no idea where to get pot from. Soon after that I found out where to get pot. So I started to hang out with college students when I was about fifteen, and that's how I got to experiment with other things. And then I started hitchhiking and getting out of the town when I was 17.
AW: Where did you go, Philadelphia?
KH: No, usually to the New Jersey shore. And one summer I ran away and lived at the Jersey shore for the whole summer because my parents refused to let me go work there. So I just did it anyway.
HALSTON: What kind of work did you do?
KH: I was a paperboy when I was little, so I was always saving money. From the time I was twelve years old, I was buying savings bonds. So years later I took a thousand-dollar savings bond, bought a half-pound of pot and moved to the shore. I spent all the money and had the best time of my life. It was really great because I learned a lot and grew up and learned how to live with people and live by myself.
HALSTON: Were you drawing all the time?
KH: Yeah, I was, but I wasn't taking it all that seriously.
HALSTON: When did you take it seriously?
KH: I guess as soon as I started thinking of art and not cartoons, when I was 17 or 18.
HALSTON: What was the first thing you sold?
KH: I sold little things when I was young.
HALSTON: How much money did you get for them?
KH: The first thing I sold I got $135. That was when I was 17. It was a little ink drawing of a map of Berks County. When I was 17 I hitchhiked to New Jersey to go to this art exhibition on the Wildwood boardwalk. I took my little portfolio with me and was in this art show. It was the kind of show they have in shopping malls with all these really tacky crafts artists. But I got a prize and was real proud and sold a few little pen and ink drawings. I was hitchhiking to Beach Haven in a car with this guy who said he was going almost all the way, and the portfolio was in the back seat. All of a sudden he changed his mind and was going a different way, so I had to get out really quick, and there was a line of traffic. I got out and left the whole portfolio of my work on the back seat. I never saw it again, and it was everything I had done up to that time. I just started all over and everything got better. Things like that happen to me a lot. I just want to go forward, forget about it and do something different. It just seemed like it kept getting better.
AW: You did the baby on Union Square, didn't you?
KH: That wasn't until 1981 or '82. I didn't start doing graffiti until two years after I got to New York. Jean Michel Basquiat

KEITH HARING PHOTOGRAPHED BY ROBERT MAPPLETHORPE.

129

Mover/shaker. While the buildings in New Canaan, Connecticut, allowed Philip to seek personal refuge in his collection, there was nothing shy or retiring in Philip's approach to art and art buying. For years following his appointment to MoMA's board, Philip acquired outstanding contemporary works at rock-bottom prices on the premise that they would later be donated to MoMA—and then occasionally declined to donate them. With collecting, Philip said, "Getting there is half the fun,"[3] and he relished the process of meeting artists and gallerists. Doling out his patronage in measured doses, using his celebrity as leverage, Philip remained a player on the New York art scene well into his (and the century's) ninth decade.

PHILIP JOHNSON PHOTOGRAPHED BY ROBERT MAPPLETHORPE.

was one of my main inspirations for doing graffiti. For a year I didn't know who Jean Michel was, but I knew his work.
AW: *And he actually went around writing poems on the street?*
KH: Yes, it was like the first literary graffiti.
AW: *What are the kinds of things that he said?*
KH: Samo became a philosophy. "Samo" supposedly stood for same old shit. That was in the Mudd Club days.
AW: *Jean Michel is a really good writer. He writes beautiful poetry.*
HALSTON: *Do you like to write, too?*
KH: Sometimes, yes. I used to keep a diary, but I stopped. I really wish I'd have kept it up. I was keeping a diary when there wasn't anything really interesting happening, and now there's so much happening and no time to sit down and write about it. Artists' diaries were always my favorite things to read. Like Rimbaud and all those people.
HALSTON: *Now you're doing things all over the world.*
KH: Yes, for the last two years.
AW: *What's so good about him is he can go and take his art with him and do it there.*
HALSTON: *You do it right on the spot? You mean if you're going to have a show in Japan or something you do it right there?*
KH: I went to Tokyo for three weeks and made everything there. I didn't even take any brushes with me. I bought everything there.
HALSTON: *Do you do commissions?*
KH: Not really. A lot of people ask me to do things inside their houses, but I rarely will do it because there are so many other chances to do things. I do commissions for the public, but in a private house it doesn't seem like it's worth the time, because not that many people will see it.
HALSTON: *What would you like to do next?*
KH: Everything. I'm working on sets now for a peformance with Bill T. Jones at the Brooklyn Academy of Music. I'm going to do a set for Roland Petit for his new ballet in Paris, which is cool, because he's had a lot of great people do sets for him. Picasso did a set for his first ballet when he was 20,

and he's used Max Ernst and Miro and Jasper Johns and David Hockney. David Hockney did his last set. That will start in the spring and probably not be in New York for two years.
HALSTON: *You want to be in the fashion business too, don't you?*
KH: I feel like I'm capable of it. You have to have either someone else working for you to set up the whole thing or you have to devote a large chunk of your time to doing it. There are endless possibilities. There's not enough time for me to do all of it. That's probably why I'm getting ripped off and imitated so much by people. I guess if I can't utilize it someone else has to. In some ways I don't really mind if people do it, because I can't do all of it myself. There are other people making jewelry and other things out of my characters without my permission. Almost every country I've been in already has Keith Haring T-shirts whether I've made them or not.
HALSTON: *You could license it. When people copy you it just makes you more known.*
KH: I guess, but then it's out of your hands and you don't really have quality control.
HALSTON: *You can do quality control.*
KH: I'm taking all that real slow because right now I'm more interested in doing children's books and animations and theater sets, expanding in lots of other directions. I'd still love to do a playground. I saw Noguchi's playground and it was so incredible. I think it's one of the best things he ever did. I know I could make an incredible playground.
HALSTON: *You should do Diana Ross' playground.*
KH: I would do it.
HALSTON: *Actually, you should get the Mayor to do that.*
KH: I'd like to make it out of huge cast rubber so you could bounce off it. It would be really sturdy, but you could climb all over it—huge sculptures.
AW: *Your sculptures were great.*
KH: The first ones were those totem poles. That was a sort of primitive attempt at doing sculpture. The headdress we made for Grace Jones was another step, really, because it deals with the inside space in-

stead of just the surface.
HALSTON: *How do you deal with the fact that you're not a starving artist anymore and your community still is starving artists?*
KH: I guess you find out quickly who your friends are. The people who were my real friends before never lost any respect for me because of what happened to me. And the people who only were acquaintances...I guess a lot of people resent it or can't handle it now. Most people want to be cool and think that as soon as something is popular that means that it's "sold out" or it's dangerous. So they have to move on to the next thing that's unpopular and still cool. I don't find any conflict between the two things. The audience I was trying to reach I'm still reaching. Those people that are upset about it aren't the people I'm interested in anyway.

[at Philip Johnson's]

KH: *Is it true you were going to make a building in Manhattan with a moat around it?*
PHILIP JOHNSON: The Trump Castle. Well, a castle has to have a moat, doesn't it? I had to set the thing back from Madison Avenue, so I put a moat around it and put a drawbridge across.
KH: *The moat would surround the entire building, the whole block?*
PJ: Not the whole block, but whatever piece of property I had. So it would give you the feeling of these great towers rising out of the moat.
KH: *How deep would the moat be?*
PJ: It wouldn't have made much difference.
KH: *Were there going to be alligators in it?*
PJ: I'd hoped to put alligators in it.
KH: *In winter that would be a problem in New York.*
PJ: Don Trump loved the idea because it's good for controlling the entrance.
KH: *Where would that building be?*
PJ: Fifty-ninth and Madison opposite General Motors. But it was much taller than General Motors, 75 stories high.
KH: *Is it just a proposal or is it going to happen?*

PJ: No, it was canceled. I told him it was too expensive. He said it wasn't, but it was.
KH: *Does that happen a lot?*
PJ: No. I very seldom work for..."mad" is not a good word for Donald Trump, but he's one of the great creative guys and he doesn't stop for a second. He's very interested in architecture. We had a lot of fun. I used to see him every day. Every day was a new idea. He would get ahead of me and say, "Well, alright, do you want to make that gold leaf or do you want to put that window up there like that?" I would say, "Well, it would look like hell," and he'd say, "It would?" He is a very exciting man.
KH: *Who canceled it, the board of directors?*
PJ: The Prudential Life Insurance Company canceled it. They would have lost an awful lot of money. But he wants to build the tallest building in the world now. I doubt if he'll get around to it.
AW: *Where is that going to be?*
PJ: That would be down at the end of Manhattan, somewhere on the East River.
AW: *Are you doing that one?*
PJ: He said I was, but I haven't heard, so I guess I'm not. But we are playing with a building down there near the South Ferry. You know the ferries that go off to Staten Island, out in the water?
KH: *In the water?*
PJ: It would be a huge tower.
KH: *I like how much the new buildings look like castles. The one in Pittsburgh, PPG Place, is really incredible, what that did to the skyline.*
PJ: Yes, that was really good, not only the skyline, but the city, now that the square is done.
KH: *I was there when it was still under construction, so I haven't seen the square. I saw a picture of the square, but you really can't see what it looks like from the picture.*
PJ: You can't see architecture *[from a picture]* because architecture is interior space. For instance, this room *[Johnson's study]* has been photographed a hundred times, but you can't get that feeling that you get of awayness here, of being totally alone. You can see that there are squirrels and things, but they don't bother you the way they do when you're outdoors. And I can get absolutely carried away. I've got all the books here, so it takes one second to find my Leonardo or my Lutyens. You can't do architecture without knowing history. You can't do any art without knowing history. So I get a lot of help from books. It's just great to have them reachable.
KH: *I have a lot of books, but right now I don't have a good library.*
PJ: You don't need them with the work you're doing now.
KH: *I don't have time to stop and think right now.*
PJ: Well, would you be changing? You don't know.
KH: *I don't think so.*
PJ: No.
KH: *I'll look at as many things as I can and absorb as much information as I can but....*
PJ: You're still evolving. I got myself in a bind because, you know, most architects, like most artists, have a style. If you change it they'll say, "Oh why is he making those awful new pictures?" Like when Jasper Johns changes, those people say the new ones are terrible—well, they're *not*. But the public gets used to it and then they don't like the *new* way he puts paint to use—and it's the same with architecture, except I'm running under the other trouble. I make a different building every single time.
KH: *But that's what's great about you.*
PJ: That's what's fun. But Mies van der Rohe, my predecessor, built one building, and then with all the rest you knew you were getting a Mies building. You were getting exactly the same building every time. That would have bored the *pants* off me. Naturally, one building has some relation to the building before; I cut a corner let's say or I have a pyramidal roof. And then my old clients come and they say, you're copying my building for that new client. Well, you can't have it both ways. You want to be a consistent architect who

KEITH HARING, UNTITLED, 1984, INK ON PAPER, 22" x 34". COURTESY OF THE ARTIST.

130

Opposite and above: "Art: from I.R.T. to ART", a newspaper article about Keith Haring, Philip, and American fashion designer Halston, December 1985. The portraits are by Robert Mapplethorpe. IRT stands for Interborough Rapid Transit and is a reference to Haring's experimental graffiti art in New York subway stations.

Top: Installation view, *Philip Johnson: Selected Gifts*, Museum of Modern Art, New York, 10 April–27 October 1985. Bottom: Selected pages of a press release for *Philip Johnson: Selected Gifts*.

Installation views, *Philip Johnson: Selected Gifts*, Museum of Modern Art,
New York, 10 April–27 October 1985.

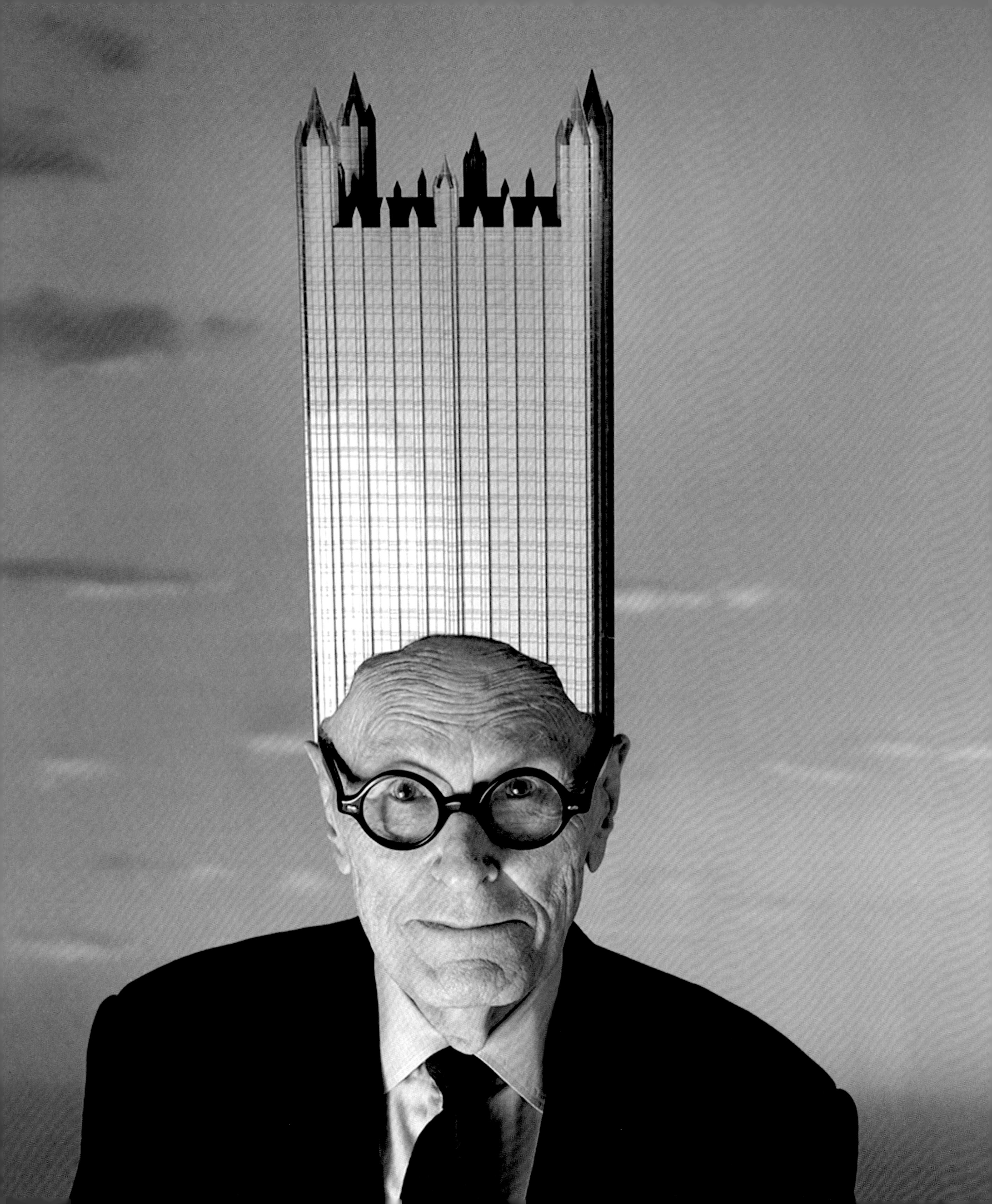

09 Postmodernist

Postmodernist

Philip's assorted architectural transformations after midcentury did not entirely satisfy him. Seeking a deeper well of inspiration, he began to look backward—and around. "You cannot not know history,"[1] he declared, and many of his younger acquaintances were arriving at similar conclusions. Rather than merely toying with the conventions of Modernism, as Philip had done for years, designers like Robert Venturi, Robert A. M. Stern, and Michael Graves had begun reintroducing explicit historical motifs into their work, bucking not just the International Style but also all of its glass, steel, and concrete cousins. Rather than try to beat them, Philip joined them and almost immediately leapt in front of the pack.

His notorious intellectual ductility made the switch a remarkably rapid one. Philip had, after all, been midwife to the postmodern movement: in 1966 he had helped fund the publication of Venturi's seminal treatise *Complexity and Contradiction in Architecture*, published by the Museum of Modern Art (MoMA). The book was an eclectic broadside, taking dead aim at what its author described as the "either/or" purity of traditional Modernist thinking; perhaps its most memorable bon mot, "Less is a bore," was a flippant inversion of the Miesian maxim that had once been Philip's credo. Now his feelings had altered, and he began to heed Venturi's call for a richer, stranger American landscape. "I am old enough to have enjoyed the International Style," said Philip. "But now the age is changing."[2]

Historical impulses had been evident in Philip's work all along. (They had never been altogether absent in Ludwig Mies van der Rohe's work, with its Grecian symmetry and Neo-Classical hierarchies.) This latest switch, such as it was, was more of a rhetorical one: while before, Philip called for a twentieth-century architecture imbued with the grandeur of the past, now he seemed to do the reverse, favoring historical forms adapted to the technical needs of the present. In his own work, the approach was evident beginning with the 1978 design of the AT&T Building, its masonry facade and grandfather-clock capital only masking a conventional corporate high-rise little different than the Seagram Building; it continued with his 1982 design for the Crescent in Dallas, a multi-use commercial complex made up to look like a French Renaissance chateau, complete with oversized mansard roof; and it grew in scale and the breadth of its references with the Deco-inspired Pennzoil Place in Houston, and the Streamline Moderne Lipstick Building in Manhattan.

The latter office tower—thirty-four stories, its nickname reflecting its elliptical plan and telescoping silhouette—would serve as the headquarters of the Johnson/Burgee office from 1986 onward, as the firm became a powerhouse of productivity. Its success came at the cost of some odium from the professional ranks: in 1982 both Philip and John Burgee participated in a conference at the University of Virginia called by the postmodernist-inclined School of Architecture dean, Jaquelin Robertson. This was a major meeting of the architectural tribes, and in front of the assembled bold-faced names, Philip delivered a presentation on Boston's One International Place, one of his office's most brazenly commercial postmodern endeavors. All sides immediately bashed it—and rather than face down the criticism, Philip owned up to the project's failings, admitting with startling candor that the building "should not be in this part of Boston."[3] Asked why he had gone ahead and designed it anyway, Philip then delivered one of his most infamous one-liners: "I am a whore," he declared, "and I am paid very well."

Rising from the architectural fringe to the big-money mainstream in an astonishingly short interval, postmodernism was to some degree a victim of its own success. Philip was instrumental in bringing about that rise, operating (as he always had) as both a maker of architecture and a maker of architects: in the mid-1970s, he secured a major house commission for Venturi and his partner, Denise Scott Brown; in 1980, even before the debut of the AT&T project, he successfully maneuvered Graves into the commission to build the Portland Building, the first completed postmodernist high-rise in America. But while the movement and many of its buildings—including many by Johnson/Burgee Architects—would fall out of favor, Philip himself did not. Fellow postmodernist Charles Moore described him as "a delightful tourist:"[4] Philip waltzed into postmodernism in the late 1970s and waltzed right out again before the next decade was out.

Left behind was a complex legacy that, as with so much of the postmodern phenomenon, has not been much dwelt upon by posterity. The distinctly fascist overtones of some of Johnson/Burgee's historicist work seem at times like a chilling wink—Philip daring his audience to catch him in the act. The style as he practiced it, big and brash and flashy, reflected a new corporate ethos for America, one embraced with singular enthusiasm by perhaps Philip's biggest postmodern client, Donald Trump. Indeed, for all its failings, its bewildering caprices, Philip's work of the period still bears consideration. His historical fantasias are evidence of a seventy-year-old architect, in the most productive period of his career, seeking to recapture the wonder of his earliest encounters with architecture.

Portrait of Philip posing with a model of his newly designed AT&T Building, May 1978.

"I like the thought that what we are to do on this earth is embellish it for its greater beauty, so that oncoming generations can look back to the shapes we leave here and get the same thrill that I get in looking back at theirs—at the Parthenon, at Chartres Cathedral."

—Philip on architecture and posterity

The postmodern moment. Philip was not alone among former card-carrying Modernists in his conversion to postmodernist work: Kevin Roche, I. M. Pei, and even Skidmore, Owings & Merrill ("the three blind Mies,"[5] as Frank Lloyd Wright had deemed them) took the same tack. The profession, to say nothing of the marketplace, seemed to reward this kind of switch: in 1979, only months after the debut of his nostalgic AT&T design, Philip took home the first-ever Pritzker Prize. Three years later, at the University of Virginia, Philip played elder statesman at a disputatious, one-time-only summit (later published as *The Charlottesville Tapes*) of twenty-five of the country's foremost practitioners; by then, at least half of them could be typified as postmodernists.

Philip with architect I. M. Pei during a gala dinner for Johnson held by the Municipal Art Society, New York, 4 December 1983.

Top: A copy of César Pelli's ceremony speech for the inaugural Pritzker Architecture Prize, which was awarded to Philip, Washington, D.C., 1979. Bottom: A copy of Philip's speech for the same ceremony, in which he describes architecture as "the primary art of our or any other culture."

Postmodernist

Top: Philip receiving a Henry Moore sculpture from César Pelli as part of the inaugural Pritzker Architecture Prize ceremony, Washington, D.C., 1979. Bottom: The Pritzker bronze medallion, based on the designs of Louis Sullivan, with the words "firmness, commodity, delight" inscribed, recalling Roman architect Vitruvius's virtues of architecture: *fimitas, utilitas, venustas*.

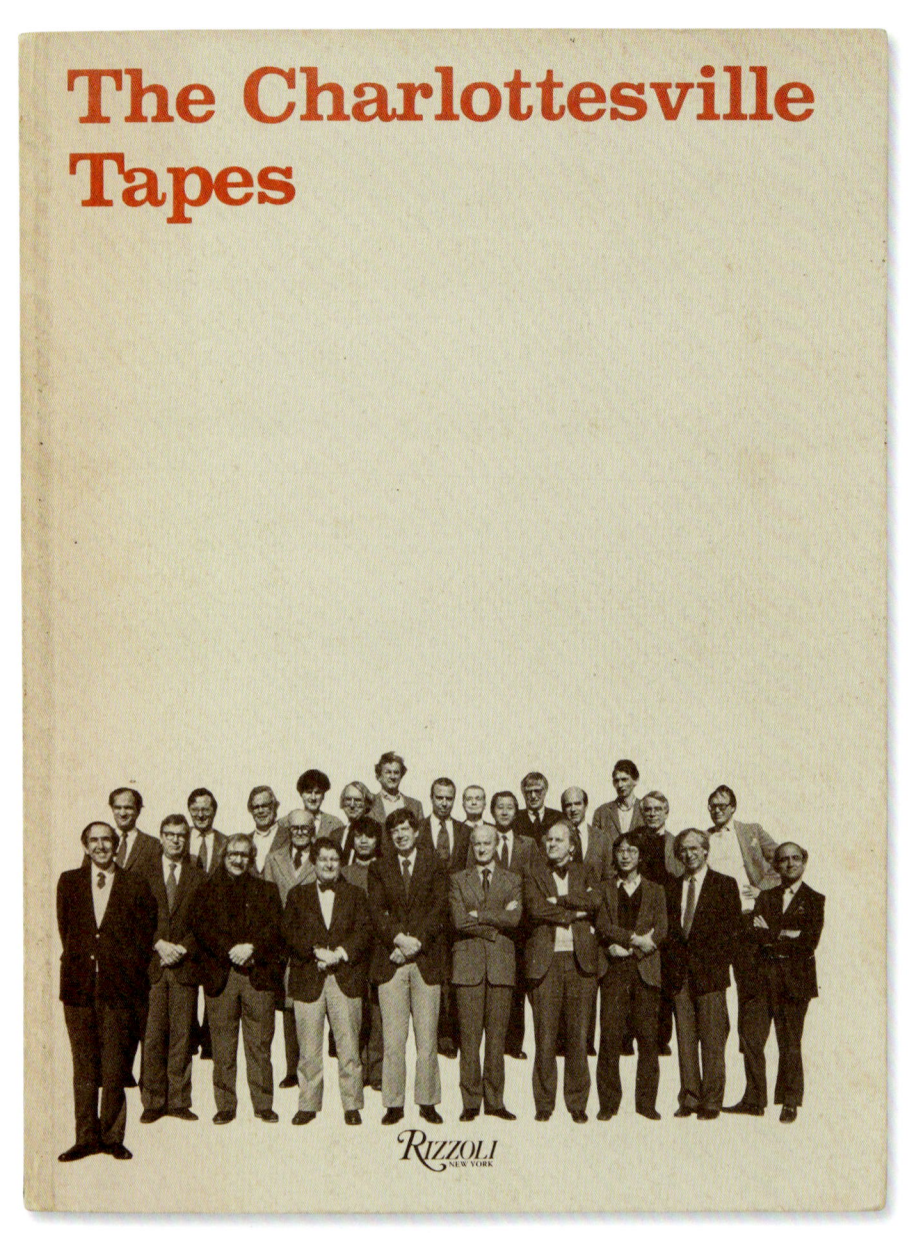

Cover of *The Charlottesville Tapes* (New York: Rizzoli, 1985).

"I do not believe in principles, in case you haven't noticed."

—Philip at the architectural conference held at the University of Virginia in 1982

Robert Siegel

Philip Johnson/John Burgee

Top: Journalist Robert Siegel (center) with Philip (right) at the conference on Modern architecture held at the University of Virginia School of Architecture, Charlottesville, Virginia, 12–13 November 1982. The recordings and transcripts became known as the Charlottesville Tapes. Bottom: Philip and John Burgee speaking at the same conference.

Crystal Cathedral, Johnson/Burgee Architects (from a concept by Eli Attia, an architect within the firm), Garden Grove, California, 1980.

Machine for praying in. Philip wasn't the first major American designer to work for televangelist Robert Schuller: Richard Neutra had designed the minister's original 1961 sanctuary. Whereas the California Modernist went for subtle, Philip went for sensation: a gleaming greenhouse, with echoes of the pioneering 1851 Crystal Palace in London, would be joined a few years later by a spiky tower, also glass clad and even more explicitly historicist in character. As extravagant as the design seemed, it suited the client's philosophy: as Schuller maintained, "A roof that comes between your eyeball and the infinity of space limits your capacity for creative imagination."[6] He had originally preached in parking lots.

Interior view of the Crystal Cathedral, Johnson/Burgee Architects (from a concept by Eli Attia, an architect within the firm), Garden Grove, California, 1980.

Philip and televangelist Robert Schuller in the newly constructed Crystal Cathedral, Garden Grove, California, 1980.

Interior of the Crystal Cathedral, Johnson/Burgee Architects (from a concept by
Eli Attia, an architect within the firm), Garden Grove, California, 1980.

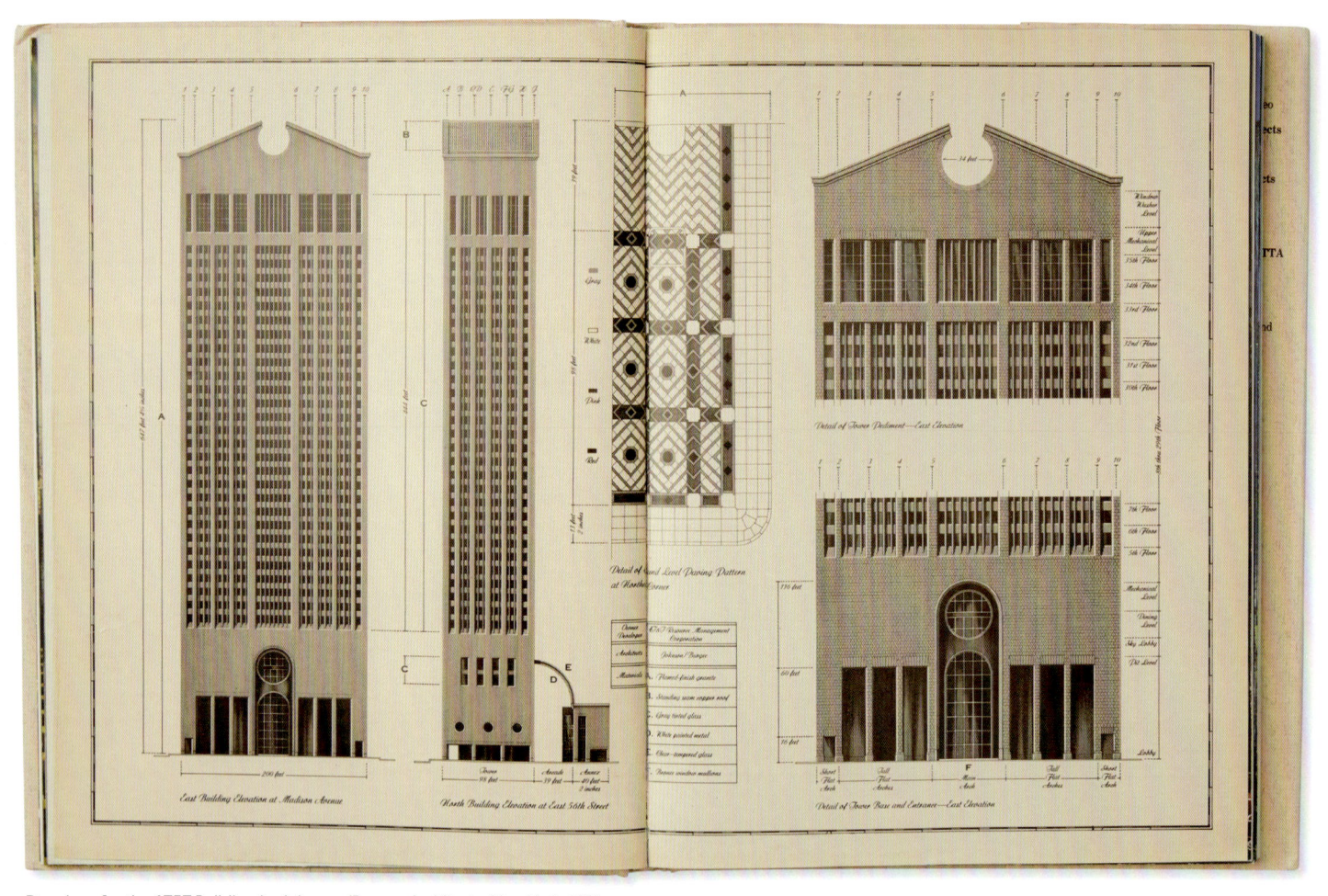

Drawings for the AT&T Building by Johnson/Burgee Architects, New York, 1984.

Chippendale on Madison. It would be "postmodernism's major monument,"[7] declared the architecture critic Paul Goldberger—and that was years before it was even built. AT&T was long in coming, almost six years between the release of the design and the completion of construction; when the building opened, it struck some as a perverse act of patricide ("Mies van der Rohe," declared the *Chicago Tribune*, "would loathe this building") and others as a remarkable success ("city reaches pinnacle as architectural leader," blared the *New York Times*). Certainly it was an unmistakable presence, with its broken-pediment crown and vast street-front loggia, the latter sadly closed off some years later and recently further threatened with an extensive recladding program. In the end, Philip's design won out, with the building declared a New York landmark in 2018.

Postmodernist

View from the west of the AT&T Building by Johnson/Burgee Architects, New York, 1984.

"It seems to me to be a bit of fun. There's nothing symbolic, nothing archaistic ..."

—Philip on the AT&T Building

Philip holding a model of the AT&T Building, 1978.

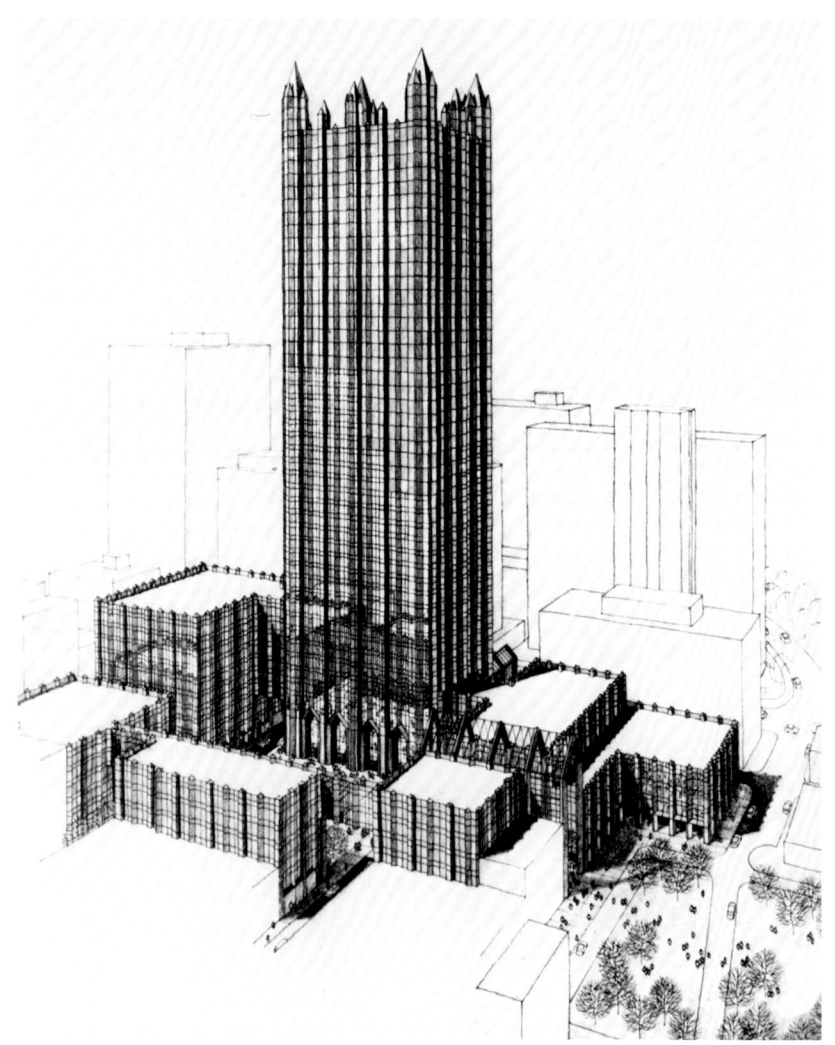

Drawing of PPG Place by Johnson/Burgee Architects, Pittsburgh, Pennsylvania, 1984.

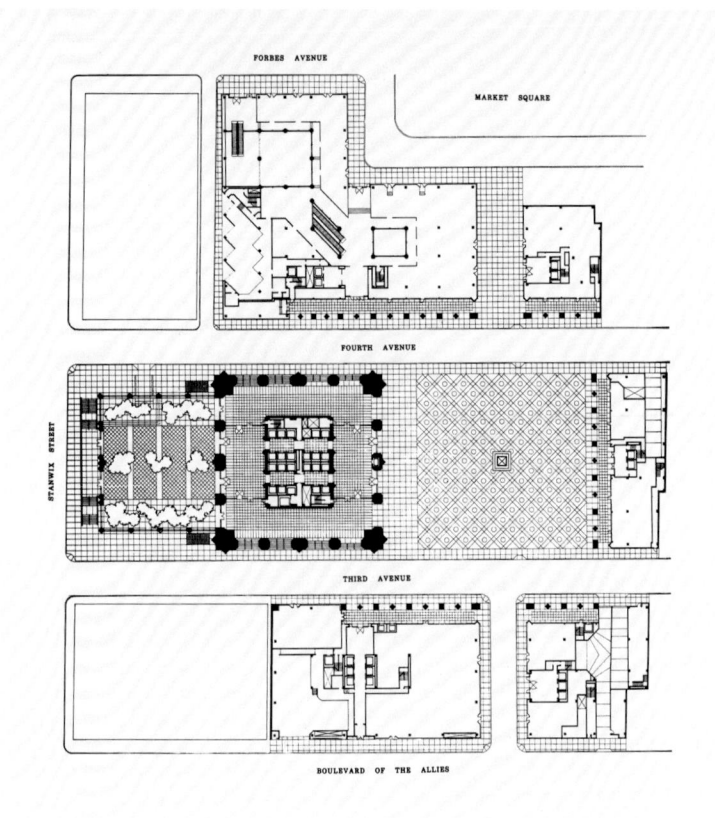

Plan of PPG Place.

Le déluge. Following the media bonanza that accompanied the AT&T project, a stream of historically inspired projects poured out of the office of Johnson/Burgee. The range of references was as broad as the list of projects was long, from Gothic—most prominently at Pittsburgh's PPG Place, headquarters of the plate glass company—to Art Deco, a surprising turn, given Philip's marked distaste for the latter when it was still in vogue. Of the several prewar-styled buildings the firm produced, the most prominent were Houston's Bank of America Center (now the TC Energy Center, a romantic cathedral of commerce replete with decorative finials) and Manhattan's Lipstick Building, the 53rd Street tower that Johnson and Burgee now called home. But despite the smooth, snazzy building, the working relationship of the senior partners had grown very rocky. "The separation," as Frank Welch described it, "was gradual," with Burgee attempting to assert greater control over the office. They finally parted ways altogether in 1991.

Postmodernist

View from the north-east of PPG Place by Johnson/Burgee Architects, Pittsburgh, Pennsylvania, 1984.

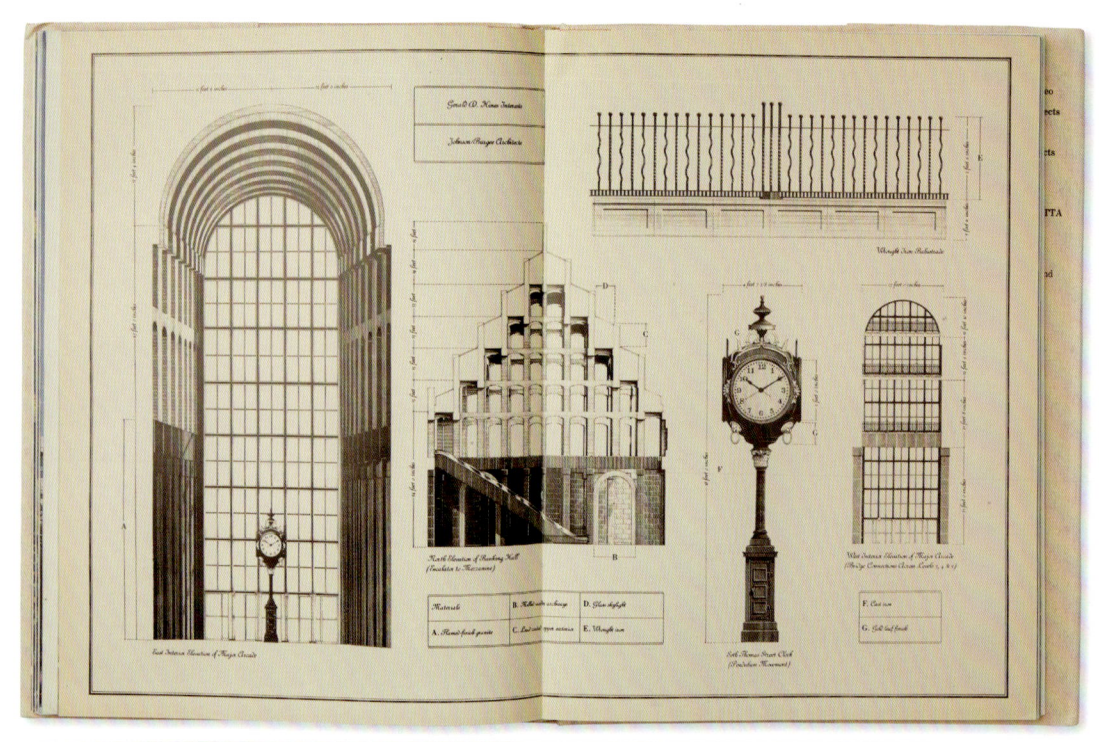

Detail and elevation plans of the Bank of America Center by Johnson/Burgee Architects, Houston, Texas, 1984.

Postmodernist 336

View from the north of the Bank of America Center by Johnson/Burgee Architects, Houston, Texas, 1984. The building to its left is Pennzoil Place, also designed by Johnson/Burgee Architects, 1976.

Interior view of the lobby atrium of the Bank of America Center by Johnson/Burgee Architects, Houston, Texas, 1984.

Bank of America Center by Johnson/Burgee Architects, Houston, Texas, 1984.

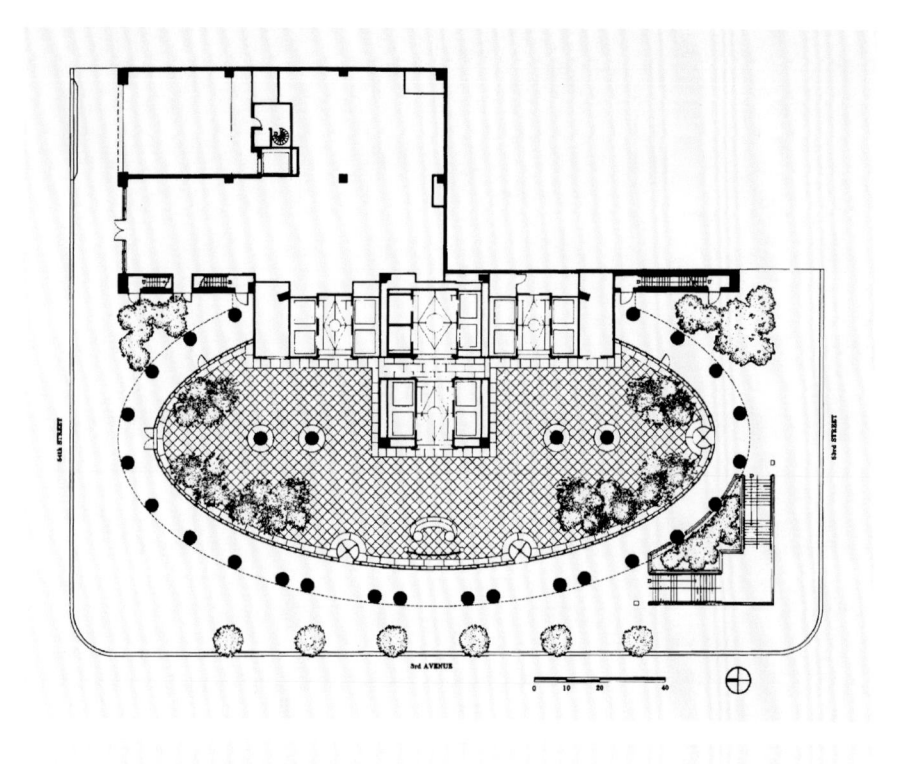

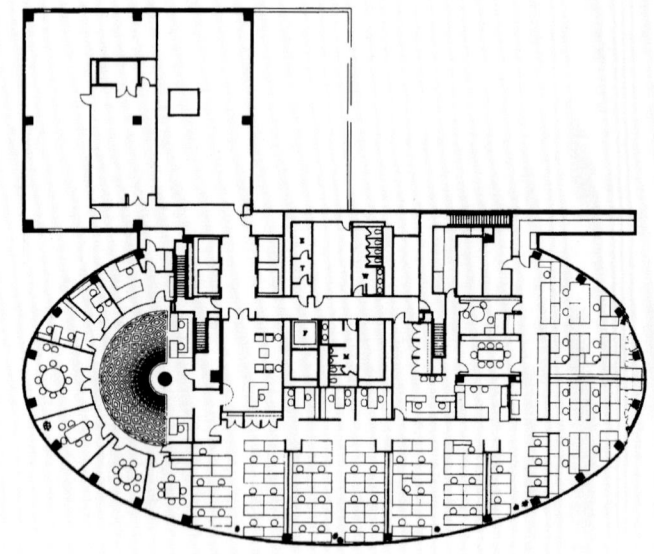

Plans of Lipstick Building by Johnson/Burgee Architects, New York, 1986.

Lipstick Building by Johnson/Burgee Architects,
New York, 1986.

"In short, I am not the 'father,' I am not the 'godfather,' I am not the 'great arbiter.'"

—Philip in correspondence with Marianne Lorenz regarding the October 1980 issue of *Domus*

Reluctant postmodernist? While he loved a good "-ism," Philip's embrace of any one mode of architectural practice was always bound to be conditional. For all his pomo enthusiasm—and as much as his historicist work helped propel his commercial success well into the 1990s—Philip was always looking for the next big thing. Eventually, he'd find it.

Johnson / Burgee   Architects

375 Park Avenue
New York, NY 10022
212/751-7440

July 15, 1980

Madame Marianne Lorenz
Domus
Via Achille Grandi 5/7
20089 Rozzano (Mi)
Italy

Dear Madame Lorenz:

Your questions are interesting.

1. "Modern; Late Modern; Post-Modernism: the new universal architectural chronology by Jencks. He claims that you slalom between these labels. What's your opinion of this"?

The fact that Jencks claims that I slalom between these labels is only a sign of the inadequacy of his labeling method. I do not admit to his simplistic categorization. I have always been a modern architect, and I am still one. The fact that many historic allusions occur in my work seems to me quite a normal development. My first direct use of historic forms was, perhaps, the pavilion in the lake at my place in New Canaan in the late fifties, more than twenty years ago. The word, Post-Modernism is a convenient label that Jencks has used to point out vast changes in architecture since the International Style of the Modern Movement became so boring. In a way, I welcome Charles Jencks categorizing since it sharpens brains and points out trends.

2. "Johnson, they say, is the father and godfather of American architecture: the great arbiter of new directions. We would be interested to hear your diagnosis and your forecast of what lies ahead for us in the 80s."

I am none of the things that I am accused of. I admit to having a quick mind, and I admit to an interest in history. I am the arbiter of a very few architects in New York, but the leaders in American architecture today are younger than I, and it would be invidious to name names. To avoid problems, I might mention Rossi and Stirling, neither of whom learned anything whatsoever from me.

You would like a forecast from me, but it is given to no one to foresee

First page of a letter from Philip to Marianne Lorenz, from New York, 15 July 1980, answering questions regarding his architectural style and influence.

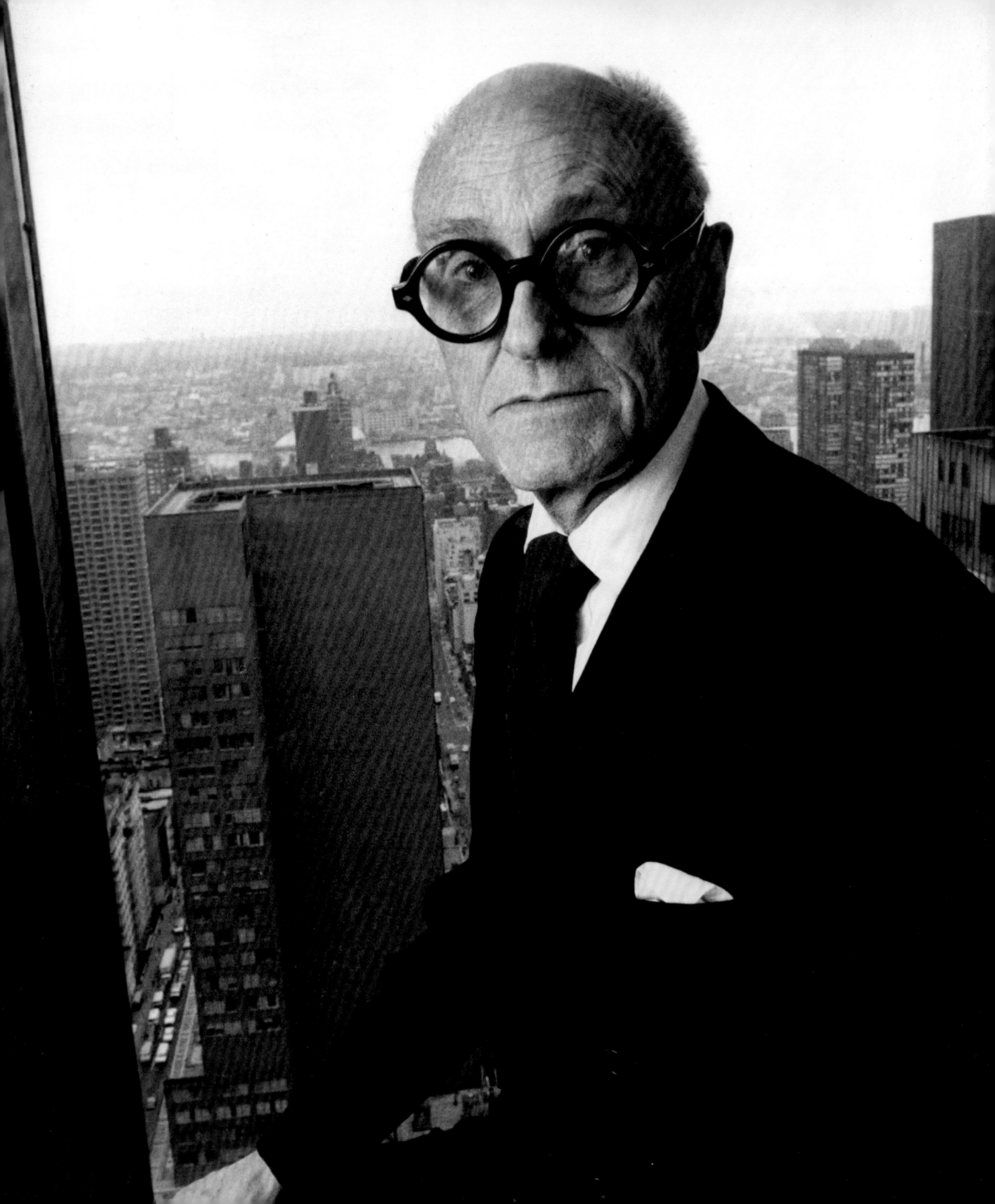

10 Icon

Icon

Just as most men of his years might have been slowing their pace, Philip demonstrated a creative afflatus and intellectual energy that shocked even many of his oldest friends (to say nothing of his enemies). In retrospect, it seems less surprising: the hallmark of Philip's personal and professional life was an almost inexhaustible capacity for change. As the twentieth century gave way to the twenty-first, the architect found himself in a world of accelerating flux and complexity, exactly the kind of environment where he had always thrived.

Even before his practice had entirely moved on from its post-modernist phase, Philip started modulating toward another, newer current in contemporary architecture. He announced the shift just as he had the International Style over five decades earlier: with a major exhibition at the Museum of Modern Art (MoMA). Opening in 1988, *Deconstructivist Architecture* was cocurated by Philip with the young New Zealand–born academic Mark Wigley; not so secretly, it was also masterminded by Peter Eisenman, who had been diligently drilling Philip in the abstruse theories of Derrida, Foucault, and their intellectual fellow travelers. The effort had succeeded, and Philip had jettisoned his previous reliance on history in favor of theory, which he now claimed (in 1990) "is an actual necessity for design"—even if, by his own admission, he found much of it "murky."[1]

Such understanding of post-structuralism and Deconstruction as Philip did possess, he owed to others, especially Eisenman and Jeffrey Kipnis, an enterprising theorist and itinerant academic who wrote about, collaborated with, and generally orbited Philip throughout the late 1980s and 1990s. On the most famous occasion, in 1987, Philip summoned those two and a group of other architects and thinkers to Century Association, one of Manhattan's oldest private clubs, explaining that they were there "for the education of Philip Johnson." To him (and some of his younger colleagues), the heady ideas filtering into architecture from the worlds of philosophy and literature suggested a daring new architecture of confusion and collapse, a frenetic vision of modernity born of emerging technologies and the cultural and social ferment of the global age. Shortly thereafter, a beaming Eisenman, clutching a set of "collagist" drawings that were plainly influenced by the new Deconstructivist thinking, approached the critic Michael Sorkin and dared him to guess the architect who made them.[2] It was Philip, of course.

In fact, Philip had begun to manifest some cognizance of emerging trends well before Eisenman clued him in. As was often the case, that awareness was first evinced in New Canaan, Connecticut, where in 1985 Philip added the so-called Ghost House, a garden pavilion whose simple chain-link construction and gabled form seemed a clear nod to the early work of Frank Gehry, specifically his own house in Santa Monica, California. In parallel with Gehry's increasingly Expressionist trajectory over the next decade, Philip designed a new gatehouse atop Ponus Ridge; completed in 1995, its irregular silhouette and almost cartoonish proportions earned it the nickname "Da Monsta." By then Philip was already exhibiting similar tendencies in his commercial projects—such as the monumental Puerta de Europa in Madrid (1989) and again in Berlin, with the Eisenmanian American Business Center (later Philip-Johnson-Haus, 1992)—favoring bold, gestural forms and gridded facades cut with slashing bolts of red. This was related to the formal recipe for Deconstructivism that Philip had described in his essay for the MoMA catalog: "the diagonal overlapping of rectangular or trapezoidal bars."

Whether such visual cues really expressed the weighty concepts that supposedly informed them was an open question. In the 1930s, Philip had successfully reduced the radical political agenda of the early Modernists into a mere "style" devoid of any impetus more profound than making an interesting image. Now he was doing the same thing to a body of thought that was never intended to be put to architectural ends, and he was doing it the same way: by handpicking a favored group of architects and using them as proof of his case. The evening gatherings at the Century Association had long been a staple of Philip's social calendar; now they—along with his birthday dinners and assorted celebrations at the Four Seasons—became an institution, a central node in New York's architecture culture. As Philip held court, a new generation of designers took their seats alongside their older confreres, proof of their host's enduring magnetism.

Susceptibility to Philip's charm was not confined to architects. In the last decade of his life, Philip became—in a way unsurpassed by any American designer since Frank Lloyd Wright—a beloved national treasure, familiar even to those who did not know his buildings as the grizzled, puckish old satyr in the owllike glasses who often appeared in magazines and on TV. "You are a 'celebrity' with 'star quality,'"[3] said John Burgee; this was by way of complaint, as the younger partner continued to be eclipsed by his older colleague's outsized persona, leading to their acrimonious split in 1991. Undaunted, Johnson kept right on working under his own name, only retreating from public life when finally (at almost the same moment as David Whitney) his health began to fail. By then, in the last of his many roles, Philip had succeeded in playing a double part: at once the foremost exponent of what would become the starchitecture phenomenon and a starchitect himself, the ultimate icon for a new, icon-obsessed age.

Cover of *Philip Johnson: The Architect in His Own Words* by Hilary Lewis and John O'Connor (New York: Rizzoli, 1994).

"Throughout his career, the otherwise mercurial Philip Johnson has remained steadfastly faithful to one principle alone: that architecture is first, foremost, and finally a visual art."

—Jeffrey Kipnis on Philip

Philip in America. With a practice that was producing both postmodernist- and Deconstructivist-inflected work through the early 1990s at least, Philip was uniquely poised to bridge the gap between American architecture's two main factions. That flexibility seemed to some like a lack of principle—though not to theorist Jeffrey Kipnis, who said that he "came to appreciate the *depth* of [Philip's] 'superficiality.'"[4] In a 1996 volume of recent work from Philip's (post–John Burgee) practice, Kipnis orchestrated a one-on-one interview with Frank Gehry, in which Philip joked to the then-sixty-seven-year-old Californian that they would have to put his name on the cover "to guarantee sales."[5] As Philip sensed, the title of America's most famous architect was about to be passed on.

Stills from a video by the Architectural Association School of Architecture, *Philip Johnson in Conversation with Jeffrey Kipnis*, London, 25 May 1994.

Philip receiving the Gold Medal at the American Institute of Architects convention, Dallas, 1978. Front row, from left to right: Frank Gehry, Charles Moore, Philip, Stanley Tigerman, and Robert A. M. Stern. Back row, from left to right: Michael Graves, César Pelli, Charles Gwathmey, and Peter Eisenman.

October 10, 1995

Telephone interview of Frank Gehry by Philip Johnson and Jeffery Kipnis

PJ   Hello Mr. Gehry

FG   Hello Mr. Johnson

JK   Hello Mr. Gehry

FG   Hello Mr. Kipnis

PJ   Apparently this interview will be used by this book in London, to help the book because you are such a good sell.

FG   I am?

PJ   Yes, we will put your name on the cover to guarantee sales.

FG   I see.

PJ   Otherwise I will assume they would never have us work like this.

FG   Philip you have created another monster.

PJ   Oh no, the German journalists were looking over my "monster" then I showed them a picture of your building - the New York Times Sunday article - then they said well we can see what you learned from Mr. Gehry.

FG   Yes, I know that article.

PJ   Now I want to know: Why did you pick me, how did you think I could possible relate to you and what does it mean to you to collaborate with me.?

FG   Oh boy, that's alot of questions. Ok, well, the obvious reason that I picked you to do the guest house is that I love you dearly, the main reason. But I had done a guest house for one of your houses in Minneapolis which you did not choose me to do and I am sure you freaked when you heard about it and so now I thought this new project was a chance for you to get even with me.

Also there was a political reason, Peter Lewis had a thing about you because he would always talk about you because you are from Cleveland and your family and things like that and I think over time he tried many times to hire you and when he tried you were busy maybe you sensed up front that none of this was going to go anywhere. He used to talk about his house as a collaboration with many different people. And I remember one day with him, it was his birthday. I called you to ask you to do a guest house for my

Transcript of a telephone interview of Frank Gehry by Philip and Jeffrey Kipnis, 10 October 1995.

"Gehry is so far the greatest architect that you almost can't talk about the rest. But the man of influence in your sense is Stern. I noticed that when he was a student of mine. I said, this is the brightest kid that ever worked for me—I didn't say 'designer'—I said [he had] an influence for the good, through his knowledge of history, his personality, everything you can come up with."

—Philip on Frank Gehry and Robert A. M. Stern

Icon

Gehry and Philip at a luncheon at the Four Seasons restaurant,
New York, c. 1999.

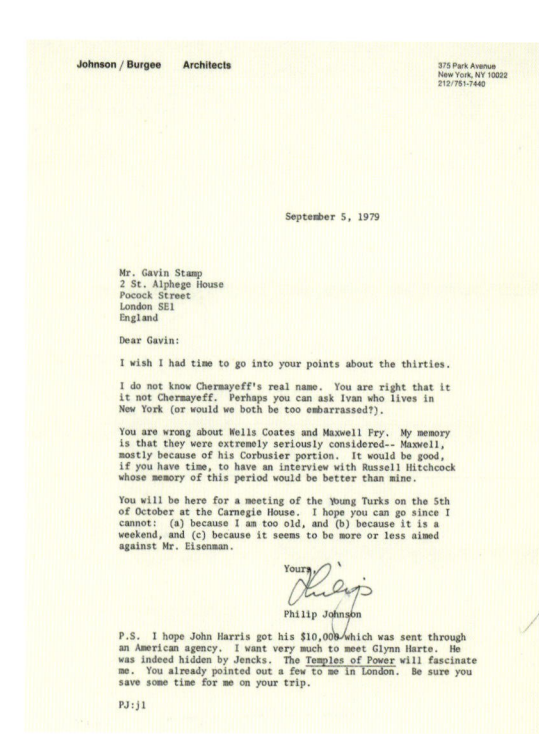

Top row, left: Philip to Gavin Stamp, from New York, 5 September 1979, in which he debates the work of architects from the 1930s. Top row, center: Jerrold Voss of Ohio State University to Stamp, from Columbus, Ohio, 27 January 1987, submitting a letter recommending Philip for an honorary degree. Top row, right: Voss to Stamp, 10 March 1987. He writes to thank Stamp for his nomination of Philip for an honorary degree.

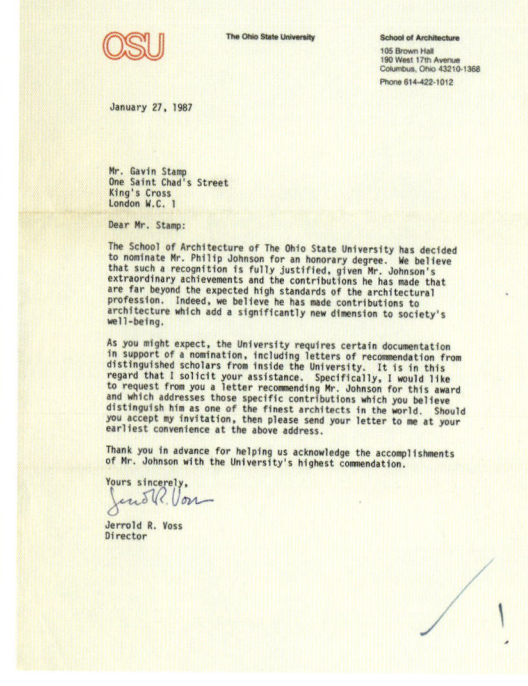

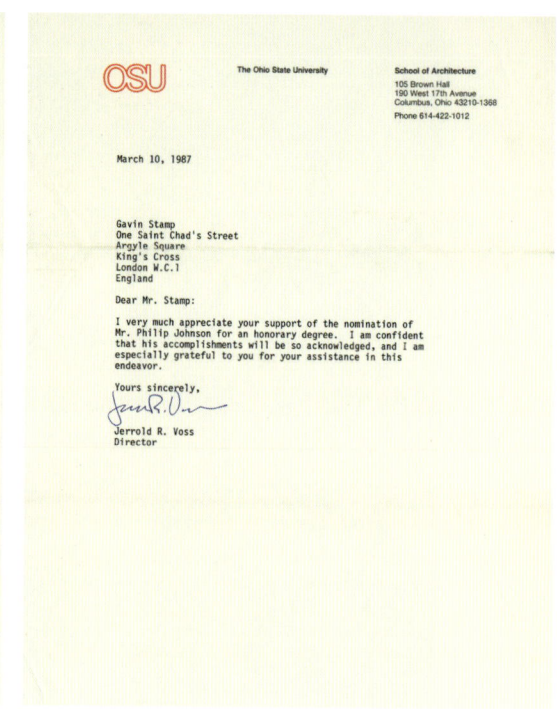

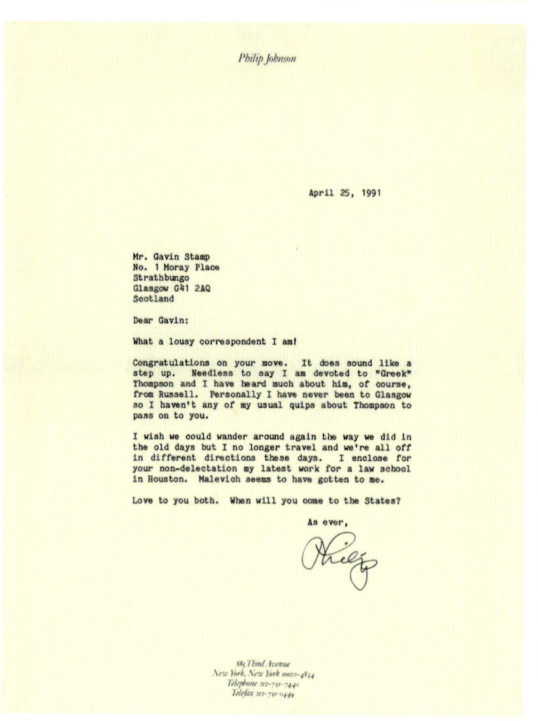

Above: Philip to British architect Gavin Stamp, from New York, 25 April 1991. Philip writes to congratulate Stamp on his move to Glasgow.

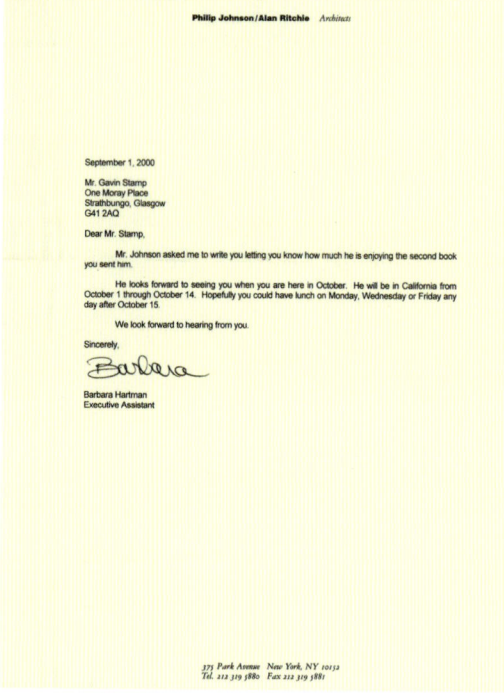

Above: Barbara Hartman, Philip's executive assistant, to Gavin Stamp, from New York, 1 September 2000. She writes to Stamp in order to set up a lunch with Philip.

Philip abroad. Though never quite as much a phenomenon as in the States, Philip was a presence overseas well before most of his colleagues had launched themselves as global architects. Neither the financial and critical failure of the Puerta de Europa project in Madrid nor the fascist echoes of the American Business Center, in Berlin, seemed to alter Europe's bemused fascination with Philip as "a good whatever-he-is," in the words of architectural historian and naturalized Englishman Charles Jencks.

Icon

Philip Johnson

Dear Gavin

I sit with my old fashioned letter head in my little library. I have just put your book right next to Speer. Stirling is next to the other side. Ah, the Alphabet!

Stirling's new Fogg Cut Museum at Cambridge: a disaster. Please a secret. Jim & I are still third friends.

First page of a letter from Philip to British architect Gavin Stamp, describing placing Stamp's book next to Speer's (likely Nazi architect Albert Speer) in his little library.

Top left: "Made in Manhattan" by British architectural historian Ken Powell in *Building Design* magazine, no. 1167, 1996. The article describes a 1993 conversation between Powell and Philip about modern architecture, postmodernism, and deconstruction. Top right and bottom left: "Johnson on Berlin." This transcript of a lecture given by Philip in 1993 recalls his impressions of Berlin since his first visit in 1929.

Above: "A Rise Out of High-rise" by David Taylor in *Punch* magazine, London, 16 May 1979. Philip discusses his own work as well as current trends in UK and U.S. architecture.

Philip Johnson Berlin Talk February 27, 1995
FINAL DRAFT 2.20.95

I feel today the way Le Corbusier must have felt coming to New York and writing about his *Voyage au Pays des Timides*. I feel the Germans today are timid. True, there are many, many cranes around town. They announce however, only the developers' dreams of money-making, not the creation of a new capital for the future Europe. The Germans have made no great plans. They are timid. It could be that it is already too late for Berlin. Yes, Berlin is building, but what is being built?

There is no use looking backward for inspiration. No use to say would it not be great to go back to Athens with its Acropolis, to Rome of Sixtus V, to Paris with Haussman's slicing of the old city, to Washington with its baroque radial streets, to Burnham with his plan of Chicago. These plans all look hopelessly ineffective in an era of 10 to 20 million people aggregations with their hopeless transportation problems, and their equally hopeless housing problems.

All simplistic plans are outmoded and impossible to impose. There is not - nor ever will be - another Sun King who can invent and impose a plan like the great spine of Paris from the Louvre through the Tuileries, Champs Elysées to la Grande Arche.

Mies van der Rohe made a statement very pertinent to this discussion: "The days of city planning are over. We must build as if in

1

a jungle!" And we do live in a veritable jungle. We have to adjust. The times are not going to adjust for us and make brand new cities possible once more. Not even Robert Moses would be possible today and even he is only remembered by his robbing New York of its waterfront by building superhighways on them.

There is no defense against the disease of the modern city, urban sprawl. How <u>can</u> we approach this gigantic problem? What advice can we three foreigners offer? We can deplore, but what would we do?

I can't speak for the other architects on the panel, only for myself. I would accept the jungle. I live in one - New York. A glorious mess with wonderful buildings. But in our great jungle there are clearings and there can be more. Historical caesuras, tiny squares, green spots, old churches - functional elements torn from the endless chaos, points of rest, islands of repose, parks, universities; interventions in the city fabric like Rockefeller Center, Lincoln Center, and greatest of all, Central Park.

Berlin has the best intervention in the Western World: the work of Schinkel. Although usually regarded as an architect and a painter, he actually was a city planner of genius, a designer whose work on the Spreeinsel is the very model of intervention in city plans: from the Packhof in the north to the Werderschekirche in the south, with the Stadtschloss in the middle. His brilliant insertion of new buildings into the old can be a shining hope for our day.

2

Top row: First two pages of final draft of Philip's "Berlin Talk" lecture, which took place on 27 February 1995. He discusses Berlin rebuilding post-reunification and the impossibility of grand simplistic plans: "the Germans today are timid … All simplistic plans are outmoded and impossible to impose." Bottom row: Likely notes taken by Gavin Stamp at a speech given by Philip at the Royal Institute of British Architects, London, 8 May 1979.

355

PETER EISEN- MAN & FRANK GEHRY

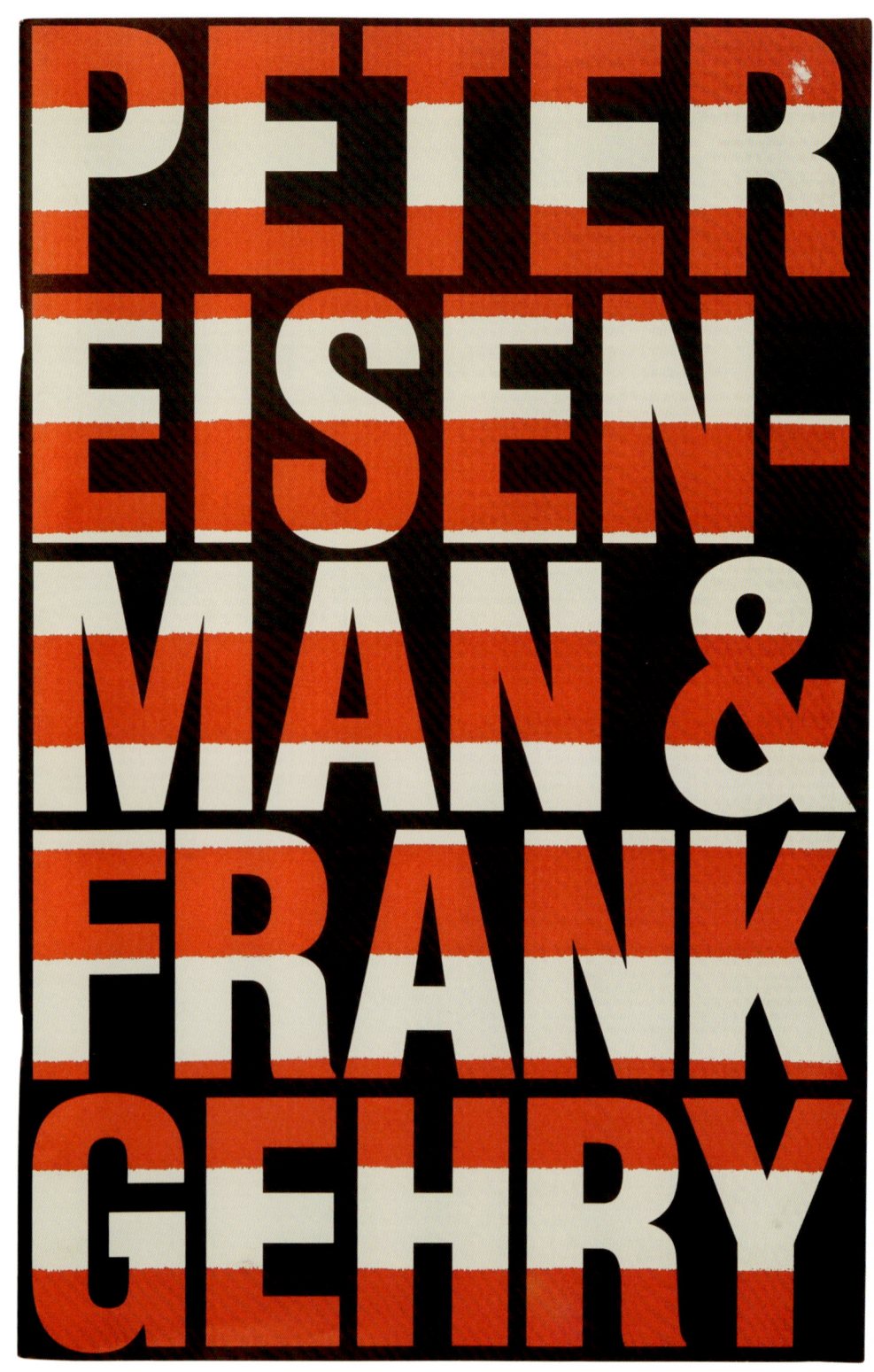

Cover of *Peter Eisenman & Frank Gehry* (New York: Rizzoli, 1991). It was created for Eisenman and Gehry's 1991 Biennale exhibition.

Mentor and oracle. Whether it was Peter Eisenman or Frank Gehry, Rem Koolhaas or Robert A. M. Stern, architects and thinkers sought out Philip as an interpreter and adviser, and he dispensed his wisdom with evident relish. Big names weren't the only ones—he received fan mail from would-be builders of all ages and stations. "I will never retire," Philip once said. "I would die without a project."[6] In a sense, in his last decade the entire profession became his project.

Icon

Introduction by Philip Johnson, Commissioner

The question of who are the most important or influential U.S. architects is endlessly debated, and there are compelling arguments for several candidates. If influence or importance were to be the criterion for making the choice for the Biennale, perhaps neither Eisenman nor Gehry would have made the short list. However, my concern was to identify those architects who were challenging their discipline most aggressively and exploiting architectural risk most successfully. On these criteria, Gehry and Eisenman are unmatched. Together, their practices leave virtually no stone unturned. They challenge every dogma; they offend every etiquette. Yet they build spectacular, troubling buildings.

Perhaps more interesting than their similarities, however, are their differences. I am not too interested in the public personae that each of these architects goes to such pains to present. Eisenman's image as East Coast intellectual extraordinaire and Gehry's role as the intuitive, anti-intellectual West Coast savant are too carefully wrought and too finely cultivated to be persuasive. I do believe, however, that these caricatures afford insight into the approach to risk each takes.

Gehry believes architecture is primarily an aesthetic endeavor, a question of the qualities of material and form. His risks, therefore, revolve around the architectural possibilities of unexplored shapes and untried materials, and his muse is Art. Eisenman, on the other hand, is convinced that architecture is primarily a matter of meaning. He takes his chances on questions of text, and his muse is Philosophy. Thus, to my mind this exhibition is a scene in which two contemporary iconoclasts engage in the classical confrontation between form and content. Seen in this light, the similarities and differences between the work of these two architects are all the more fascinating. However history may assess the results, for the time being, this is where the action is.

The opening pages of an introduction written by Philip for *Peter Eisenman & Frank Gehry* (New York: Rizzoli, 1991). Philip asserted that Eisenman and Gehry were "unmatched" in U.S. architecture and claimed the fundamental difference between them was that Gehry's muse was art while Eisenman's was philosophy.

Philip with Gehry on a trip to visit Gehry's Guggenheim Museum Bilbao, Spain, 1998.

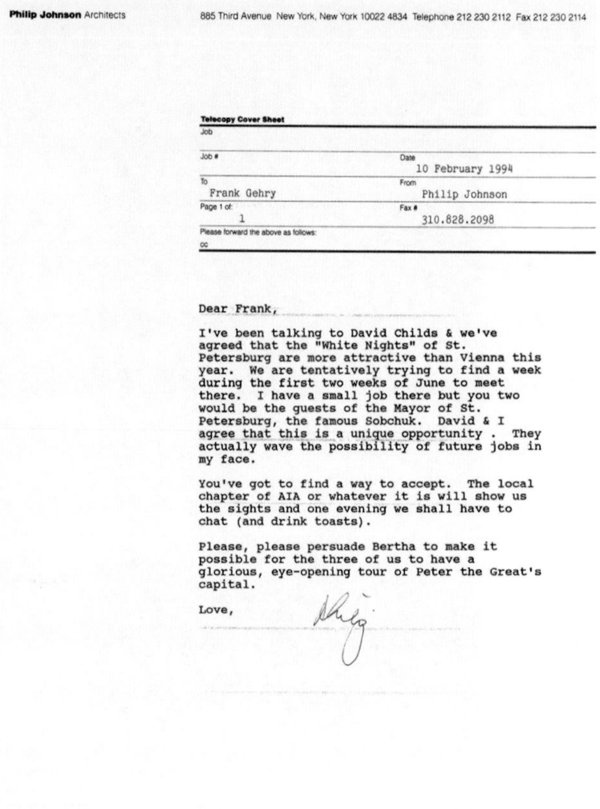

Philip to Gehry, from New York, 10 February 1994. He writes to try to persuade Gehry to join him on a trip to St. Petersburg with architect David Childs.

Dear Frank,

I've been talking to David Childs & we've agreed that the "White Nights" of St. Petersburg are more attractive than Vienna this year. We are tentatively trying to find a week during the first two weeks of June to meet there. I have a small job there but you two would be the guests of the Mayor of St. Petersburg, the famous Sobchuk. David & I agree that this is a unique opportunity. They actually wave the possibility of future jobs in my face.

You've got to find a way to accept. The local chapter of AIA or whatever it is will show us the sights and one evening we shall have to chat (and drink toasts).

Please, please persuade Bertha to make it possible for the three of us to have a glorious, eye-opening tour of Peter the Great's capital.

Love,

Philip

Icon

Plan of Orientation Pavilion, intended for the grounds of the Glass House,
1991–93. This pavilion was never constructed.

"Philip Johnson may be the last architect of the Enlightenment."

—Peter Eisenman

Top (from left to right): Peter Eisenman, Phyllis Lambert, and Philip in conversation at the opening of *Cities of Artificial Excavation: The Work of Peter Eisenman, 1978–1988*, Canadian Centre for Architecture, Montreal, 1994. Bottom (from left to right): Robert A. M. Stern, Philip, and Peter Eisenman, 1991.

Philip at the opening of *Cities of Artificial Excavation: The Work of Peter Eisenman, 1978–1988*, Canadian Centre for Architecture, Montreal, 1994.

Rem Koolhaas

If I had had his temptations, I am not sure I would have been better.

If I had had his money, I am not sure I would have spent it more altruistically.

If I had had his clients, I am not sure I would have built better buildings.

If I had had his power, I am not sure I would have used it.

If I had had his schedule, I am not sure I would have spent so much time on others.

If I had his age, I am not sure I would still be "there."

Dutch architect Rem Koolhaas and Philip inside the Glass House, reflected on the glass, with a quotation from Rem about Philip.

Icon

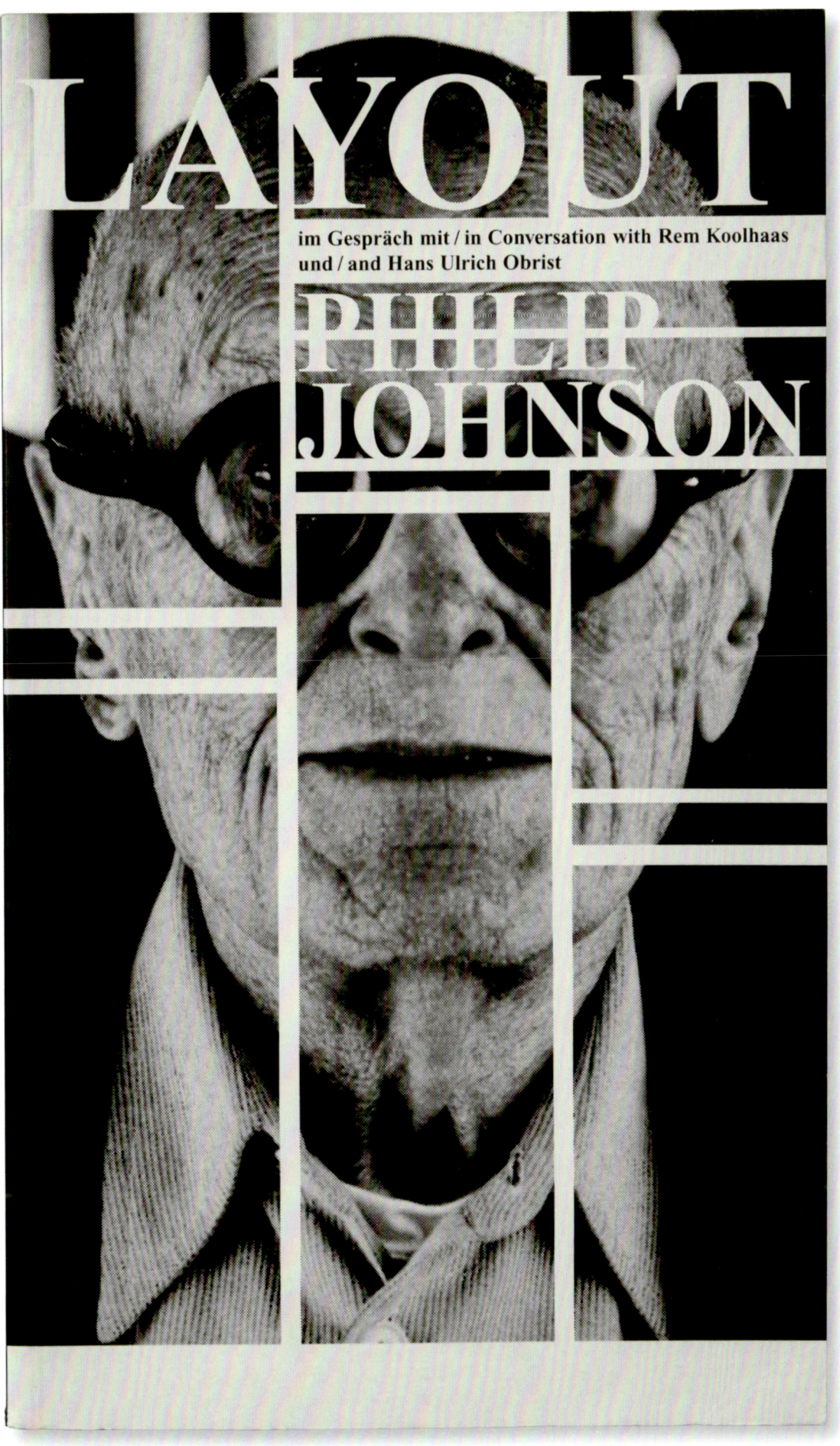

Cover of *Layout: Philip Johnson in Conversation with Rem Koolhaas and Hans Ulrich Obrist* (Cologne: Walther König, 2003).

February 9, 1993

Chris Smith
1262 West Swartzville Road
Reinholds, PA 17569-9609

Dear Chris Smith:

I hope you are sure you want to become an architect, it is a very tough profession.

I think my favorite building is the church in California that I enclose.

It doesn't make any difference where you go to college, it's what you bring to the work that counts.

Sincerely,

enc.

March 1, 1993

Ms. Vicki Ferro
POBox 435
Lynbrook, NY 11563

Dear Ms. Ferro:

Thank you for your very flattering letter of February 11.

I would love to have you build a glass house for yourself but, I urge you not to copy mine. I think the cost might be frightening to you and the design not work if you move the fireplace.

The steel was very carefully detailed and executed and would cost a fortune. I should think that $600,000 to $1 million would cover it but, I doubt that is what you had in mind.

Best of luck.

Yours sincerely,

This page: Two examples of fan mail received by Philip. Above: Philip to Chris Smith, from New York, 9 February 1993, asserting his favorite building and offering advice.

Philip to Vicki Ferro, from New York, 1 March 1993, urging her not to copy his Glass House.

Philip being interviewed by filmmaker Nathaniel Kahn for the documentary *My Architect*, New Canaan, Connecticut, 2003. In the film, Philip expresses his respect and affection for Nathaniel's father, architect Louis Kahn.

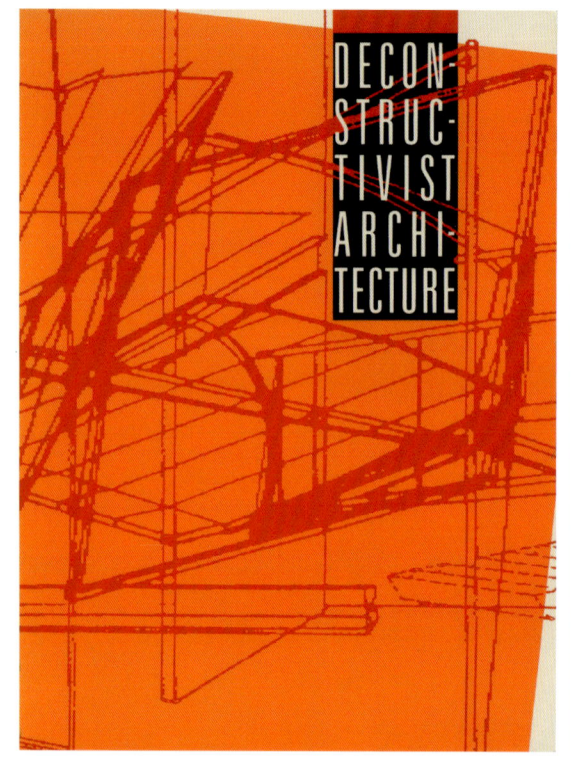

Cover of catalog for *Deconstructivist Architecture* edited by Philip and Mark Wigley, published by the Museum of Modern Art, New York, 1988. The cover illustration shows a detail of a project sketch by architecture firm Coop Himmelb(l)au, transmitted by fax.

Installation view, *Deconstructivist Architecture*, Museum of Modern Art, New York, 23 June–30 August 1988.

Show of shows. The *Deconstructivist Architecture* exhibition was mired in controversy from the start: Michael Sorkin, Philip's journalistic bête noire, exposed a lengthy and distasteful process that had seen Philip effectively rip off the show's premise from younger thinkers and would-be curators. One of them, critic Joseph Giovannini, roasted Philip, telling Sorkin that "Johnson's receptive to ideas because he hasn't got any"—a view that seemed to be borne out by the show's negative reception.[7] The exhibition was meant to be a kind of successor to the International Style show, and yet the only real parallel might be that few participants identified themselves with the label. Nonetheless, it crystallized a moment at the very beginning of a new chapter in architecture and canonized a few of its most important players.

Icon

Installation views, *Deconstructivist Architecture*, Museum of Modern Art, New York, 23 June–30 August 1988.

"All architects want to live beyond their deaths."

—Philip on leaving a legacy

Bookends. Philip's first full-dress biography, Franz Schulze's *Philip Johnson: Life and Work* (1996), came about only after a long back-and-forth between subject and author about when it could be published and under what terms. In the end, despite having originally held out for a posthumous release, Philip conceded to having it published while he was still alive; the book delivered on Schulze's promise of a "warts and all" treatment, and it seemed like there could be nothing more to be said. But there was—much more: *Dallas Morning News* architecture critic Mark Lamster's *The Man in the Glass House: Philip Johnson, Architect of the Modern Century* (2018) was chock full of fresh insights on Philip's work and his political trajectory. The two biographies now form the cornerstones of a burgeoning catalog of texts on Philip.

December 12, 1986

Mr. Franz Schulze
c/o George Sheanshang, Esq.
315 West 57th Street
New York, New York 10019

Dear Franz:

I understand that you are writing a biography of me ("the Work") to be published by Alfred A. Knopf, Inc. I agree to cooperate with you in the preparation of the Work as follows:

1. I will make available to you, in New York City, either originals or copies of materials relevant to my work, such as diaries, memoranda, correspondence, personal papers, photographs, etc. Any originals supplied by me to you shall be returned promptly to me upon my request.

2. I will make myself reasonably available, in New York City, for consultation with you.

3. I agree to introduce you to those persons, (friends, relatives, colleagues, employees, etc.) who may be able to provide you with useful information and other materials, for inclusion in the Work.

4. I will use my best efforts to gain access for you to archives at Columbia University and elsewhere which

---

PAUL, WEISS, RIFKIND, WHARTON & GARRISON

December 29, 1986

George Sheanshang, Esq.
315 West 57th Street
New York, New York 10019

Dear George:

I have been asked by Philip Johnson to review the letter from Franz Schulze to Mr. Johnson with respect to the biography which Mr. Schulze proposes to write. I have discussed this letter with Mr. Johnson. Our main concern is with the exclusivity of the arrangements suggested by you. Unquestionably there will be many biographies of Mr. Johnson and he cannot make available to Mr. Schulze papers and other materials on an exclusive basis.

We also have a few other (less important) problems with your draft.

August 22, 1988

Philip:

In haste --

This is all I have found, and it's more than my alleged research assistant came up with. I cannot guarantee on my life that it is all about or by you that ever appeared in Social Justice. The periodical was a weekly, as you know, and it lasted for well over half a decade. That means a lot of print to wade through -- a task not lightened by the fact that one is confined to aging microfilm. I may have missed something.

But I doubt it. I have slogged through the stuff -- and would grow quite tedious -- several times, discovering these enclosures on the first go round and nothing more since. My assistant, blurry-eyed little thing, found even less.

In any case, there are two articles here that refer to you and your radio broadcasts. Both are from 1937. One may be by you or by Blackburn. That is not clear. It refers to "another in the series," as if SJ had published others. I have not found them.
The other four are under your byline, dated 1939, all from the European war zone. Four bylines plus two other articles may equal the six Peter Eisenman keeps referring to, but there remain, so far as I can see, only four byline articles.

Will you please ask him to show you what he says he has, so that you can compare?

Best,

Franz

Sorry about the poor copier. The microfilm looked all cataracted.

P.S. Latest from the F.B.I. has just arrived. Here's a copy. What is means is several more month's delay.

Top row, left: Philip to Franz Schulze, from New York, 12 December 1986, in which he lays out how he can assist the process of writing his biography. Top row, right: Philip's lawyers to Schulze via his lawyer, George Sheanshang, from New York, 29 December 1986, debating the terms of Schulze's biography of Philip. Bottom: Schulze to Philip, 22 August 1988. The letter accompanied material Philip wrote for the anti-Semitic newspaper *Social Justice* between 1937 and 1939.

Detail of a bookshelf in the library at the Glass House.

Philip in his library at the Glass House, 1980.

The last of Mr. Johnson. The final two buildings on the Glass House property were the library (1980), or Studio, and Da Monsta (1995). The former was a subdued, hermit-like shelter, and the latter was an almost menacing bit of Expressionism. The pair showed Philip modulating between his last architectural preoccupations: history and invention. Speaking in 1998, Philip speculated that he had eight more years to live, adding that he just wanted "to finish some more buildings." He died, just shy of his estimate, the night of January 25, 2005, lying in bed inside the Glass House.

Icon

The Studio, a one-room workspace and library, in the grounds of the Glass House, New Canaan, Connecticut, 1980.

Da Monsta, New Canaan, Connecticut, 1995.

"To me there was only one comment about Da Monsta that mattered. Eisenman said, 'Philip, that's the first time you've made something for the history books.'"

—Philip on Da Monsta

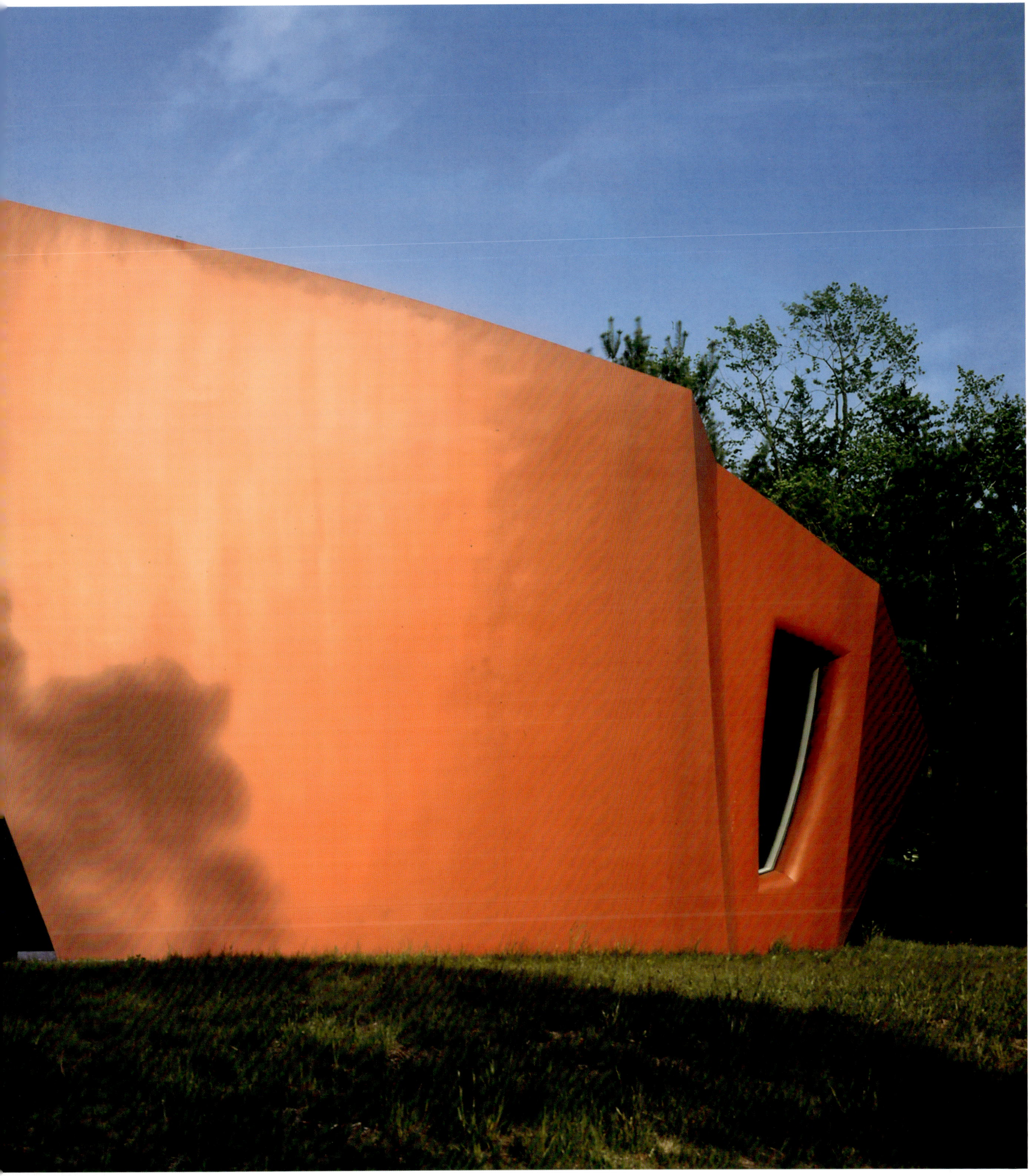

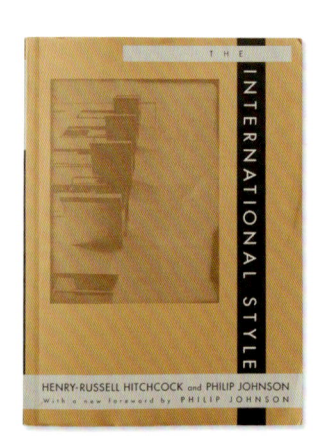

The International Style: Architecture Since 1922 by Henry-Russell Hitchcock, Jr. and Philip Johnson (New York: W. W. Norton, 1932).

Philip Johnson: Makers of Contemporary Architecture by John M. Jacobus, Jr. (New York: George Braziller, 1962).

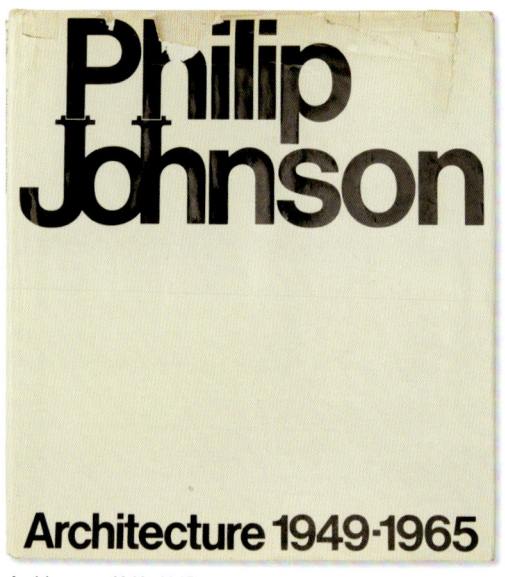

Architecture 1949–1965 by Philip Johnson (New York: Holt Rinehart Winston, 1966).

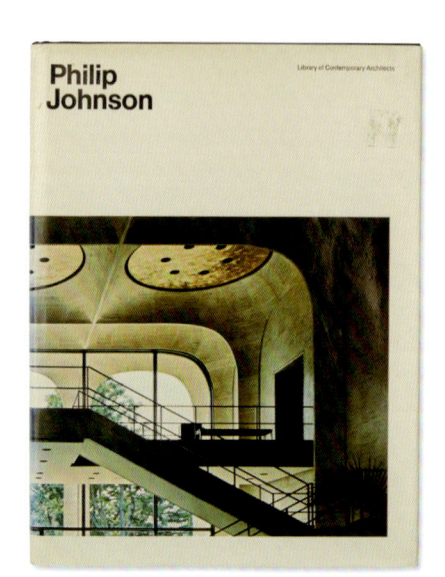

Philip Johnson (Library of Contemporary Architects) by Charles Noble (New York: Simon & Schuster, 1972).

Johnson/Burgee: Architecture. The Buildings and Projects of Philip Johnson and John Burgee by Nory Miller and Richard Payne (New York: Random House, 1979).

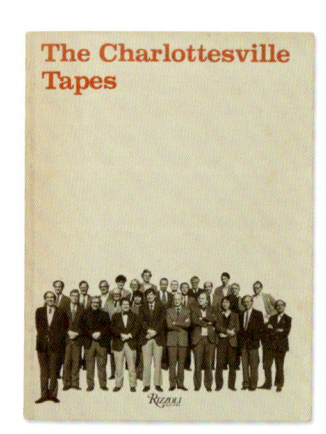

The Charlottesville Tapes (New York: Rizzoli, 1985).

Icon

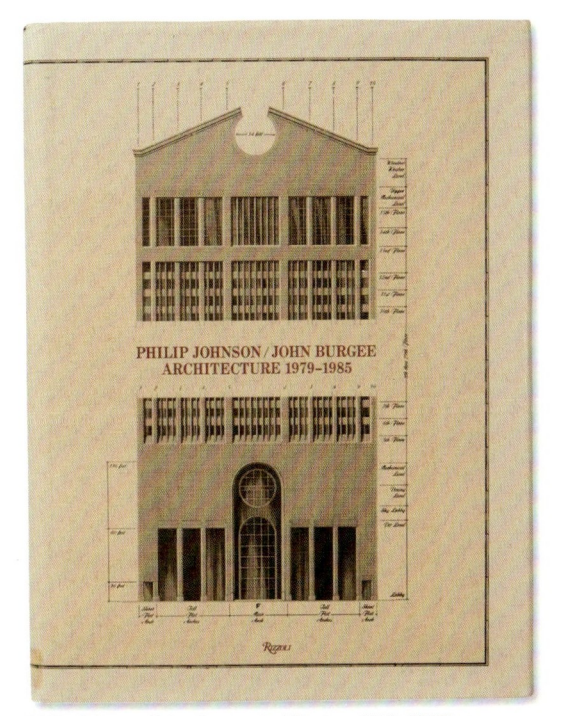

Philip Johnson/John Burgee Architecture 1979–1985 by Ivan Zaknic, ed. (New York: Rizzoli, 1985).

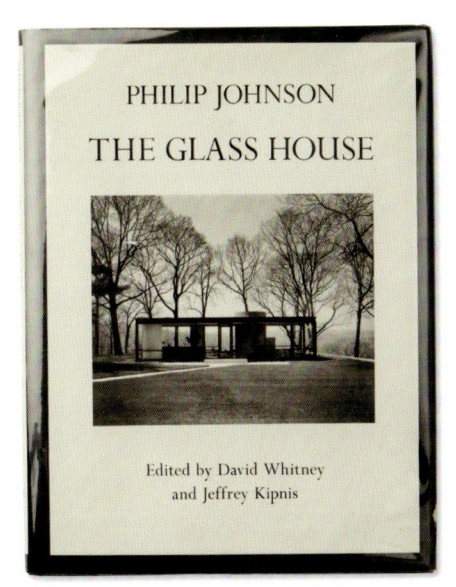

Philip Johnson: The Glass House by Jeffrey Kipnis and David Whitney, eds. (New York: Pantheon Books, 1993).

Philip Johnson: Life and Work by Franz Schulze (Chicago: University of Chicago Press, 1994).

Philip Johnson: The Architect in His Own Words by Hilary Lewis and John O'Connor (New York: Rizzoli, 1994).

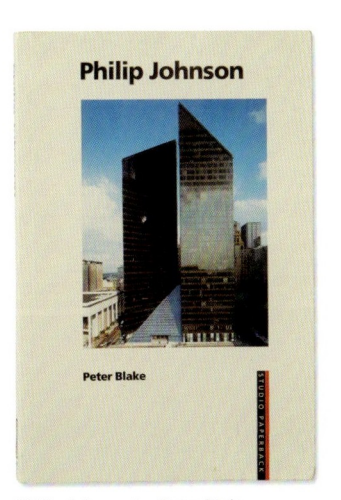

Philip Johnson by Peter Blake (Basel: Birkhäuser, 1996).

Architectural Monographs No 44: Philip Johnson Recent Work by Jeffrey Kipnis (New York: John Wiley & Sons, 1996).

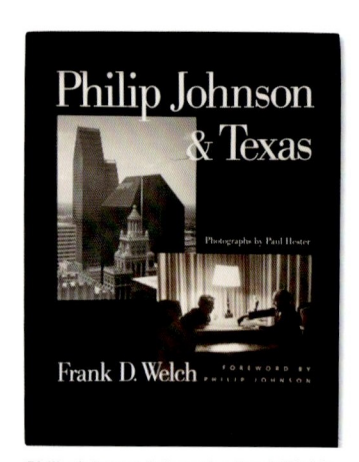

Philip Johnson & Texas by Frank Welch (Austin, Texas: University of Texas Press, 2000).

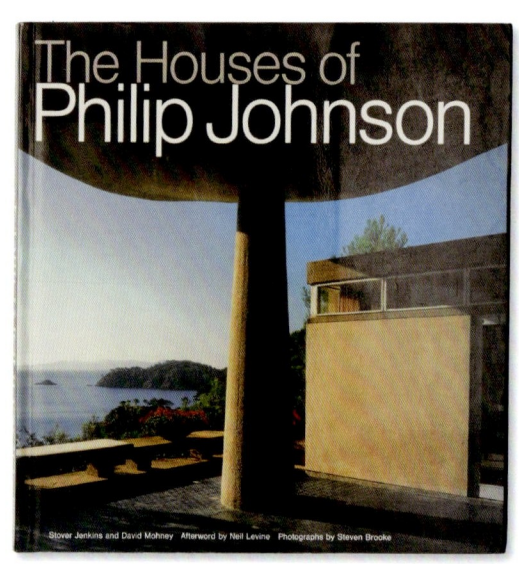

The Houses of Philip Johnson by Stover Jenkins (New York: Abbeville Press, 2001).

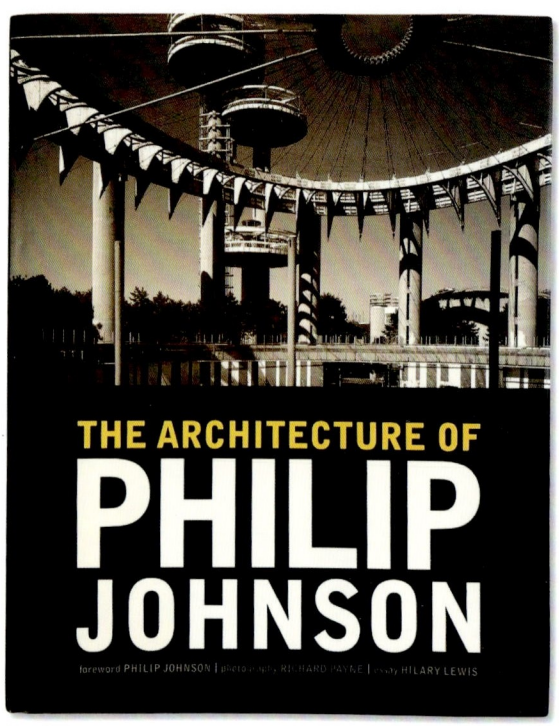

The Architecture of Philip Johnson by Hilary Lewis and Richard Payne (Boston: Little, Brown & Company, 2002).

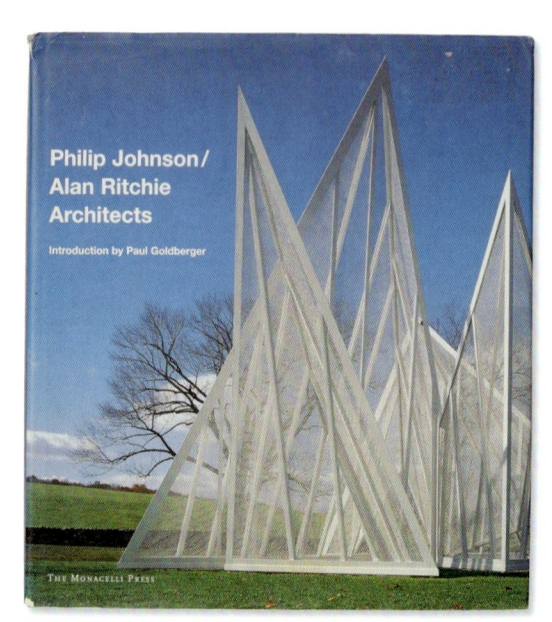

Philip Johnson/Alan Ritchie Architects by Paul Goldberger (New York: Monacelli Press, 2002).

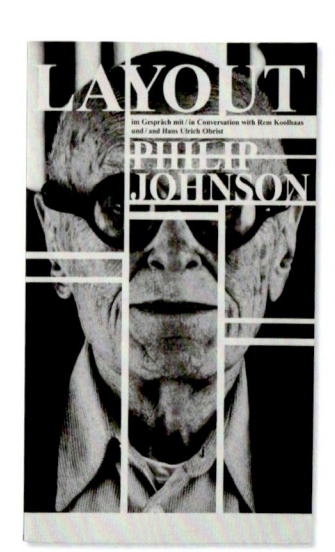

Layout: Philip Johnson in Conversation with Rem Koolhaas and Hans Ulrich Obrist by Thomas Bayrle and Andreas Zybach (Cologne: Walther König, 2003).

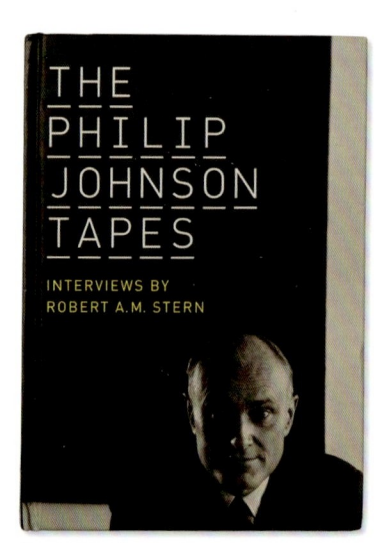

The Philip Johnson Tapes: Interviews by Robert A. M. Stern (New York: Monacelli Press, 2008).

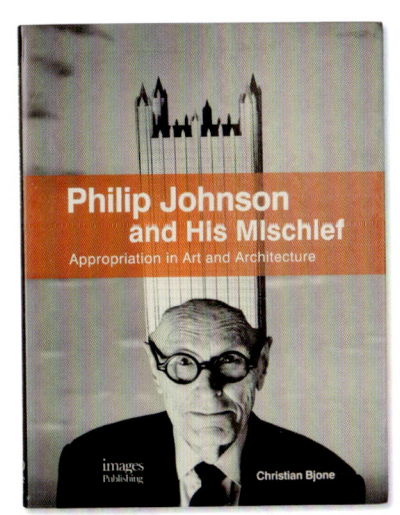

Philip Johnson and His Mischief: Appropriation in Art and Architecture by Christian Bjone (Melbourne: Images Publishing Group, 2014).

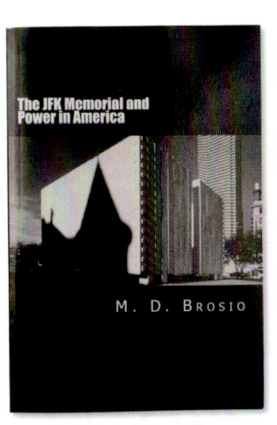

The JFK Memorial and Power in America by M. D. Brosio (Scotts Valley: CreateSpace Self Publishing, 2016).

Partners in Design: Alfred H. Barr, Jr. and Philip Johnson by David Hanks, ed. (New York: Monacelli Press, 2015).

Dream House: An Intimate Portrait of the Philip Johnson Glass House by Adele Tutter (Charlottesville, Virginia: University of Virginia Press, 2016).

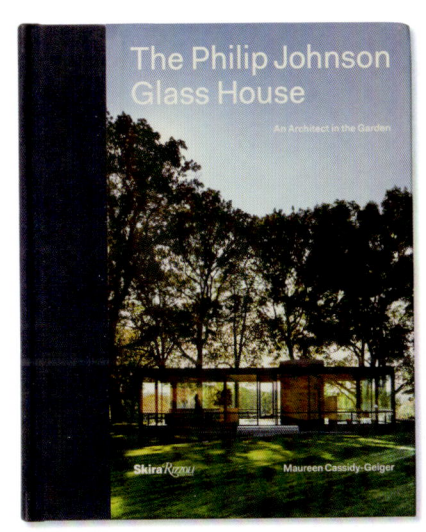

The Philip Johnson Glass House: An Architect in the Garden by Maureen Cassidy-Geiger (New York: Skira Rizzoli, 2016).

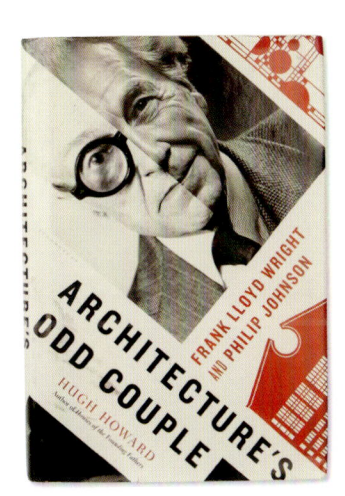

Architecture's Odd Couple: Frank Lloyd Wright and Philip Johnson by Hugh Howard (London: Bloomsbury, 2016).

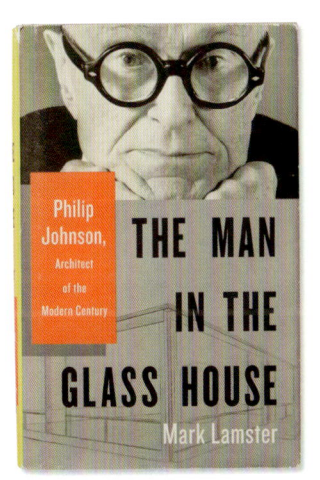

The Man in the Glass House: Philip Johnson, Architect of the Modern Century by Mark Lamster (Boston: Little, Brown and Company, 2018).

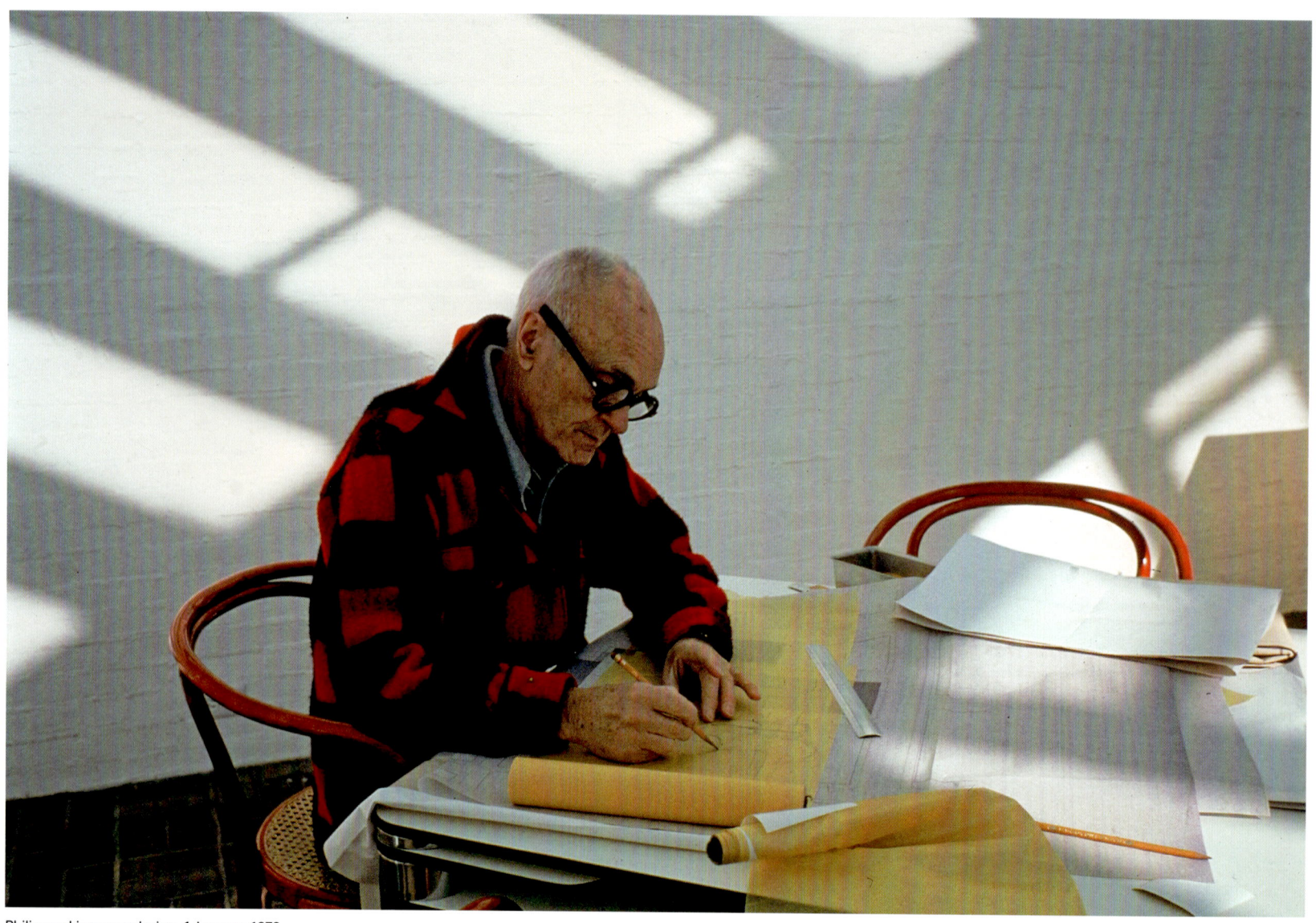

Philip working on a design, 1 January 1979.

Philip with his two dogs at the Glass House, 1998.

"Philip Johnson, who has died aged 98, was for half a century the doyen of architectural opportunists. When Modernist austerity was an aesthetic cause, he was in the vanguard. When the business of American architecture seemed to be business, he was its slickest salesman. Postmodernism was partly of his making. When Deconstruction hit New York, there was Johnson in his 80s in the thick of the theorists, networking, promoting favourites and talking, always talking … If Johnson was always ahead of the architectural game, he never actually invented it. A second-class creative figure with a first-class brain and boundless wealth, charm and wit; in personality, he was half monster, half paragon of urbanity."

Andrew Saint, "Philip Johnson: Flamboyant Postmodern Architect Whose Career Was Marred by a Flirtation with Nazism." *Guardian*, 29 January 2005

"His long career was a study in contradictions. He first became famous as an impassioned advocate of Modern architecture, and his early writings helped establish the reputation of European Modernists like Mies van der Rohe and Walter Gropius in this country. He began his architectural career as Mies's leading acolyte. But what fascinated him most was the idea of the new, and once he had helped establish Modernist architecture in the United States, he moved on, experimenting with decorative Classicism, embracing the reuse of historical elements that would become known as postmodernism, and finally returning again to Modernism, yet one with an expressive and highly emotional energy."

Paul Goldberger, "Philip Johnson, Architecture's Restless Intellect, Dies at 98." *New York Times*, 27 January 2005

"Philip Johnson was unquestionably the most influential American architect of the 20th century. Although he built on a considerable scale and in a variety of styles during a career that extended over 60 years, Johnson will be remembered as much for his activities as propagandist, patron, educator, and orchestrator, as for those as practitioner. He was variously described as 'the dean of American architects' and 'the godfather of American architecture,' roles which he filled with gusto."

Kenneth Powell, "Philip Johnson: Godfather of American Architecture." *Independent*, 28 January 2005

Icon

"Johnson's combination of mercurial brilliance, a flair for publicity, vast erudition and skilful power-broking established him in an impregnable position at the top of the architectural tree, first as critic and then as creator. Always fastidiously well-dressed and with his trademark round black glasses giving him a slightly sinister aspect, Johnson was the most recognisable and influential figure in post-war US architecture."

"Philip Johnson: Authoritative Elder Statesman of US Architecture Whose Designs Moved from Modernist Minimalism to Capitalist Flamboyance." *The Times*, 28 January 2005

"The Cleveland native brought glass-box modernism to America, then led the postmodern revolt against that style with a skyscraper shaped like a Chippendale highboy. He then championed another stylistic shift, popularizing the fragmented forms of such notable contemporary architects as Frank Gehry. He was, at the height of his influence, known as much for his understated elegance, disarming wit and towering prestige as for his multi-million-dollar skyscrapers. In 1979 *Time* magazine put him on its cover, with Johnson clutching an image of his then-revolutionary AT&T building in New York, the so-called 'Chippendale skyscraper,' and gazing down as if he were Moses holding the tablets of the Ten Commandments."

Blair Kamin, "Philip Johnson." *Chicago Tribune*, 27 January 2005

"Whatever the contradictions of a life designed to provoke and dazzle, Philip Johnson ceaselessly promoted architecture as the art that has shaped the great monuments and cities of history, and he sincerely believed that we owe the future a legacy of equal value. He led the march against the destruction of Pennsylvania Station and was quick to lend his prestige to any worthy architectural cause. He kept the subject of architecture on a front burner over a high flame, and if there was no excitement, he made it. He loved celebrity and controversy, but most of all he loved being at the center of it."

Ada Louise Huxtable, "Philip Johnson: Short of Attention Span, Long on Aesthetic." *Wall Street Journal*, 10 February 2005

Notes

Son

1. Franz Schulze, *Philip Johnson: Life and Work* (Chicago: University of Chicago Press, 1994), 41.
2. Ibid., 40.
3. Friedrich Nietzsche, *Beyond Good and Evil*, trans. Judith Norman (Cambridge: Cambridge University Press, 2002), 69. Originally published in 1885.

Traveler

1. Calvin Tomkins, "Forms Under Light." *New Yorker*, May 23, 1977.

Modernist

1. *Princeton Alumni Weekly* 32 (July 8, 1949), 5.
2. Mark Lamster, *The Man in the Glass House: Philip Johnson, Architect of the Modern Century* (New York: Little, Brown and Company, 2018), 65.
3. Terrence Riley, "Portrait of the Curator as a Young Man." In *Philip Johnson and The Museum of Modern Art*, ed. John Elderfield (New York: Museum of Modern Art, 1998), 36.
4. Schulze, *Philip Johnson*, 70.

Politician

1. Schulze, *Philip Johnson*, 106.
2. Ibid., 103.
3. The phrase referred to an advertisement for a washing powder brand. It was commonly used to describe two talented individuals working closely together or, as in this case, as derisive parody.
4. Schulze, *Philip Johnson*, 138.

Architect

1. Lamster, *The Man in the Glass House*, 187.
2. Thomas S. Hines, *Architecture and Design at the Museum of Modern Art: The Arthur Drexler Years, 1951–1986* (Los Angeles: Getty Research Institute, 2019), 27.
3. Schulze, *Philip Johnson*, 198.
4. Nicholas Fox Weber, *Patron Saints: Five Rebels Who Opened America to a New Art, 1928–1943* (New Haven: Yale University Press, 1992), 242.
5. Patrick Sisson, "21 First Drafts: Philip Johnson's 9 Ash Street House." *Curbed*, August 20, 2015. <www.curbed.com/2015/8/20/9928560/21-first-drafts-philip-johnsons>.
6. Robert Andrews, "Architecture." In *The Columbia Dictionary of Quotations* (New York: Columbia University Press, 1994), 48.
7. Joseph Giovannini, "Johnson and His Glass House: Reflections." *New York Times*, July 16, 1987.
8. Tomkins, "Forms Under Light."

Socialite

1. Robert A. M. Stern, *The Philip Johnson Tapes: Interviews by Robert A. M. Stern* (New York: Monacelli Press, 2008), 64.
2. Lamster, *The Man in the Glass House*, 313.
3. Ibid., 216.

Transformer

1. Schulze, *Philip Johnson*, 359.
2. Philip Johnson, interview by Eleanor Devens, Franz Schulze, Jeffrey Shaw, and Frank Sanchis, *Walking Tour with Philip Johnson, The Glass House*, 1991. <www.theglasshouse.org/explore/pavilion-in-the-pond>.
3. Paul Goldberger, "Bobst Library: An Emphasis on Space." *New York Times*, November 7, 1973.
4. Philip Johnson, interview by the Academy of Achievement, *Maestro of Modernism*, February 28, 1992. <www.achievement.org/achiever/philip-johnson/#interview>.
5. Schulze, *Philip Johnson*, 255.
6. Ada Louise Huxtable, "And It's Big and Beautiful: Redesigned Museum is Good Architecture, Fine Cityscape." *New York Times*, May 31, 1964.

Collector

1. Schulze, *Philip Johnson*, 442.
2. James E. B. Breslin, *Mark Rothko: A Biography* (Chicago: University of Chicago Press, 1993), 466.
3. Philip Johnson, interview by Sharon Zane, *Museum of Modern Art Oral History Program*, December 18, 1990. <www.moma.org/momaorg/shared/pdfs/docs/learn/archives/transcript_johnson.pdf>.

Postmodernist

1. Schulze, *Philip Johnson*, 333.
2. John Jacobus, *Philip Johnson: Makers of Contemporary Architecture* (New York: George Braziller, 1962), 121.
3. *The Charlottesville Tapes* (New York: Rizzoli, 1985), 15.

4. Robert Hughes, "U.S. Architects: Goodbye to Glass Boxes and All That." *Time*, January 8, 1979.
5. Paul Goldberger, "House Proud." *New Yorker*, July 2, 2001.
6. *Architectural Record* 168 (December 1980): 78.
7. Paul Goldberger, "A Major Monument of Postmodernism." *New York Times*, March 31, 1978.

Icon

1. Schulze, *Philip Johnson*, 402.
2. Michael Sorkin, *Exquisite Corpse: Writing on Buildings* (London: Verso, 1991), 257.
3. Schulze, *Philip Johnson*, 390.
4. Frank D. Welch, *Philip Johnson & Texas* (Austin: University of Texas Press), 258.
5. Jeffrey Kipnis, *Architectural Monographs No 44: Philip Johnson Recent Work* (New York: John Wiley & Sons, 1996).
6. Welch, *Philip Johnson & Texas*, 271.
7. Mark Lasswell, "People Who Need People." *Spy*, April 1988.

Bibliography

Archives

Andy Warhol Foundation for the Visual Arts, New York, NY
Avery Architectural & Fine Arts Library, Columbia University, New York, NY
Canadian Centre for Architecture, Montreal, QC
Carol M. Highsmith Archive, Library of Congress, Washington, D.C.
CBS Photo Library, New York, NY
Condé Nast Archive, New York, NY
Dumbarton Oaks Museum, Washington, D.C.
Getty Research Institute, Los Angeles, CA
Hulton Archive, London
J. Paul Getty Trust, Los Angele, CA
LIFE Picture Collection, New York, NY
Museum of Modern Art, New York, NY
New York Daily News Archive, New York, NY
New York Post Archives, New York, NY
New York Times Photo Archive, New York, NY
RIBA Collections, London
Underwood Photo Archive, Woodside, CA
Walker Evans Archive, Metropolitan Museum of Art, New York, NY

Published sources

"Architect Philip Johnson Dies." *CBS News* (January 26, 2005). www.cbsnews.com/news/architect-philip-johnson-dies

Thomas Bayrle and Andreas Zybach, *Layout: Philip Johnson in Conversation with Rem Koolhaas and Hans Ulrich Obrist* (Cologne: Walther König, 2003).

Christian Bjone, *Philip Johnson and His Mischief: Appropriation in Art and Architecture* (Melbourne: Images Publishing Group, 2014).

Peter Blake, *Philip Johnson* (Basel: Birkhäuser, 1996).

Mike Brosio, *The JFK Memorial and Power in America* (Scotts Valley California: CreateSpace Self Publishing, 2016).

Tom Buckley, "Philip Johnson: The Man in the Glass House." *Esquire*, December, 1983.

Maureen Cassidy-Geiger, *The Philip Johnson Glass House: An Architect in the Garden* (New York: Skira Rizzoli, 2016).

The Charlottesville Tapes (New York: Rizzoli, 1985).

Mason Currey, "Philip Johnson on Power, Modern Architecture, and the Guggenheim Bilbao." *Metropolis*, August 26, 2013.

David Dalton, *A Year in the Life of Andy Warhol* (London: Phaidon, 2003).

Lee Eisenberg, "America's Most Powerful Lunch." *Esquire*, October 1979.

———, *Fifty Who Made the Difference* (New York: Villard Books, 1984).

Peter Eisenman, *Eisenman Inside Out: Selected Writings, 1963–1988* (New Haven: Yale University Press, 2004).

Kenneth Frampton, *Philip Johnson: Processes* (New York: Institute for Architecture and Urban Studies, 1980).

Joseph Giovannini, "Johnson and His Glass House: Reflections." *New York Times*, July 16, 1987.

Paul Goldberger, "Bobst Library: An Emphasis on Space." *New York Times*, November 7, 1973.

———, *Philip Johnson/Alan Ritchie Architects* (New York: Monacelli Press, 2002).

David Hanks, ed. *Partners in Design: Alfred H. Barr Jr. and Philip Johnson* (New York: Monacelli Press, 2015).

Thomas S. Hines, *Architecture and Design at the Museum of Modern Art: The Arthur Drexler Years, 1951–1986* (Los Angeles: Getty Research Institute, 2019).

Hugh Howard, *Architecture's Odd Couple: Frank Lloyd Wright and Philip Johnson* (London: Bloomsbury, 2016).

Ada Louise Huxtable, "And It's Big and Beautiful: Redesigned Museum is Good Architecture, Fine Cityscape." *New York Times*, May 31, 1964.

Ada Louise Huxtable and Garth Huxtable, "The Four Seasons: Collaboration for Elegance." *Progressive Architecture*, December 1959.

John Jacobus, *Philip Johnson: Makers of Contemporary Architecture* (New York: George Braziller, 1962).

Stover Jenkins, *The Houses of Philip Johnson* (New York: Abbeville Press, 2001).

Philip Johnson, *Architecture 1949–1965* (New York: Holt Rinehart Winston, 1966).

———, *Philip Johnson: Writings* (Oxford: Oxford University Press, 1979).

———, "Johnson on Berlin." *Building Design*, 1996.

Philip Johnson and Henry-Russell Hitchcock, *The International Style* (New York: W. W. Norton & Company, 1995). Originally published in 1932.

Philip Johnson and Mark Wigley, eds. *Deconstructivist Architecture* (New York: Museum of Modern Art, 1988).

Jeffery Kipnis, *Architectural Monographs No. 44: Philip Johnson Recent Work* (New York: John Wiley & Sons, 1996).

———, *A Question of Qualities: Essays in Architecture* (Cambridge, MA: MIT Press, 2013).

Jeffery Kipnis and David Whitney, eds. *Philip Johnson: The Glass House* (New York: Pantheon Books, 1993).

Phyllis Lambert, "*Stimmung* at Seagram: Philip Johnson Counters Mies van der Rohe." *Grey Room* 20 (Summer 2005).

———, "Save New York's Four Seasons." *New York Times*, May 15, 2015.

Mark Lamster, "A Personal Stamp on the Skyline." *New York Times*, April 3, 2013.

———, *The Man in the Glass House: Philip Johnson, Architect of the Modern Century* (New York: Little, Brown and Company, 2018).

Alexandra Lange, "Philip Johnson's Not Glass Houses." *New York Times Style*, February 13, 2015.

Hilary Lewis and John O'Connor, *Philip Johnson: The Architect in His Own Words* (New York: Rizzoli, 1994).

Hilary Lewis and Richard Payne, *The Architecture of Philip Johnson* (Boston: Bulfinch Press, 2002).

David McCabe, "Warhol at the Glass House: The Story Behind the Photograph." *Telegraph*, November 1, 2011.

Detlef Mertins, *Mies* (London: Phaidon, 2014).

Nory Miller and Richard Payne, *Johnson/Burgee: Architecture. The Buildings and Projects of Philip Johnson and John Burgee* (New York: Random House, 1979).

"More Elegance at the House of Seagram." *Architectural Record*, November 1959.

Friedrich Nietzsche, *Beyond Good and Evil*. Judith Norman, trans. (Cambridge: Cambridge University Press, 2002). Originally published in 1885.

Charles Noble, *Philip Johnson (Library of Contemporary Architects)* (New York: Simon & Schuster, 1972).

Ruth Peltason and Grace Ong-Yan, eds. *Architect: The Work of the Pritzker Prize Laureates in Their Own Words* (New York: Black Dog & Leventhal, 2010).

Peter Eisenman & Frank Gehry (New York: Rizzoli, 1991).

Ken Powell, "Made in Manhattan." *Building Design*, 1996.

John H. Richardson, "Philip Johnson: What I've Learned." *Esquire*, February 1999.

Terrence Riley, "Portrait of the Curator as a Young Man." In *Philip Johnson and the Museum of Modern Art*, John Elderfield, ed. (New York: Museum of Modern Art, 1998).

Barbara Rose, "8 Gamblers on Young Artists: Art Dealers in New York." *Vogue*, February 1970.

Franz Schulze, *Philip Johnson: Life and Work* (Chicago: University of Chicago Press, 1994).

Robert A. M. Stern, *The Philip Johnson Tapes: Interviews by Robert A. M. Stern* (New York: Monacelli Press, 2008).

David Taylor, "A Rise Out of High-rise." *Punch*, May 16, 1979.

Calvin Tomkins, "Forms Under Light." *New Yorker*, May 23, 1977.

Adele Tutter, *Dream House: An Intimate Portrait of the Philip Johnson Glass House* (Charlottesville, VA: University of Virginia Press, 2016).

Nicholas Fox Weber, *Patron Saints: Five Rebels Who Opened America to a New Art, 1928–1943* (New Haven, CT: Yale University Press, 1992).

Frank Welch, *Philip Johnson & Texas* (Austin: The University of Texas Press, 2000).

Ivan Zaknic, ed. *Philip Johnson/John Burgee Architecture 1979–1985* (New York: Rizzoli, 1985).

Index

Page numbers in *italics* refer to illustrations

9 Ash Street, Cambridge 122, 126, *130*, *131–3*
42DP office towers, New York *285*

A

Abby Aldrich Rockefeller Sculpture Garden, Manhattan 258, *258–3*
AGBANY (Action Group for Better Architecture in New York) 274–5
Aillaud, Émile *291*
Alan Ritchie Architects *212*
Albers, Anni *296*
Albers, Josef *296*
   catalog covers *83*
American Architecture Now *217*
American Business Centre, Berlin *346*
American Institute of Architects *350*
American Steel & Wire Co. *84*
ANY magazine *224*
Architectural Association School of Architecture *349*
Architectural Forum *126*
Architectural League of New York 62
Architecture *89*
Arp, Hans (Jean) *247*, *248*
Art Deco 62, *334*
ARTnews 64
Asplund, Erik Gunnar, Paradise Restaurant *52*
AT&T Building, New York 318, 320, 330, *331*, *334*
   drawings of *330*
   model of *319*, *333*
   sketch by Michael Graves *220*
Attia, Eli *289*
   Crystal Cathedral *326–9*

B

Balanchine, George *197*
Balmori, Diana *219*
Bank of America Center, Houston *336–9*
Baroque *232*
Barr, Alfred H. Jr. 58, 60, 92, 122
   German travels with Johnson 33, 38, 52, 53
   Johnson's art collection *294*
Barr, Marga Scolari 32, 52, 53, 58
Bauer, Margaret *158*

Bauhaus 58
   Bauhaus Dessau *38*, *39*
   Bauhaus Stairway (Schlemmer) *103*, *294*, *296*, *314*
   Johnson's art collection *294*, *296*
   Modern Architecture: International Exhibition (1932) *70*
Beaubourg competition *291*
Beck House *230*
Belluschi, Pietro *250*
Benson, Elizabeth P. *243*
Berlin, Isaiah *192*
Bernstein, Roberta *299*
Blackburn, Alan 92, 96, 100, *100*, *101*
Booth House, Bedford *122*
Boston Public Library *230*
Breuer, Marcel *128*
Brick House, New Canaan 152, *152–3*, *230*, *308*
Brock, H. I. 65
Bronfman, Samuel *166*
Brown, Denise Scott *318*
Brutalism *230*
Buckminster Fuller, Richard *238*
Building Design magazine *354*
Building Sights (BBC) *216*
Burgee, John *219*, *231*, *325*, *346*
   partnership with Johnson 230, 284, 318, *346*
   see also Johnson/Burgee Architects

C

Cage, John *192*
Cairo, Egypt 34
Canadian Centre for Architecture, *Cities of Artificial Excavation: The Work of Peter Eisenman* (1994) *360–1*
Carter, Jimmy *211*
Carter, Rosalynn *211*
Castello Plan of New Amsterdam *21*
Celmins, Vija *299*
Central Harlem, New York 76
Centre Pompidou, Paris *291*
Century Association, Manhattan *346*
Chamberlain, John *294*
The Charlottesville Tapes *324–5*, *374*
Chase Brass & Copper Co. *86*
Chast, Roz, *A Visit From the Relatives* *158*
Christy, Francis *296*
Cleveland, Ohio 22, *22–3*
Cobb, Eliza Bliss Parkinson *206–7*
Coop Himmelb(l)au *366*

388

Cooper, Paula *299*
Costas Kondylis & Partners *212*
Coughlin, Charles Edward 92, 96, *97*
Crescent, Dallas *318*
Crommelynck, Aldo *299*
Cross, James *77*
Crystal Cathedral, Garden Grove 326, *326–9*
Cunningham, Merce *192*

D

Dalton, Dr. John *302*
Daniels, Jimmie 76, *77*, *192*
David H. Koch Theater (New York State Theater), New York *251–7*, *306*
David Whitney Gallery, New York *298*
de Menil family *286*
Deconstructivism 346, 348
Deconstructivist Architecture, MoMA (1988) 346, 366, *366–7*
Dennis, Lawrence 96, *97*
Diamonstein-Spielvogel, Barbaralee *217*
Distillers Products Corp. *87*
Dix, Otto *294*
　Dr. Mayer-Hermann 102
Dubuffet, Jean *263*
Dumbarton Oaks, Washington, D.C. *238–43*

E

Early Modern Architecture: Chicago 1870–1910, MoMA (1933) *74–5*
Edward M. M. Warburg Apartment 124, *125*
Eimer & Amend *86*
Eisenman, Peter *360*
　American Institute of Architects *350*
　Cities of Artificial Excavation: The Work of Peter Eisenman (1994) *360–1*
　Deconstructivist Architecture 346
　Johnson biography *108*
　Johnson's protégé *230*
　Peter Eisenman & Frank Gehry (1991) 356, *356–7*
Eliot, T. S. *110*
Eriksson, Nils Einar, Paradise Restaurant *52*

exhibitions
　Cities of Artificial Excavation: The Work of Peter Eisenman, Montreal (1994) *360–1*
　Deconstructivist Architecture, MoMA (1988) 346, 366, *366–7*
　Early Modern Architecture: Chicago 1870–1910, MoMA (1933) *74–5*
　The Island Nobody Knows, MoMA (1969) *282–3*
　Machine Art, MoMA (1934) 58, 78, *82–7*
　Mies van der Rohe, MoMA (1947–8) 122, 164, *164–5*
　Modern Architecture: International Exhibition, MoMA (1932) 58, 59, *63–73*, 78
　Modern Painting and Sculpture, MoMA (1950) *296*
　Objects: 1900 and Today, MoMA (1933) 78, *78–81*
　Philip Johnson, Architect: The First Forty Years, Municipal Arts Society (1983) *198*
　Philip Johnson: Selected Gifts, MoMA (1985) *314–15*
　Rejected Architects: Models, Projects, Photos, New York (1931) 62, *62*
　The Work of Young Architects in the Middle West, MoMA (1933) 78
Expressionism 346, 370

F

Felsen, Sidney *299*
Ferro, Vicki *364*
Flechtheim, Alfred *296*
Fort Belvoir 104, *107*
Fort Worth Water Gardens *286–7*
Foster, Richard
　Kreeger House (Kreeger Museum) *244–9*
　New York State Pavilion *264–9*, *304*, *304*
　New York University Bobst Library *276–7*
Fostoria Glass Co. *87*
Franchini, Gianfranco *291*
Francis, Frank *291*
Frankl, P. T. *86*
Frankl Galleries *86*
Futurism *230*

G

Gehry, Frank 346, *348*, *351*, *358*
　American Institute of Architects *350*
　Johnson's birthdays *219*, *227*
　Peter Eisenman & Frank Gehry (1991) 356, *356–7*
　sketch by *219*
Ghost House, New Canaan *346*
Giacometti, Alberto
　Man Pointing 162
　Night *146–7*

Gill, Brendan *218*
Giuliani, Rudy *213*
Glass House, New Canaan 126, *134–59, 150, 220, 378–9*
   artwork at *146–7,* 294, 306, *306–7*
   Brick House 152, *152–3,* 230, *308*
   Da Monsta 370, *372–3*
   furniture *60*
   Ghost House 346
   Glass House Conservancy 156
   Lake Pavilion *156–7,* 230, 234, *234–7,* 238
   media success of 146
   modifications to 152
   monument to Lincoln Kirstein 196, *196*
   Orientation Pavilion *359*
   Painting Gallery 306, *309–10*
   parties at 192, *193–5, 194, 221, 302*
   Sculpture Gallery *295,* 306, *311*
   The Studio 370, *370, 371*
   views of *122*
Glass House Conservancy 156
Goebbels, Joseph *94*
Goldberger, Paul 230
Goodwin, Philip 258
Goodyear family 92
Gores, Landis 122
Gotham magazine 215
Graves, Michael *220, 221,* 230, *318, 350*
Greek Revival 24
Griffith, Bill, *Zippy the Pinhead 158*
Groffsky, Maxine *299*
Gropius, Walter 58, 122
   Bauhaus Dessau *38, 38*
   Modern Architecture: International Exhibition (1932) 66, 70
Gwathmey, Charles *219,* 230, *350*

H

Hackley School, Tarrytown, New York 26, *26, 27*
Hadid, Zaha *227*
Halle, Kay *107*
Halston *312–13*
Haring, Keith *312–13*
Harrison, Wallace 250
Hart, Kitty Carlisle *192*
Hartman, Barbara *352*

Harvard Graduate School of Design (GSD)
   Johnson at 122, *123,* 124, *124, 127–9,* 196
   Lincoln Kirstein at 196
   Walter Gropius at 122
Harvard Society for Contemporary Art 296
Hejduk, John 230
Hemingway, Ernest 110
Herald Tribune 101
Hines, Gerald D. *198, 209,* 212
Hitchcock, Henry-Russell 63
   The International Style: Architecture Since 1922 58, *63, 374*
   Johnson's description of 64
   travels with Johnson 37
Hitler, Adolf 92, 98, *98*
Hoppold, Ted *291*
Hound & Horn 96
Howe, George 95
Hudnut, Joseph 122
Hughes, Robert *99*
Huxtable, Ada Louise 258

I

IDS Center, Minneapolis 230, *288*
Institute for Architecture and Urban Studies (IAUS) 230
International Competition Jury *290*
International Style 230, 318, 346, 366
The International Style: Architecture Since 1922 58, 63
The Island Nobody Knows exhibition, Metropolitan Museum of Art (1969) *282–3*
Isozaki, Arata *227*
Israel Emergency Fund of the United Jewish Appeal 110

J

Jacobs, Jane 274
Jeanneret, Pierre
   Single House and Double House 41, *43*
   Villa Savoye *37*
Jencks, Charles 352
John Burgee Architects *284*
John F. Kennedy Memorial, Dallas *200–5*
Johns, Jasper *298, 299, 308*
Johnson, Alfred (Philip Johnson's brother) 20, *23*
Johnson, Homer (Philip Johnson's father) 20, *23, 100*
   career 24, 25
   early life 24

Index

Johnson, Jeannette (Philip Johnson's sister) 20, *23*, 25
   letters from Johnson 28, *28*
   travels with Johnson 36
Johnson, Louise (Philip Johnson's mother, née Pope) 20, 25
   letters from Johnson 28, *28-9*, *37*, *38*, *48*, *64*
Johnson, Philip Cortelyou
   art collection 292-315
   books on 374-7
   chameleon-like persona 32
   death 370
   depression 20, 28
   early life 20-9
   education 26, *27*
   the icon 344-79
   the Modernist 32, 56-89, 158
   partnership with Burgee 230, 284, 318, 346
   politics 90-119
   postmodernism 316-43, 348
   relationships 76, 192, 298, *300*
   the socialite 190-227
   travels 30-55
Johnson, Theodate (Philip Johnson's sister) 20, *25*
   Johnson's Germanophilia 92
   letters to *107*
Johnson/Burgee Architects
   AT&T Building 220, 318, *319*, 320, 330, *330-1*, *333*, 334
   Bank of America Center 336-9
   Crystal Cathedral 326, *326-9*
   Fort Worth Water Gardens *286-7*
   IDS Center *288*
   Lipstick Building 318, 334, *340-1*
   New York State Theater 251-7, *306*
   Pennzoil Place *289*, *337*
   PPG Place 334, *334-5*
Johnson House, Pinehurst 48, *50-1*, 78
Judd, Donald *311*

K

Kahn, Louis 230
Kahn, Nathaniel 365
Katz, Bill *299*
Kawanishi, Hiroshi *299*
Kelly, Ellsworth 294
Kennedy, John F. *200-5*
Ker-Seymer, Barbara *77*
Kipnis, Jeffrey *227*, 346, 348, *350*
Kirstein, Lincoln 58, 192, 196, *196*, *197*

Klee, Paul 294
Kline Biology Tower, Yale University 230, *272-3*
Kline Geology Laboratory, Yale University *270-1*
Kneses Tifereth Israel Synagogue, Port Chester 110, *112-15*
Knoblauch, Eduard, Kroll's Establishment 44
Koch, Ed 199
Koolhaas, Rem *227*, 356, 362
Kreeger, Carmen 246-9
Kreeger, David Lloyd 246-9
Kreeger House (Kreeger Museum) 244-9
Kunstbunker 294
Kusama, Yayoi, *Narcissus Garden 156-7*

L

Lake Maggiore 33
Lake Pavilion, New Canaan *156-7*, 234, *234-7*, 238
Lalance & Grosjean Mfg. Co. *87*
Lambert, Phyllis *227*, 360
   Seagram Building 166, *166-71*, 186
Lamster, Mark 192, 368
Lancaster, Mark *299*
Landmarks Preservation Foundation 213
Layout: Philip Johnson in Conversation with Rem Koolhaas and Hans Ulrich Obrist 363, *376*
Le Corbusier 36, 58, 92
   Modern Architecture: International Exhibition (1932) 66
   Single House and Double House *41*, *43*
   Villa Savoye *37*
   Weissenhofsiedlung 36, *40-1*, 43
Leonhardt, Robert 122
Leonhardt House 122
Les Halles, Paris *290*
Lethbridge, Julian *299*
Lewis, Hilary *214*, *347*
Lichtenstein, Roy 294
Lincoln Center Plaza, New York 250, *250*
Lincoln Center's State Theater, New York 230
Lindsay, John 192, 198, *208*
Lipchitz, Jacques 232, *247*, *248*
Lipstick Building, Manhattan 318, 334, *340-1*
Long, Huey 92, *97*
Long, Lois *299*
Lorenz, Marianne 343
Luckman, Charles 230
Lynes, George Platt, *Jimmie Daniels, Singer at Le Ruban Bleu 77*

391

M

McAndrew, John *38*
McCaughey, Betsy *213*
Machine Art, MoMA (1934) 58, 78, *82–7*
McIlroy, Glen *296*
Maguire, Sharon *214*
Maillol, Aristide *246*, *294*
　Pomona 246
Manera, Livia *198*
Manhattan Magazine 76
Manley, John *264*
Mapplethorpe, Robert *312–13*
Massachusetts Institute of Technology *167*
Mayo, James *243*
Meier, Richard *230*
Merce Cunningham Dance Company *193*
Mies van der Rohe, Ludwig 92, *296*
　Farnsworth House *156*
　friendship with Johnson 46, 58
　furniture 146, *149*
　historical impulses *318*
　influence on Johnson 70, 98, 122, 126, 230
　Mies van der Rohe, MoMA (1947–8) 122, 164, *164–5*
　Philip Johnson Apartment 58, 60, *60–1*, *296*
　portraits of *40*, *46*
　Seagram Building *166–87*
　Tugendhat House *46*, 46, *47*, 66
　view of Glass House 122, *138*
　Weissenhofsiedlung *42*
Mies van der Rohe, MoMA (1947–8) 122, 164, *164–5*
Minimalism *294*
Miró, Joan *294*
Modern Architecture: International Exhibition, MoMA (1932) 58, 59, *63–73*, *78*
Modernism 32, 56–89, 98, 122, 126, *129*, 230, *274*, *289*, *294*
Moholy-Nagy, László *296*
Moholy-Nagy, Sibyl *296*, *297*
Mondrian, Piet *294*, *296*, *296*
Moore, Charles *318*, *350*
Moore, Henry *247*, *248*, *323*
Moran, Michael *214*
Moses, Robert *264*, *304*
Moses Research Tower, New York *278–9*
Mumford, Lewis 58, 70
The Municipal Art Society *321*
　Philip Johnson, Architect: The First Forty Years (1983) *198*
Muschamp, Herbert *176*

Museum of Modern Art (MoMA), New York 52, 58, *206*
　Deconstructivist Architecture (1988) *346*, *366*, *366–7*
　Early Modern Architecture: Chicago 1870–1910 (1933) *74–5*
　East Wing *258*, *258–9*, *261*
　Johnson appointed to Board of Trustees *263*, *312*
　Johnson resigns from 92, 100
　Johnson returns to 122
　Johnson's art collection *294*, *296*
　Machine Art (1934) *78*, *82–7*
　Mies van der Rohe (1947–8) 122, 164, *164–5*
　Modern Architecture: International Exhibition (1932) 58, 59, *63–73*, *78*
　Modern Painting and Sculpture (1950) *296*
　Objects: 1900 and Today (1933) *78*, *78–81*
　Philip Johnson: Selected Gifts (1985) *314–15*
　Work of Young Architects in the Middle West (1933) *78*
My Architect 365
Mycenae, Greece *34*
Myerson, Bess *199*

N

Nadelman, Elie *257*, *306*
National Party 92, 100
National Socialist movement 92
Nazism 92–9
Neo-Classicism *89*
Neues Volk 96
Neutra, Richard *326*
New Amsterdam, Castello Plan of *21*
The New York Five *219*, *220*, *221*
New York State Pavilion *264*, *264–9*, *304*, *304*
New York State Theater *251–7*, *306*
New York Sun 78
New York Times 100, *111*
New York University *264*
　Bobst Library *276–7*
Newman, Barnett *311*
Niemeyer, Oscar *291*
Nietzsche, Friedrich 20
　Beyond Good and Evil 92
Nubia, Egypt *34*
Nuremberg Rally *94*

O

Objects: 1900 and Today, MoMA (1933) *78*, *78–81*

O'Connor, John *214*, *347*
Oculus 275
Ohio State University 352
Onassis, Jacqueline Kennedy 192, *198*, *199*
One International Place, Boston 318
Orientation Pavilion 359
Oud, J. J. P.
    friendship with Johnson 48, *48*, 58, 296
    Johnson House, Pinehurst 48, *50–1*
    Kiefhoek Housing Development 49
    Modern Architecture: International Exhibition,
        MoMA (1932) 66
    Weissenhofsiedlung *41*, 48
    Workers' Housing Estate 49
Owen, Jane Blaffer 232

P

Paintings and Sculptures 110
Paley, Bill 192
Panorama 198
Pei, I. M. 320, *321*
Pelli, César
    American Institute of Architects 350
    Pritzker Prize Award *211*, *322*, *323*
    sketch by Pelli for Johnson *219*
Penn Station, New York 274, *274*
Pennzoil Place, Houston *284*, *289*, 318, *337*
Peres, Shimon 110, 192
Persius, Ludwig 44
    Heilandskirche 44
    Kroll Opera House 44
    Orangery Palace 45
    Wirtshaus Moorlake 45
Philip Johnson Apartment 58, 60, *60–1*, 296
Philip-Johnson-Haus, Berlin 346
Piano, Renzo *291*
Picasso, Pablo 294
Pinehurst, North Carolina 25, 26
Ponus Ridge 346
Pop art 294
Pope, John Russell *89*
Portland Building 318
Postmodernism 316–43, 348
Poussin, Nicolas 294, *307*
Powell, Ken 354
PPG Place, Pittsburgh *334*, *334–5*

Pre-Columbian Pavilion, Dumbarton Oaks,
    Washington, D.C. *238–43*
Pritzker, Cindy *211*
Pritzker, Jay *211*
Pritzker Architecture Prize *211*, *320*, *322*, *323*
Prouvé, Jean *291*
Puerta de Europa, Madrid 346
Punch magazine 354

R

Rauschenberg, Robert 294, *298*
Read, Helen Appleton 94
Reagan, Nancy *210*
Reagan, Ronald *210*
Reed, Lou 192
Reich, Lilly 58, *70*
    Philip Johnson Apartment 58, 60, *60–1*, 296
Reich, Party Congress, Nuremburg (1938) *93*, *95*
Rejected Architects: Models, Projects, Photos exhibition,
    New York (1931) 62, *62*, *70*
Renaissance 230
Rice, Peter *291*
Riverbank State Park *280–1*
Riverside Boulevard *212–13*
Robert Woods Bliss Collection of Pre-Columbian Art 243
Robertson, Jaquelin 318
Roche, Kevin 230, 320
Rockefeller, Blanchette Ferry Hooker 162, *162*
Rockefeller, John D. III 22, *162*
Rockefeller, Nelson 198, *208*
Rockefeller family 58, 92, 122, 192, 250
Rockefeller Guest House 162, *162–3*
Rogers, Richard *291*
Rogers, Su *291*
Rome, Italy 35
Roofless Church, New Harmony 232, *232–3*
Roosevelt Island (Welfare Island), New York *282–3*
Rosenthal, Ruth *216*
Rothko, Mark 294
Royal Institute of British Architects 355
Rudolph, Paul 230
Ruhtenberg, Jan 38

S

Saarinen, Eero 230, 250
Saks Fifth Avenue *87*

Sandberg, Willem *291*
Schinkel, Karl Friedrich 44
Schlemmer, Oskar, *Bauhaus Stairway 103*, 294, *296*, *314*
Schlesinger, Arthur M. 192
Schuller, Robert 326, *328*
Schulze, Franz 92, *214*
   Philip Johnson: Life and Work 368, *369*
Seagram Building, Manhattan 122, 166, *166–87*, *176*, 318
Sheanshang, George 369
Sheldon Memorial Art Gallery 230
Short, Bobby *213*
Siegel, Robert 325
Simms Campbell, E., Harlem nightclubs *76*
Skidmore, Owings & Merrill 320
Smith, Carlton *211*
Smith, Chris 364
Snider, Grant, *Iconic Houses 159*
Soane, Sir John 152
Social Justice 369
Somaini, Francesco *247*
Soreq Nuclear Research Centre, Rehovot 110, *116–19*
Sorkin, Michael 108, *108–9*, 346, 366
Speer, Albert 98, *98*, 353
   interview with 99
   Welthauptstadt Germania *98*
Spy magazine 108, *108–9*
Stamp, Gavin *352*, 353, *355*
Standard Oil 22
Stein, Gertrude 192, *197*
Stella, Frank *311*
Stern, Robert A. M. *302*, 356, 360
   American Institute of Architects *350*
   historical motifs 318
   Johnson's 90th birthday *227*
Stevenson, Ruth Carter 286
Stone, Edward Durell 230, 258
Streamline Moderne 318
Sullivan, Louis *297*, 323
Sullivan Shipyards *84*

T

Thomson, Virgil 192, *197*
Tigerman, Stanley *350*
Townsend Farm, New London, Ohio 24, *24*
Tremaine family 294

Trump, Donald 192, 318
   Riverside Boulevard 212, *212*, 213
   Trump International Hotel and Tower *213*
Twombly, Cy *299*

U

U.S. Army 95, *96*
U.S. Naval Reserves 104, *105*
University of Virginia School of Architecture *324–5*

V

Velvet Underground *193*
Venice Biennale (1966) *156*
Venturi, Robert *274*, 318
Vidal, Gore 216
Vidler, Anthony 156
Vignelli, Massimo *222–3*
Vitruvius 323
Voss, Jerrold *352*
Vyas, Ujjval *214*

W

Walters, Barbara 192
Warburg, Edward 92, 124, *125*, 192
Warhol, Andy 192, 294, *298*, 302–3
   13 Most Wanted Men 304, *304*
   David Whitney 301
   Philip Johnson 305
   Philip Johnson and David Whitney 300
Weil, Joni *299*
Weissenhofsiedlung, Stuttgart 36, *40–3*, 48
Welch, Frank D. 264
Welfare Island (Roosevelt Island), New York *282–3*
Wellesley College 58
Welling, James
   0158 (2006) 154
   0696 (2006) 154
   0806 (2006) 155
   0865 (2006) 155
Welthauptstadt Germania *98*
Whitney, David *299*, 302, 346, 358
   Andy Warhol's pictures of *300–1*
   David Whitney Gallery *298*
   relationship with Johnson 192, 294, 298

Wigley, Mark 346, 366
Wiley House, New Canaan 122, *220*
Wilmot, Chester 98
Wintour, Anna *215*
World War II (1939–45) 94, 122
World's Fair, New York (1964) 264, 294, 304
Wright, Frank Lloyd 58, 92, 346
   Louise Johnson (née Pope) 20
   Modern Architecture: International Exhibition (1932) 70
   Skidmore, Owings & Merrill 320
   view of Glass House 122

Y

Yale School of Architecture 230
Yale University 264
   Kline Biology Tower 230, *272–3*
   Kline Geology Laboratory *270–1*
Young Nationalists 100, *100*

Picture credits

Every reasonable effort has been made to acknowledge the ownership of copyright images inlcuded in this volume. Any errors or omissions are inadvertent, and will be corrected in subsequent editions provided notification is sent in writing to the publisher.

AA School of Architecture 349 (t); Joan Adlen via Getty Images 328; AIA 350 (l); akg-images 44 (b), 44 (t), 45 (b), 45 (t), 98 (l), 98 (r); © The Andy Warhol Foundation for the Visual Arts, Inc./Artists Rights Society (ARS), New York 2012 305 (r); © The Andy Warhol Foundation for the Visual Arts, Inc./DACS/Artimage 2019 300 (l), 300 (r), 301 (l), 301 (r); AP Photo/Jim Colburn 320; AP Photo/John Rooney 257 (b); © ARS, NY and DACS, London 2019 193; Associated Press 344; © Josef Astor 316; © Austrian Archives/Corbis 94 (tl); Philip Johnson architectural drawings, 1943-1994, Avery Architectural & Fine Arts Library, Columbia University 112 (b), 112 (t), 112, 113, 116 (b), 116 (t), 116, 118, 119, 163 (b), 232, 250, 251 (b), 251 (m), 251 (t), 252 (l), 252 (r), 258, 264, 270 (b), 270 (t), 272, 283 (b), 283 (t), 334 (r), 334 (l), 340 (b), 340 (t); Patrick Batchelder/Alamy Stock Photo 341; Bauhaus-Archiv Berlin 46 (l); The Beinecke Rare Book & Manuscript Library at Yale University 76; Bettmann via Getty Images 56, 210, 253, 304, 323 (t), 326, 198 (l); © Jennifer Calais Smith 185; Photographs in the Carol M. Highsmith Archive, Library of Congress, Prints and Photographs Division 289; Photo by CBS Photo Archive via Getty Images 120; Courtesy CCA © Architectural Association 349 (b); © Roz Chast, used by permission of The Wylie Agency LLC. 158 (br); Collection Centre Canadien d'Architecture/Canadian Centre for Architecture, Montréal 50-1 (t), 51 (b); © Corbis 94 (tr); Corbis/VCG via Getty Images 182-3; © DACS 2011. Courtesy Netherlands Architecture Institute, Rotterdam 49 (bl); Emelie Danielson/Conde Nast via Getty Images 125; Walter Daran/Hulton Archive via Getty Images 274; Walter Daran/The LIFE Images Collection via Getty Images 200 (l); © Bruce Davidson/Magnum Photos 235; All images courtesy Philip Dempsey 34 (bl), 34 (r), 34 (tl), 35, 298 (bl), 298 (r), 298 (tl), 299 (b), 299 (t); Jan Derwig/RIBA Collections 49 (t); Courtesy of Dr. Barbaralee Diamonstein-Spielvogel, materials provided by the Barbaralee Diamonstein-Spielvogel Collection, David M. Rubenstein Rare Book & Manuscript Library, Duke University 217; © Dumbarton Oaks Museum, Washington, D.C. 238 (b), 238 (t), 239, 240, 241, 243; Courtesy of Zvi Efrat 117; Everett Collection Inc/Alamy Stock Photo 200 (r), 266 (r), 365; Nora Feller 370 (r); © Fondation Le Corbusier, Paris 37 (t), 40 (tr), 43; Ron Galella/Ron Galella Collection via Getty Images 212 (tr); James Garrett/NY Daily News Archive via Getty Images 208 (l); Used with permission of The George Platt Lynes Estate 77 (b); Getty Images/Joan Woolicombe Collection 40 (br); Getty Research Institute, Los Angeles (2012.R.4) 53 (b), 104; Getty Research Institute, Los Angeles (980060) 23 (br), 24, 25 (l), 25 (r), 26, 27 (b), 27 (tl), 27 (tm), 27 (tr), 28 (l), 28 (r), 29 (l), 29 (r), 30, 36, 37 (b), 38 (l), 39 (b), 48, 54, 55 (b), 55 (tl), 55 (tr), 64, 64, 90, 99, 99, 100 (l), 105 (bl), 105 (br), 105 (tl), 105 (tr), 106 (l), 107 (bl), 107 (br), 107 (tl), 107 (tr), 123, 124 (l), 124 (r), 127 (b), 127 (t), 128, 129, 130 (b), 137, 18, 198 (m), 201, 208 (r), 209, 211, 212 (tl), 214, 216 (l), 218, 219 (bl), 219 (br), 219 (tl), 219 (tr), 220 (l), 220 (r), 221, 222-3, 225 (r), 226, 227, 284 (br), 284 (l), 284 (tr), 286 (l), 296 (b), 343, 350 (r), 358 (l), 358 (r), 359, 364 (l), 364 (r), 369 (b), 369 (tl), 369 (tr); The Glass House 351; © Bill Griffith 158 (t); Harry Harris/AP/Shutterstock 199 (t); Horst P. Horst/Condé Nast via Getty Images 244, 242 (b); Hulton Archive via Getty Images 97 (tr); © Hulton-Deutsch Collection/Corbis 95 (b); The Hyatt Foundation/Pritzker Architecture Prize 322 (b), 322 (b), 322 (t), 323 (b); © J. Paul Getty Trust. Getty Research Institute, Los Angeles (2004.R.10) 140-1, 143, 180, 234 (l), 234 (r), 236, 237; Hugo Jaeger/Timepix/The LIFE Picture Collection via Getty Images 93; Hugo Jaeger via Getty Images 95 (t); Derek Jensen 335; © The estate of Barbara Ker-Seymer/Collection: Tate 77 (t); The Kroul Collection at Hofstra University, Special Collections 106 (r); Courtesy Phyllis Lambert 166, 360 (t), 361; Phyllis Lambert, Montréal 170, 171; Landesmedienzentrum Baden-Württemberg (LMZ) 42; James Leynse/Corbis via Getty Images 338, 339; Library of Congress 22-3 (t); Manuel Litran/Paris Match via Getty Images 290 (b), 290 (t); LOC 162; Lowell Williams Design 336 (b), 336 (t), 330; Copyright Notice: © Lucia Moholy Estate/Artists Rights Society (ARS), New York/VG BildKunst, Bonn Rights Holder: Lucia Moholy Estate 38 (r), 39 (t); © David McCabe 302; Thomas McDonald 379; Gift of Susan and Peter MacGill in honor of Phyllis Lambert 168 (r); Norman McGrath 196, 311; David McLane/NY Daily News via Getty Images 148, 149 (t), 150, 151, 153 (t), 306, 308; Christopher Makos, 1978/makostudio.com 303; Ben Martin via Getty Images 281; © Peter Mauss/Esto 331; © Maddy Miller 295; Michael Moran 372-3; Guillermo Murcia via Getty Images 265; © 2019. Digital image, The Museum of Modern Art, New York/Scala, Florence 33, 40 (l), 46 (br), 46 (tr), 47, 53 (t), 59, 60, 61 (b), 61 (t), 62, 66, 67 (b), 67 (t), 68, 69, 70, 71, 72-3, 72-3, 72-3, 72-3, 74, 74, 75 (l), 75 (r), 78 (l), 78 (r), 79, 80, 81 (b), 81 (t), 82, 82, 83, 84 (l), 84 (r), 85 (b), 85 (t), 86 (l), 86 (r), 87 (bl), 87 (br), 87 (tl), 87 (tr), 89, 102, 103, 110, 111, 130 (t), 134, 135 (b), 135 (t), 136 (b), 136 (t), 164 (l), 164 (r), 165 (b), 165 (t), 168 (l), 190, 198 (r), 206-7, 215, 224, 224, 224, 261, 262, 263 (b), 263 (t), 280, 282, 296 (tl), 296 (tm), 296 (tr), 297 (bl), 297 (bm), 297 (br), 297 (t), 297 (t), 312-3, 312-3, 314 (b), 314 (b), 314 (t), 315 (b), 315 (t), 362, 366 (r), 367 (bl), 367 (br), 367 (t), 367; The New York Times/PARS 65; New York Times Co. via Getty Images 197 (tr); © Arnold Newman/Getty Images/2012 Arnold Newman 194-5; Michael O' Neill/Collection Centre Canadien d'Architecture/Canadian Centre for Architecture, Montréal 186-7; © Richard Payne, FAIA 213, 287, 288, 331; Bill Pierce/The LIFE Images Collection via Getty Images 319; Robin Platzer/The LIFE Images Collection via Getty Images 199 (b); © Jan Van Raay/www.janvanraay.com 286 (r); Courtesy of Raptis Rare Books 63; RIBA Collections 50 (b); Frank Scherschel/The LIFE Picture Collection via Getty Images 167; © Roberto Schezen/Esto 231; Julius Shulman 327; © Grant Snider 159; Michael Sorkin/Spy magazine 108, 109; Francis Specker/New York

Post Archives/(c) NYP Holdings, Inc. via Getty Images 212 (b); Spy Magazine 360 (b); Gavin Stamp 329, 352 (bl), 352 (br), 352 (tl), 352 (tm), 352 (tr), 353, 354 (br), 354, 354, 355 (b), 355 (b), 355 (t), 355 (t); Charles E. Steinheimer/The LIFE Images Collection via Getty Images 97 (tl); © Ezra Stoller/Esto 114, 115, 131, 132, 133, 138–9, 142, 144, 145, 146–7, 152, 172, 173, 175, 176, 177, 177, 178, 179, 202, 203, 204, 205, 233, 242 (t), 254–255, 256, 257 (t), 259, 266, 267, 268, 269, 271 (b), 271 (t), 278, 279, 276 (b), 276 (t), 277, 245 (b), 245 (t), 246, 247, 248, 249 (b), 249 (t), 292, 309, 310; Ramin Talaie/Corbis via Getty Images 371; Ted Thai/The LIFE Picture Collection via Getty Images 285, 333, 378; Time Life Pictures/Pictures Inc./The LIFE Picture Collection via Getty Images 97 (b); Underwood Archives via Getty Images 94 (b); © Walker Evans Archive, The Metropolitan Museum of Awrt 197 (bl); Bob Wands/AP/Shutterstock 228, 228; © James Welling jameswelling.net 155 (b); Wikimedia 21; ZUMA Press, Inc./Alamy Stock Photo 225 (bl), 225 (tl); Courtesy of US Modernist, 275; Courtesy of The Virgil Thomson Foundation, Ltd., 197 (br).

Book photography

Philip Johnson and Henry-Russell Hitchcock, *The International Style* (New York: W. W. Norton & Company, 1995). Originally published in 1932. 41; *The Charlottesville Tapes* (New York: Rizzoli, 1985) 325; Ivan Zaknic, ed., *Philip Johnson/John Burgee Architecture 1979–1985* (New York: Rizzoli, 1985) 330, 336.

Acknowledgments

The author would like to thank Sarah Sherman, Virginia Mokslaveskas, and the staff at the Getty Research Institute; Christina Eliopoulos and all the archivists at the Museum of Modern Art; Janet Parks and the staff at the Avery Architectural and Fine Arts Library at Columbia University; Rachel Gracey for her help organizing images; Peter Eisenman, Martin Filler, Paul Goldberger, Robert A.M. Stern, and Terry Riley for their input; and of course Emilia Terragni, Belle Place, Tom Wainwright, and the whole team at Phaidon for all their support and dedication.

—Ian Volner

Phaidon Press Limited
Regent's Wharf
All Saints Street
London N1 9PA

Phaidon Press Inc.
65 Bleecker Street
New York, NY 10012

phaidon.com

First published 2020
© 2020 Phaidon Press Limited

ISBN 978 0 7148 7682 5

A CIP catalogue record for this book is available from the British Library and the Library of Congress.

All rights reserved. No part of this publication may be reproduced, stored in a retrieval system or transmitted, in any form or by any means, electronic, mechanical, photocopying, recording or otherwise, without the written permission of Phaidon Press Limited.

Commissioning Editor: Emilia Terragni
Project Editors: Belle Place and Tom Wainwright
Production Controller: Adela Cory
Design: Philipp Hubert, Hubert & Fischer, Berlin, New York

Printed in China

The publisher wishes to thank Katherine M. Prater and Mathieu Pomerleau, Avery Architectural and Fine Arts Library; Caroline Dagbert, Canadian Centre for Architecture; Erica Stoller and Caroline Hirsch, Esto; Virginia Mokslaveskas and Ted Walbye, Getty Research Institute; Hilary Lewis and Christa Carr, the Glass House; Tara Gruchalski; Amy Ladner; Phyllis Lambert; and Valentina Bandelloni, Scala for their generous assistance and allowing access to their archives.

The publisher would also like to thank Vanessa Bird, Clare Churly, Alex Darby, Robert Davies, Lisa Delgado, and João Mota for their contributions to the making of this book.

Jacket: © Roberto Schezen/Esto